Scott's Last Journey

SCOTT'S
Last Journey

Edited by Peter King

Duckworth

First published in 1999 by
Gerald Duckworth & Co. Ltd.
61 Frith Street, London W1V 5TA
Tel: 0171 434 4242
Fax: 0171 434 4420
Email: enquiries@duckworth-publishers.co.uk

ISBN 0 7156 2938 7

Designed and typeset by Tony Hart, Isle of Wight
Printed and bound in Great Britain by Bath Press, Bath

Contents

Long commentaries by the editor are distinguished from Scott's Journals by being in boxed rules; they sometimes extend for several pages. The captions, with subject and date by Ponting, are in italics, sometimes followed by editorial notes. The separate editor's notes are in normal typeface to distinguish them from the captions.

Foreword

Some years ago the British Broadcasting Corporation interviewed Tryggve Gran, then in his eighties; sixty years before, a sub-lieutenant in the Norwegian navy and an expert on skis, he had been a member of Captain Robert Falcon Scott's 1910 Antarctic expedition to the South Pole. Speaking in a heavily accented and quavering voice, and against a background of what seemed to be a howling wind, he recounted his memories of that day in 1912 when the Polar search party stumbled upon the tent in which lay the bodies of Scott and his two companions, Edward 'Uncle Bill' Wilson and Henry 'Birdie' Bowers. The three men had frozen to death on their return journey from the South Pole, holed up eleven miles from the food and fuel deposited at One Ton camp, prevented from reaching safety by the ferocity of an Antarctic blizzard.

'We saw the mound of snow . . . we knew it was Scott's tent. I stayed outside . . . as a Norwegian it was not my place. The others undid the tent flaps and went inside. Wilson was lying quite peacefully, his feet towards the entrance . . . Bowers, the other direction. Wilson had died peacefully . . . Scott was between them, half sitting up, one hand reached out to Wilson. Then I heard a noise . . . like a pistol shot . . . I was told this was Scott's arm breaking as they raised it to take away the journals strapped under his arm. Scott had died dreadfully . . . his face contorted with frostbite. We covered up the tent with snow and made a cairn on top. I shall never forget . . . we stood and sang Scott's favourite hymn, "Onward Christian Soldiers".'

Robert Falcon Scott was born on June 6th 1868, in the parish of Stoke Damerel, Devonport, England. He was the first son and third child of John Scott, member of the middle classes, brewer by profession and morose by nature, the latter disposition brought about (in part) by ill health and the belief that he was a failure. In constitution, his son took after him, being undersized for his age and delicate from infancy; as for temperament, all his life he was to suffer from bouts of moodiness and self-doubt.

At the age of thirteen Robert Scott sat the examination for a cadetship in the Royal Navy and joined the training ship *Britannia*. Two years later he became a midshipman. In 1887 he was transferred to the *Rover*, one of the four ships of the navy's training squadron exercising in the waters of the West Indies. It was here that he encountered the geologist Clements Markham, who, at the age of twenty, had been a member of the search party sent to look for the vanished ships of Sir John Franklin, lost while trying to find a north-west passage to India. It was a meeting that was to shape Scott's destiny.

Nine years later the two met again, in Vigo, north-west Spain. Popular with his fellow officers, generous-hearted, often absent-minded and sometimes hot-tempered, Scott was now serving as a torpedo officer. Markham, recently knighted, had become

Opposite: *Capt. Scott at the ice crack. Oct 8th 1911. Ponting, the expedition photographer, described Scott as 'a man of splendid physique: five feet, nine inches in height, broad and deep-chested, and slender in the flanks. His eyes were deep blue, and his face was a faithful index to the resolution and courage that dominated his soul.'*

president of the prestigious Royal Geographical Society; more important, he was obsessed with the idea of a British expedition to explore the unknown continent of Antarctica.

There was to be a third chance meeting, three years afterwards, when, home on leave in London and walking down Buckingham Palace Road, Scott caught sight of Markham on the opposite pavement. They had tea together, during which Markham told him that an expedition to Antarctica was now in the planning stages. Two days later, backed by Markham, Scott applied to lead it; in due course he was given command, though it was not until July 10th 1901 that he boarded the *Discovery* and set sail down the Thames on the first leg of his first journey to the Great White South. On deck, acknowledging the cheers of the onlookers, stood two men who were to perish with him on his last and fatal journey—the saintly Edward 'Uncle Bill' Wilson and the hard-drinking Edgar 'Taff' Evans, who was to hit his head on a rock while descending the Beardmore Glacier and who died ranting and raving. 'I fear Evans is becoming stupid,' reads the original entry in Scott's journal, changed out of respect for Evans' family into 'I fear he is becoming dull.' Also among the company was Ernest Shackleton, a junior officer in the merchant service.

By most accounts, Markham's in particular, that first expedition was judged a success, though later detractors declared the so-called 'scientific' discoveries to be minimal, badly written up and lacking in serious intent. No one, however, doubted the hardships endured or the courage needed to meet such extremes of cold and physical exertion.

In the years following his return Scott was determined to set out once more for Antarctica and, in 1907, again backed by Markham, an appeal was launched for funds to underwrite a second expedition. It was then that Shackleton announced his intention of making his own bid for the Pole. Historians have since claimed that Scott was incensed at Shackleton's 'poaching' of territory he considered his. Certainly in his diaries he expresses dismay when his daily marches compare unfavourably with those of Shackleton's party. In 1909 Shackleton got within 100 miles of the Pole and turned back because his three companions were unable to continue further.

This same year, dining with James Barrie, the playwright who wrote that adult fairy tale, *Peter Pan*, Scott met his future wife. It says much for the complex character of the man that he should be attracted to the vivid and talented sculptress, Kathleen Bruce. It says even more that she should immediately single him out as her destined mate. In her own words he was 'not very young, not very good looking, but he looked very healthy and alert, and I glowed rather foolishly. I had to leave immediately to catch a train . . . he strode behind me . . . he would have swooned with embarrassment at that time could he have foreseen how soon he would be wheeling the perambulator of this tiresomely independent young woman's baby.' Kathleen had always wanted a son and had instinctively marked out Scott to be its father. They were married the following year: their son, the naturalist Peter Scott, was born ten months later. Kathleen wrote to her mother-in-law that with the arrival of Peter she had fallen madly in love with her husband.

For the next two years Scott devoted all his energies to raising funds for the expedition. It was a hard slog. Patriotism was appealed to in order to sway the emotions. Though the exploration was primarily to be of a scientific and geological nature, it was, he urged, a matter of pride that the Union Jack should be the first flag to fly at the Pole. 'If we don't get there soon,' Scott warned, 'the Americans will.'

Finally, on June 10th 1910, an old, patched-up whaling ship named the *Terra Nova* left West India Dock, London, on the start of her voyage to Antarctica. Scott paid out £100 to have her registered as a yacht, which enabled her to dodge the attentions of Board of Trade officials who would most certainly have pronounced her unseaworthy. By November she was berthed at Lyttelton, New Zealand. When she sailed away there were almost sixty men crowded aboard, among them Captain 'Titus' Oates, seconded from the Fifth Royal Inniskilling Dragoons, and Lieutenant 'Birdie' Bowers, temporarily released from the Royal Indian Marine. Both men had paid a thousand pounds to join the expedition.

They spent their first winter at Cape Evans in a hut built on one of the dark spurs of the volcanic Mount Erebus. Even before it was completed Scott set off to visit the old hut he had made his home in 1902. He was disgusted to find the windows had been left open, turning the interior into a block of ice, and blamed Shackleton and his expedition party of 1909. When he returned the new hut was ready for occupation. There was a dark room for Ponting the photographer, space for the scientific instruments and stables to house the ponies. Scott instructed a partition to be built down the middle of the living quarters to separate the men's space from that of the Officers. From a distance of eighty years it is easy to draw the wrong inference; it was not that he considered the men inferior, rather that he felt both groups would be more comfortable with such an arrangement.

On midwinter's day, which fell on June 22nd, they celebrated Christmas and had what Bowers innocently termed an orgy; they drank champagne, ate roast beef, Yorkshire pudding, anchovy pie, crystallised fruits and plum pudding flaming with brandy. Oates, who usually spent his time in the stables with the ponies, drank a little too much, danced the Lancers with the Russian stable groom and ran about shooting at everybody with a toy pop-gun. Finally Scott, rather in the manner of a head prefect at an English public school, told him to call it a day.

At this stage Scott was despondent. He found inactivity irksome and was upset at the poor performance of the motorised sledges by which he had set so much store. One had fallen through the ice during the unloading from the *Terra Nova*, and the other three had proved unreliable. Added to that he had little faith in either the ponies or the dogs, the former being in particularly bad shape after their storm-ridden passage south. Worse, though he had only confided in his good friend, Wilson, before leaving New Zealand, he had learnt the shocking news that the Norwegian explorer, Amundsen, thought to be going north, had announced his intention of turning south and making a dash for the Pole.

On November 1st 1911, the British expedition started out on its terrible 800-mile journey. On January 4th Scott made his selection of the men who were to accompany him on the final stage – Evans, Bowers, Wilson and Oates – and turned back the support party. On the 16th, some ten miles from their goal, Bowers detected a black speck on the horizon. Soon after they came across sledge and ski tracks and the imprints of dogs' paws. Amundsen had beaten them, and indeed was already retracing his steps. It was a cruel blow to the five men who had struggled so valiantly to be first. Scott wrote in his journal that night – 'Great God! this is an awful place and terrible enough for us to have laboured to it without the reward of priority.'

From the start of the return journey, Evans was weakening. He was the largest of them in size and on the same meagre rations. Unknown to the others he had cut his hand some weeks before on one of the sledge runners and it was now the size of a melon and gangrenous. He died on the Beardmore Glacier.

The last entry in Scott's journal, dated March 29th 1912, reads:

We had fuel to make two cups of tea apiece and bare food for two days on the 20th. Every day we have been ready to start for our depot eleven miles way, but outside the doors of the tent it remains a scene of whirling drift. I do not think we can hope for any better things now. We shall stick it out to the end, but we are getting weaker, of course, and the end cannot be far. It seems a pity, but I do not think I can write more.

R. Scott.
For God's sake look after our people.

Three days before, on the dawning of the 17th day of the month, the fourth occupant of that blizzard-bound tent, Captain 'Titus' Oates, driven half-crazy from the pain of frost-bitten feet and longing for oblivion, quit the tent murmuring that memorable phrase, 'I'm just going outside . . . and may be some time.'

Modern readers of these journals, acquainted with contemporary accounts of polar exploration, in which men clad in the latest insulated clothing, equipped with radios, lightweight sledges, and with the knowledge that an aeroplane could rescue them, will find Scott's account of the terrible hardships endured and the bravery with which they met death well-nigh unbelievable. Peter Pan, that lost boy created by James Barrie, faced with the prospect of fighting Hook, cries out 'To die must be an awfully big adventure.' Amen to that.

Beryl Bainbridge
London

Introduction

When my illustrated edition of Shackleton's *South* was published in 1991 one critic suggested that I had been hard on my subject; and the explorer's son, the late Lord Shackleton, told me that he rather objected to my drawing attention, once again, to Shackleton's peccadillos. The fact was that the publication of Roland Huntford's biography five years earlier had made their hair stand on end, because in that justly popular book no stone had been left unturned to reappraise the great man.

Huntford had written in his earlier book, *Scott and Amundsen* (1979), a sentence that will surprise most of my readers. 'It is a little ironic that Shackleton, who is half forgotten today, was the better able to enjoy contemporary success.' *Half-forgotten* then, perhaps, but certainly not so today. What an astonishing *volte-face*. Shackleton has had a major exhibition in New York, shortly it is said to move to Washington DC and perhaps elsewhere. He is the subject of at least two books in English. His exploits have been taken up in newspaper and magazine articles, even by such exotica as the *New Yorker*. The work of his photographer, Frank Hurley, has played a key role in this renaissance of interest. Hurley's splendid *South* has been re-edited by the British Film Institute, re-issued as a video, and shown extensively in the cinema and on television. A full-length feature film is talked about.

Although my edition contained, for the first time, many more pictures by Hurley than had previously been published in *South,* I can make no claims to have brought about this change in attitude to Shackleton, because my book went out of print here soon after Century published it and although it was available in the USA it did not really enjoy wide sales until it came out in paperback there in 1998. In England, my publishers did not get around to reissuing it until the end of 1999, again in paperback.

If I can take a little credit for having foreseen that Shackleton deserved a wider audience, I was much influenced by the encouragement of my friend Richard Kossow, who first drew my attention to the Hurley photographs, of which he had a collection. What I did not foresee was that renewed interest in Shackleton would result in a denigration of Scott. Let me give examples:

'Unlike Scott, Shackleton thought survival more important than glory.'

The Observer, 18 April 1999

'Shackleton didn't play it like Scott with flags and salutes, officers and men divisions. Americans see Scott as a bit of a twit, whereas Shackleton was a natural leader with incredible charisma.'

Jeff Rubin, author of Lonely Planet's *Guide to Antarctica*,
quoted *Weekend Telegraph*, 12 September 1998

'Defining himself against Scott, Shackleton threw gentlemanliness to the winds . . . [Scott's] death in the Antarctic had turned him into a national symbol of patriotic self-sacrifice . . . a more convenient hero for the times than Shackleton . . . Today, however, Shackleton has emerged as the most admirable and glamorous of the twentieth-century explorers . . . Scott is at present in partial eclipse.'

The Guardian, quoting *New York Review of Books,* 29 May 1999

'After more than half a century during which he [Scott] was looked on as the quintessential English hero, it was inevitable that some would itch to besmirch the image.'

Professor G. E. Fogg, *The Exploration of Antarctica,* 1990

'Unlike his contemporary Scott . . . Shackleton placed the safety of his men above personal ambition.'

Washington Post (USA)

'Shackleton summed up [his journey] with characteristic plainness: "Not a life lost and we have been through Hell".'

New Yorker, 4 January 1999

This last quotation, extended to a global claim that 'not a life' was lost by Shackleton on his 1914 expedition is, to put it at its very kindest, a misconception. It is not true. And to make it the basis for a contrast with Scott doubles the offence.

Since the myth that no one died on Shackleton's expedition is so widespread, and is so generally used to demean Scott, the matter has to be clarified here, in the hope of seeing it withdrawn. (The latest American book on Shackleton dismisses the subject in four words—*Three lives were lost*—as if it were some kind of uncontrollable bad luck. The author gives no names or details, her only intention appearing to be to minimise the 'loss' to the point of extinction.)

Those who wish to read the full terrible story should study Shackleton's *South*, Huntford's biography of him, and if they can find a copy, *The South Pole Trail,* the illustrated log of Ernest Joyce (Duckworth 1929).

The facts are as follows: Shackleton's 1914 expedition was made up of two parties, and he had two ships, both of which he owned, to convey them to their separate destinations. He himself led the *Endurance* party from the Weddell Sea, while he appointed Captain Æneas Mackintosh to take his other vessel *Aurora* to the Ross Sea base on the other side of the Pole. His plan was for this Ross Sea Party (so styled) to lay depôts of stores southwards to the foot of the Beardmore Glacier. They would be picked up later by the party making for the Pole itself, led by Shackleton.

The *Aurora* also carried materials for a hut, equipment for landing and sledging parties, stores and clothing, sledges, dog teams and one of the motor tractors—this is Shackleton's list. Like the *Endurance,* the Ross Sea Party vessel was fitted up for scientific work. She had a complement of 28 men.

On the debit side, commentators agree that Captain Mackintosh would probably not

Left: *Capt. Robert Falcon Scott, C.V.O., R.N. on the bridge of the* Terra Nova. *Ponting probably took this picture as he stood near Scott on the poop as the ship steamed out of London Dock and down the Thames. Ponting remarked on the splendid send-off, but Scott replied that 'he cared nothing for that sort of thing'. All he desired, he said, was to complete the work begun seven years earlier and get back to the Navy.*

Right: *Roald Amundsen was quite different – a 'driven soul' who for 30 years returned again and again to polar regions, finally disappearing in the Arctic in 1928. He was born in 1872, four years after Scott, the son of a shipowner. From his early teens he had decided to become a polar explorer.*

have been put in charge of *Aurora* but for the fact that he had lost an eye during the earlier Shackleton attempt and his leader was sorry for him as he felt in some way responsible. Huntford indeed calls him incompetent, impetuous and erratic; and a member of crew labelled him 'not exactly a dependable leader'. However, the men he found waiting for him when he arrived in Australia, chosen by Shackleton, were disorganised and he had to discharge several of them because they were drunk. Other members were made of sterling stuff, notably Ernest Joyce and Arnold Spencer-Smith, the latter a young parson turned photographer to the party, the opposite number to Hurley on *Endurance*.

Other tribulations facing Mackenzie were that Shackleton had appropriated all available funds ear-marked for *Aurora* for his own party on *Endurance*, so as the former required a complete refit, the captain had to arrange a mortgage. Worse still, the ship was not insured and left port without papers.

There is not room here to describe the many setbacks which dogged the voyage, nor the terrible conditions the men faced once they left ship and began to lay supplies along the route Shackleton had chosen. Shackleton asserts that despite their deprivations they 'achieved the object of this side of the expedition', though he had arranged things so that only Mackenzie and Joyce had sledging experience and there were no dependable dogs. So man-hauling was once again the order of the day.

It was all a supreme effort wasted – but one unknown to the Ross Sea men. Shackleton did not succeed in landing and could only complain, 'if only we had been able to cross the Weddell Sea we would have found the assistance vital to the success of our undertaking'.

Worse was to follow. So many of the party suffered from scurvy that the fitter men had to pull the dying on the sledges. Mackintosh was at one point left behind in a tent alone with three weeks' food while his men went to Hut Point for fresh meat to stop scurvy. Spencer-Smith was also left behind at one point, and it would be interesting to compare his spirit of self-sacrifice with that of Oates earlier. He was pulled, lying helpless, for 40 days over 300 miles in a wet sleeping bag. He died on the sledge.

Mackintosh's death may have been worse; we shall never know. On May 8th 1916 he announced at breakfast at Hut Point that he proposed to set off for Cape Evans across the thin ice. Hayward, described by Huntford as a nondescript Londoner of 25 years of age who served as a dog-driver, volunteered to accompany him. Neither man had yet recovered from scurvy, and they set off to travel 13 miles over dangerously thin ice, forgetful of the effort their companions had expended to get them to the safety of Hut Point. They were never seen again.

On January 10th 1917, when *Aurora* finally reached the McMurdo Sound to rescue the men left behind, Huntford describes how 'Shackleton was profoundly shocked by what he saw . . . Filthy, ragged and unkempt. Bloodshot eyes . . . Beards impregnated with grease and blubber-soot.' They spoke in an unmodulated way that revealed mental strain. Cope, their so-called medical officer, had been 'quite irrational', and Richards, one of the Australians, had collapsed mentally and physically. These men, the survivors, were astonished when Shackleton and his two *Aurora* companions, after counting them, lay down upon the ice. Their leader explained that this was a prearranged signal to the Aurora at its moorings to tell the Captain how many of the original party were missing.

I noted in *South* that Shackleton's attitude to these deaths in his record was 'a curious one'. The fate of the party must have been on his mind ever since he failed to make his landfall on the South Polar continent, yet he never mentioned them in the earlier part of the book and by pretending, perhaps subconsciously, that this was a separate expedition outside his control, he was able to perpetuate the myth that he 'never lost a man', concentrating on the epic journey which helped save the main party. True, he did not directly contrast his record with that of Scott, whose loss of comrades was all too apparent to the reading public.

All this criticism of Scott seemed to me to be over the top, exacerbated by the fact that when most of it was written no edition of *Scott's Last Expedition* was in print in the UK. Beryl Bainbridge's introduction to the edition published in the USA by Carroll and Graf (1996) was more balanced, and she has kindly consented to its being reprinted in my edition, which is shorter but much more extensively illustrated. It was, therefore, with a view to presenting a more balanced view of Scott's expedition that, encouraged once more by Richard Kossow, I persisted in the task of preparing a similar version of Scott's book to that I had prepared for *South* some ten years earlier. It took some time.

The question we are asked to consider now while reading this new book is 'Was Scott alone responsible for the failure of the 1910-12 expedition?' I suggest that the answer to this question, a complex one, is to be found from a study of Scott's own record here, and in the data left by his companions and others who have studied the evidence.

If I were called to the bar and forced to answer the question myself, the answer would be—No, he was ably abetted by Sir Clements Markham, who chose him for a position of responsibility for which he was not fitted, and by the Royal Geographical Society and the Royal Navy, who allowed him to take up a task for which he was not adequately suited – and without supervision.

Finally, if it is asked whether it is reasonable to base such a judgement on an incomplete version of Scott's text, with deletions by his editors, my reply would be – Yes, for three reasons: (1) the originally published text was itself full of deletions and editorial additions; (2) where they are of significance, many such deletions have been restored in my marginal notes; (3) by using the shorter version it has been possible to print some 150 photographs by Ponting, plus a small amount of additional illustrated material, which could not have been contained within the covers of a complete transcript of the Journals.

I leave the final judgement to the readers, only asking that it be remembered that Ponting was an unrepentant fan of Scott.

Peter King
Oxfordshire, 1999

Note

In some parts of this narrative, passages will be found in quotation marks. These are not parts of Scott's original Journal but additions taken from his private letters. Passages from Dr Wilson's Journal are enclosed in square brackets and acknowledgment is made to George Seaver's Edward Wilson of the Antarctic.

The photographs and the photographer

Scott's widow wrote that Herbert Ponting's great artistry with the camera was very widely known, but 'to find him also writing with such lucidity and beauty is delightful'. Ponting had returned to England before the news of Scott's death reached there, and he printed the photographs and made them up in to albums for Kathleen Scott, for various members of the expedition, for their families and for sponsors. The pictures in this book are mostly taken from two such albums, which Ponting bound up for Captain Oates' mother. She in turn gave them to the Royal Geographical Society, where they are carefully kept today. Similar albums are in the Scott Polar Research Institute at Cambridge.

Ponting wrote brief captions to these 'album' photographs, which in most cases included the date when each picture was taken. He was also working on an autobiographical book, *The Great White South,* published by Duckworth in 1921. Its 132 illustrations are mostly photographs similar to, or identical with, those that appear in the albums. Each of Ponting's pictures in this book is therefore printed alongside his brief captions which are usually expanded with a sentence or two

Ponting with his cinematograph camera in the Antarctic. The film was of great importance to him, because he would rely on the income from film shows and lectures when he returned from the expedition.

taken from the appropriate pages of his book. In effect, therefore, the photographs are Ponting's and so are the captions. Occasionally I have edited out or added a few words.

Scott and Ponting had many discussions about photography, and the latter was listed as a member of the Scientific Staff of the Expedition and described as its 'camera artist'. But he was more than that. Scott wrote that he was a 'great asset' because of the lectures he gave the crew about his travels and about his art; he added that 'his value as pictorial recorder of events becomes daily more apparent. No expedition has ever been illustrated so extensively.' Scott also admired Ponting's enthusiasm. He said that the photographer had acquired 'a mastery' of 'ice subjects' and was so 'enraptured' that he 'uses expressions which in anyone else and alluding to any other subject might be deemed extravagant'.

The text and the author

Although Scott and his widow were both enthusiastic about Ponting's descriptive powers, the fact is that to our current tastes he is at times prolix, prone to cliché and somewhat quaint. It was natural that he should be proud of being chosen by the explorer from the 8,000 (some say 10,000) applicants who wanted to join the expedition. It was natural, too, that after the event, he should be pleased that he had shown the good judgement to give up writing a book about his own travels in the east, plus a sponsored two-year tour of the British Empire, in order to set off for the Pole. This pride shows up clearly in his text. Unlike Scott he had time to edit his diaries and turn them into book form, as he had returned on the *Terra Nova* on April 1st 1912. He therefore took nearly a decade to assess what his readers wanted from another book about Scott. He also had the advantage of having read the newly issued Scott *Journals*, rushed out by the publishers in 1913 when the manuscript had been returned to London.

That 1913 edition is taken mostly from Scott's journals, hand-written by him in large manuscript books in moments snatched from the day's activities, usually during the lunch-time break. Although there was only the one source, this text has variously been called his 'Personal Journals' and his 'Diaries'. Much later, in 1968, a facsimile edition was published (University Microfilms Ltd, Buckinghamshire).

The first publication, referred to above, was called *Scott's Last Expedition, being the journals of Captain F. Scott R.N., C.V.O. arranged by Leonard Huxley* (1913) and the name *Scott's Last Expedition* has stuck to it ever since. The publishers were Smith, Elder & Co of London. This, it should be noted, was not a transcript of the 'pure' journals, since the editors added passages in inverted commas which were taken from his private letters, many to his wife. Also the term 'arranged by' instead of 'edited by' is rather quaintly employed. In addition, it was sold in two volumes, the second dealing with scientific aspects, much from Dr. Wilson's own diaries (not printed until 1972) from the 1930s. Later single volume reprints also contained passages in square brackets which were taken from Wilson too.

This present editor's main text was first published in 1923, with later editions and imprints appearing with a Foreword by the explorer's son Peter (later, Sir Peter) Scott, the eminent ornithologist. It is reasonable to assume that Peter Scott and/or his editors took the opportunity to remove many longer passages which had appeared in 1913, though nothing is said about this in his Foreword. The fact is that this edition consists of about half the number of words of the first volume of the 1913 *Journals*. Some of them I have put back in this new edition because I believe them to be relevant to the action; the fact that they were deleted is made clear in the marginal notes in which they appear.

I have taken the view that this shorter edition should be republished with 141 photographs instead of the 20 or so which appeared in earlier editions of *Scott's Last Journey*. This has enabled me to set the pictures in more or less chronological order of exposure, which is unique in any edition I have seen. Finally, for the reasons explained in my Introduction, it allows me to print extended comments in the margins of the pages, explaining what recent commentators have had to say about Scott's conduct of his expedition, also giving other information or comment which I consider may be helpful to readers.

One reviewer of a recent book about Scott described it as 'blowing like a polar gale through the musty air of a too-long enclosed national sanctuary'. My aim has not been to introduce any hurricanes but to expose readers to a breath of fresh air, enabling them, I hope, to make up their own minds on the vexed matter of whether Scott was or was not a polar hero.

Scott's Last Journey has been out of print (except in the USA) for some time, and Ponting's photographs have only recently been readily available here, for example as 'fine art prints' at £40 per print, or in a reprint. I believe Scott's text now needs to be read in the light of the views of such modern commentators as Savours, Preston, Huntford and Bainbridge for readers to obtain a balanced picture. This edition makes it possible for the first time to do so.

Members of the British Antarctic Expedition 1910

Shore Parties

Robert Falcon Scott. *Captain, C.V.O., R.N.*

Edward R. G. R. Evans (Teddie). *Lieutenant, R.N.**

Victor L. A. Campbell (The Mate, Mr Mate). *Lieutenant, R.N. (Emergency List).*

Henry R. Bowers (Birdie). *Lieutenant, R.I.M.*

Lawrence E. G. Oates (Titus, Soldier). *Captain 6th Inniskilling Dragoons.*

G. Murray Levick (Toffarino, the Old Sport). *Surgeon, R.N.*

Edward L. Atkinson (Jane, Atchison). *Surgeon, R.N., Parasitologist.*

Scientific Staff

Edward Adrian Wilson (Bill, Uncle Bill). *B.A., M.B.(Cantab.), Chief of the Scientific Staff, and Zoologist.*

George C. Simpson (Sunny Jim). *D.Sc., Meteorologist.*

T. Griffith Taylor (Griff, and Keir Hardie). *B.A., B.Sc., B.E., Geologist.*

Edward W. Nelson (Marie, Brontë). *Biologist.*

Frank Debenham (Deb). *B.A., B.Sc., Geologist.*

Charles S. Wright (Silas, Toronto). *B.A., Physicist.*

Raymond E. Priestley (Raymond). *Geologist.*

Herbert G. Ponting (Ponco). *F.R.G.S., Camera Artist.*

Cecil H. Meares. *In Charge of Dogs.*

Bernard C. Day. *Motor Engineer.*

Apsley Cherry-Garrard (Cherry). *B.A., Asst. Zoologist.*

Tryggve Gran. *Sub-Lieutenant, Norwegian N.R., B.A., Ski Expert.*

Men

W. Lashly. *Chief Stoker, R.N.*

W. W. Archer. *Chief Steward, late R.N.*

Thomas Clissold. *Cook, late R.N.*

Edgar Evans. *Petty Officer, R.N.**

Robert Forde. *Petty Officer, R.N.*

Thomas Crean. *Petty Officer, R.N.*

Thomas S. Williamson. *Petty Officer, R.N.*

Patrick Keohane. *Petty Officer, R.N.*

George P. Abbott. *Petty Officer, R.N.*

Frank V. Browning. *Petty Officer, 2nd Class, R.N.*

Harry Dickason. *Able Seaman, R.N.*

*To prevent confusion between the officer and the seaman on the expedition who both have the name of Evans, it should be noted that the former is referred to as Lieutenant E. or E. R. Evans and 'Teddie' Evans; the latter as Seaman, Petty Officer (P.O.), or Edgar Evans.

F. J. Hooper. *Steward, late R.N.*

Anton Omelchenko. *Groom.*

Dimitri Gerof. *Dog Driver.*

Ship's Party

Harry L. L. Pennell (Penelope). *Lieutenant, R.N.*

Henry E. de P. Rennick (Parnie). *Lieutenant, R.N.*

Wilfred M. Bruce. *Lieutenant, R.N.R.*

Francis R. H. Drake (Francis). *Asst. Paymaster, R.N. (Retired). Secretary and Meteorologist in Ship.*

Denis G. Lillie (Lithley, Hercules). *M.A., Biologist in Ship.*

James R. Dennistoun. *In Charge of Mules in Ship.*

Alfred B. Cheetham. *R.N.R., Boatswain.*

William Williams. *Chief Engine-room Artificer, R.N., Engineer.*

William A. Horton. *Engine-room Artificer, 3rd Class, R.N., 2nd Engineer.*

Francis E. C. Davies. *Leading Shipwright, R.N.*

Frederick Parsons. *Petty Officer, R.N.*

William L. Heald. *Late P.O., R.N.*

Arthur S. Bailey. *Petty Officer, 2nd Class, R.N.*

Albert Balson. *Leading Seaman, R.N.*

Joseph Leese. *Able Seaman, R.N.*

John Hugh Mather. *Petty Officer, R.N.V.R.*

Robert Oliphant. *Able Seaman.*

Thomas F. McLeod. *Able Seaman.*

Mortimer McCarthy. *Able Seaman.*

William Knowles. *Able Seaman.*

Charles Williams. *Able Seaman.*

James Skelton. *Able Seaman.*

William McDonald. *Able Seaman.*

James Paton. *Able Seaman.*

Robert Brissenden. *Leading Stoker, R.N.*

Edward A. McKenzie. *Leading Stoker, R.N.*

William Burton. *Leading Stoker, R.N.*

Bernard J. Stone. *Leading Stoker, R.N.*

Angus McDonald. *Fireman.*

Thomas McGillon. *Fireman.*

Charles Lammas. *Fireman.*

W. H. Neale. *Steward.*

Through Stormy Seas – 1910

Scott's Journals begin as *Terra Nova* leaves New Zealand on Nov. 26th. By now they had covered 110 miles.

Scott's first choice had been his old ship, *Discovery* (alas sold to the Hudson Bay Company), but he made the best of *Terra Nova*, a Dundee whaler built in 1884, which had proved itself in the Antarctic pack ice. He secured her for £5,000 down, with the balance of £7,500 to be paid later. (Although both men had government funding, they had largely to finance their expeditions by their own fund-raising efforts; Amundsen went to the extent of mortgaging his house.) On paper, Amundsen's *Fram*, carrying 19 men to *Terra Nova*'s 65 (described by Wilson as 'shoved together at random'), was the superior vessel, and, according to Huntford, the first modern ship to be specifically designed for a polar winter, round-bottomed to avoid being crushed by the ice. She had been four years in the Canadian Arctic before being acquired by Amundsen. *Fram*'s diesel engine, served by one man, was a huge success, whereas *Terra Nova*'s steam engine consumed coal at a furious rate and needed two or three stokers to keep the boiler going.

Thursday, December 1. – The month opens well on the whole. During the night the wind increased; we worked up to 8, to 9, and to 9.5 knots. Stiff wind from N.W. and confused sea. Awoke to much motion.

The ship a queer and not altogether cheerful sight under the circumstances.

Below one knows all space is packed as tight as human skill can devise – and on deck! Under the forecastle fifteen ponies close side by side, seven one side, eight the other, heads together and groom between – swaying, swaying continually to the plunging irregular motion.

One takes a look through a hole in the bulkhead and sees a row of heads with sad, patient eyes come swinging up together from the starboard side, whilst those on the port swing back; then up come the port heads, whilst the starboard recede. It seems a terrible ordeal for these poor beasts to stand this day after day for weeks together, and indeed though they continue to feed well the strain quickly drags down their weight and condition; but nevertheless the trial cannot be gauged from human standards. There are horses which never lie down, and all horses can sleep standing; anatomically they possess a ligament in each leg which takes their weight without strain. Even our poor ani-

mals will get rest and sleep in spite of the violent motion. Some 4 or 5 tons of fodder and the ever watchful Anton take up the remainder of the forecastle space.

There are four ponies outside the forecastle and to leeward of the fore hatch, and on the whole, perhaps, with shielding tarpaulins, they have a rather better time than their comrades. Just behind the ice-house and on either side of the main hatch are two enormous packing-cases containing motor sledges, each 16 x 5 x 4; mounted as they are several inches above the deck they take a formidable amount of space. A third sledge stands across the break of the poop in the space hitherto occupied by the after winch. All these cases are covered with stout tarpaulin and lashed with heavy chain and rope lashings, so that they may be absolutely secure.

The petrol for these sledges is contained in tins and drums protected in stout wooden packing-cases which are ranged across the deck immediately in front of the poop and abreast the motor sledges. The quantity is 2½ tons and the space occupied considerable.

Round and about these packing-cases, stretching from the galley forward to the wheel aft, the deck is stacked with coal-bags forming our deck cargo of coal, now rapidly diminishing.

We left Port Chalmers with 462 tons of coal on board, rather a greater quantity than I had hoped for, and yet the load mark was 3 inches above the water. The ship was over 2 feet by the stern, but this will soon be remedied.

Upon the coal sacks, upon and between the motor sledges, and upon the ice-house are grouped the dogs, thirty-three in all. They must perforce be chained up, and they are given what shelter is afforded on deck, but their position is not enviable. The seas continually break on the weather bulwarks and scatter clouds of heavy spray over the backs of all who must venture into the waist of the ship. The dogs sit with their tails to this invading water, their coats wet and dripping. It is a pathetic attitude, deeply significant of cold and misery; occasionally some poor beast emits a long pathetic whine. Such a life is truly hard for these poor creatures.

We manage somehow to find a seat for every one at our cabin table, although the wardroom contains twenty-four officers. There are generally one or two on watch, which eases matters, but it is a squash. Our meals are simple enough, but it is really remarkable to see the manner in which our two stewards, Hooper and Neale, provide for all requirements—washing up, tidying cabin, and making themselves generally useful in the cheerfullest manner.

With such a large number of hands on board, allowing nine seamen in each watch, the ship is easily worked, and Meares and Oates have their appointed assistants to help them in custody of dogs and ponies, but on such a night as the last with the prospect of dirty weather, the 'after guard' of volunteers is awake and delightfully enthusiastic: some lend a hand if there is difficulty with ponies and dogs, others in shortening or trimming sails, and others again in keeping the bunkers filled with the deck coal.

The choice of the ponies had been a muddle. Oates had been recruited as the horse expert, but Scott sent Meares, the dog expert, to Russia to buy the horses as well. Meares deputed a friend to buy the ponies at a fair, with the help of a Russian jockey, Anton Omelchenko, who later joined the party. On Shackleton's expedition, the dark ponies had died before the white ones, so Scott insisted on using only white ponies as superior in Antarctic conditions. When Oates saw them, he was horrified by their appearance– much later he said that they were 'without exception the greatest lot of crocks I've ever seen that were seriously meant for use'.

Scott had been keen on motor sledges since 1902 and had played a part in their design and testing, having secured financial support from Lord Howard de Walden. But they were half a century before their time, only finally proving their worth on Fuchs' and Hillary's polar expedition of 1958.

Nansen persuaded Scott to take dogs in addition to ponies and motor sledges. In Greenland, where the most suitable types came from, Amundsen bought 100 dogs. Meares bought just 33 from Siberia, and so got the worse bargain. Scott, however, wrote, 'Dogs finest ever got together.'

The Terra Nova *in heavy weather. (Undated, presumably late Dec 1910.) After this the ship ran into hurricane-force gales and Ponting had his work cut out to save his photographic gear from ruin. He had to bale day and night to keep it dry.*

Teddie Evans wrote of Oates' behaviour during the storm: 'He was a fine, powerful man and on occasion he seemed to be actually lifting the poor little ponies to their feet as the ship lurched.'

Friday, December 2. – A day of great disaster. From 4 o'clock last night the wind freshened with great rapidity, and very shortly we were under topsails, jib, and staysail only. It blew very hard and the sea got up at once. Soon we were plunging heavily and taking much water over the lee rail. Oates and Atkinson, with intermittent assistance from others, were busy keeping the ponies on their legs. Cases of petrol, forage, etc., began to break loose on the upper deck; the principal trouble was caused by the loose coal-bags, which were bodily lifted by the seas and swung against the lashed cases. 'You know how carefully everything had been lashed, but no lashings could have withstood the onslaught of these coal-sacks for long'; they acted like battering rams. 'There was nothing for it but to grapple with the evil, and nearly all hands were labouring for hours in the waist of the ship, heaving coal sacks overboard and re-lashing the petrol cases, etc., in the best manner possible under such difficult and dangerous circumstances. The seas were continually breaking over these people and now and again they would be completely submerged. At such times they had to cling for dear life to some fixture to prevent themselves being washed overboard.

'No sooner was some semblance of order restored than some exceptionally heavy wave would tear away the lashing and all the work had to be done again.'

The night wore on, the sea and wind ever rising, and the ship ever plunging more distractedly; we shortened sail to main topsail and staysail, stopped engines and hove to, but to little purpose. Tales of ponies down came frequently from forward, where

22

Oates and Atkinson laboured through the entire night. Worse was to follow, much worse – a report from the engine-room that the pumps had choked and the water risen over the gratings.

From this moment, about 4 a.m., the water gained in spite of every effort. Lashly, to his neck in rushing water, stuck gamely to the work of clearing suctions. For a time with donkey engine and bilge pump sucking, it looked as though the water would be got under; but the hope was short lived: five minutes of pumping invariably led to the same result – a general choking of the pumps.

The outlook appeared grim. The amount of water which was being made, with the ship so roughly handled, was most uncertain. 'We knew that normally the ship was not making much water, but we also knew that a considerable part of the water washing over the upper deck must be finding its way below; the decks were leaking in streams. The ship was very deeply laden; it did not need the addition of much water to get her waterlogged, in which condition anything might have happened.' The hand pump produced only a dribble, and its suction could not be got at; as the water crept higher it got in contact with the boiler and grew warmer – so hot at last that no one could work at the

At the pumps in a gale in the Antarctic Ocean. Early in Dec 1910, Lieut. Evans had wriggled over the coal to the pump shaft and succeeded in clearing it. Now it was working well each day.

Group in wardroom of Terra Nova *1910? These were the officers and the scientists, who messed separately from the 'men'. Scott is at the far end of the table, a little aloof as always.*

Specialists in the expedition.

Top left:
Lieut. H. E. de P. Rennick.

Top right:
Lieut. H. Pennell.

Lower left:
Bo'sun A. Cheetham.

Lower right:
Lieut. W. Bruce.

On Terra Nova *'At the hand pumps' Dec 2nd/ 3rd 1910. Ponting notes that twice daily, plus once in the night watches, some 16 of the company, ratings and officers, would have to man the pumps and, singing to a chanty, clear the bilges of water. 'There was nothing inspiring about this work,' he says, which, when the ship returned to New Zealand, was found to be due to a badly-fitting bolt in her timbers. The leak 'ate heavily into our precious coal reserves'.*

suctions. Williams had to confess he was beaten and must draw fires. What was to be done? Things for the moment appeared very black. The sea seemed higher than ever; it came over lee rail and poop, a rush of green water; the ship wallowed in it; a great piece of the bulwark carried clean away. The bilge pump is dependent on the main engine. To use the pump it was necessary to go ahead. It was at such times that the heaviest seas swept in over the lee rail; over and over [again] the rail, from the forerigging to the main, was covered by a solid sheet of water which swept aft and high on the poop. On one occasion I was waist deep when standing on the rail of the poop.

The scene on deck was devastating, and in the engine-room the water, though really not great in quantity, rushed over the floor plates and frames in a fashion that gave it a fearful significance.

The after guard were organised in two parties by Evans to work buckets; the men were kept steadily going on the choked hand-pumps–this seemed all that could be done for the moment; and what a measure to count as the sole safeguard of the ship from sinking, practically an attempt to bale her out! Yet strange as it may seem the effort has not been wholly fruitless–the string of buckets which has now been kept going for four hours, together with the dribble from the pump, has kept the water under–if anything there is a small decrease.

Meanwhile we have been thinking of a way to get at the suction of the pump: a hole

Bowers later commented: 'Captain Scott was simply splendid, he might have been at Cowes.' But Scott was given to moods of euphoria, alternated with inner worry and bouts of depression – the 'black thundercloud', as his wife Kathleen called them.

is being made in the engine-room bulkhead, the coal between this and the pump shaft will be removed, and a hole made in the shaft. With so much water coming on board, it is impossible to open the hatch over the shaft. We are not out of the wood, but hope dawns, as indeed it should for me, when I find myself so wonderfully served. Officers and men are singing chanties over their arduous work. Williams is working in sweltering heat behind the boiler to get the door made in the bulkhead. Not a single one has lost his good spirits. A dog was drowned last night, one pony is dead and two others in a bad condition – probably they too will go. 'Occasionally a heavy sea would bear one of them away, and he was only saved by his chain. Meares with some helpers had constantly to be rescuing these wretched creatures from hanging, and trying to find them better shelter, an almost hopeless task. One poor beast was found hanging when dead; one was washed away with such force that his chain broke and he disappeared overboard; the next wave miraculously washed him on board again, and he is now fit and well.' The gale has exacted heavy toll, but I feel all will be well if we can only cope with the water. Another dog has just been washed overboard. Thank God, the gale is abating. The sea is still mountainously high, but the ship is not labouring so heavily as she was. I pray we may be under sail again before morning.

[**From Dr Wilson's Journal. Dec. 2.** – It was a weird night's work with the howling gale and the darkness and the immense sea running over the ship every few minutes, and no engines and no sail, and we all in the engine-room black as ink, singing chanties as we passed slopping buckets full of bilge, each man above slopping a little over the heads of all of us below him; wet through to the skin, so much so that some of the

Detail of pack. Dec 11th 1910. This was two days after they had entered the ice, and were then a few hours short of three weeks among the floes, 'steadily working our way south for over 400 statute miles'. As he wrote the words, Ponting said he could almost feel the shocks that made the ship stagger 'as her iron shod prow forced aside the floes or split them silently asunder'.

26

party worked altogether naked like Chinese coolies; and the rush of the wave backwards and forwards at the bottom grew hourly less in the dim light of a couple of engine-room oil-lamps whose light just made the darkness visible – the ship all the time rolling like a sodden lifeless log, her lee gunwale under water every time.

. . . Just about the time when things looked their very worst – the sky was like ink and water was everywhere and everyone was as wet inside their oilskins as the skins were wet without – there came out a most perfect and brilliant rainbow for about half a minute or less and then suddenly and completely went out. If ever there was a moment when such a message was a comfort it was just then; it seemed to remove every shadow of doubt not only as to the present but as to the final issue of the whole expedition. And from that moment matters mended, and everything came all right.]

Cinematographing the pack-ice. With the help of two or three crew members Ponting rigged some planks on which he spread-eagled himself, hanging ten feet out over the side. Ponting hung on as the ship bumped into the ice, clinging to his precious cine camera with one hand while he turned the handle with the other – 'one of the most thrilling moving picture records of the Expedition'.

Saturday, December 3. – Yesterday the wind slowly fell towards evening; less water was taken on board, therefore less found its way below, and it soon became evident that our baling was gaining on the engine-room. The work was steadily kept going in two-hour shifts. By 10 p.m. the hole in the engine-room bulkhead was completed, and (Lieut.) Evans, wriggling over the coal, found his way to the pump shaft and down it. He soon cleared the suction 'of the coal balls (a mixture of coal and oil) which choked it', and to the joy of all a good stream of water came from the pump for the first time. From this moment it was evident we should get over the difficulty, and though the pump choked again on several occasions the water in the engine-room steadily decreased. It was good to visit that spot this morning and to find that the water no longer washed from side to side. In the forenoon fires were laid and lighted – the hand pump was got into complete order and sucked the bilges almost dry, so that great quantities of coal and ashes could be taken out.

Now all is well again, and we are steaming and sailing steadily south within two points of our course. Campbell and Bowers have been busy relisting everything on the upper deck. This afternoon we got out the two dead ponies through the forecastle skylight. It was a curious proceeding, as the space looked quite inadequate for their passage. We looked into the ice-house and found it in the best order.

Though we are not yet safe, as another gale might have disastrous results, it is wonderful to realise the change which has been wrought in our outlook in twenty-four hours. The others have confessed the gravely serious view of our position which they shared with me yesterday, and now we are all hopeful again.

As far as one can gather, besides the damage to the bulwarks of the ship, we have lost two ponies, one dog, '10 tons of coal', 65 gallons of petrol, and a case of the bio-

Furling the Terra Nova's *main-sail in the pack. Dec 10th 1910. Ponting recorded that the ship entered the Antarctic Circle, surrounded to the horizon by ice floes. From the crow's nest on the main top mast, the officer of the watch would shout directions to the helmsman on the poop below. He was looking for openings in the ice known as leads, invisible to those on deck. If none appeared the ship would try to make one by charging a mass of ice, sometimes an acre or more in size. Even though the hull of the* Terra Nova *was built to battle with the ice, the shock would make her tremble from stem to stern.*

logists' spirit – a serious loss enough, but much less than I expected. 'All things considered, we have come off lightly, but it was bad luck to strike a gale at such a time.' The third pony which was down in a sling for some time in the gale is again on his feet. He looks a little shaky, but may pull through if we don't have another gale. Osman, our best sledge dog, was very bad this morning, but has been lying warmly in hay all day, and is now much better. 'Several more were in a very bad way and needed nursing back to life.' The sea and wind seem to be increasing again, and there is a heavy southerly swell, but the glass is high; we ought not to have another gale till it falls.

I would record here a symptom of the spirit which actuates the men. After the gale the main deck under the forecastle space in which the ponies are stabled leaked badly, and the dirt of the stable leaked through on hammocks and bedding. Not a word has been said; the men living in that part have done their best to fend off the nuisance with oilskins and canvas, but without sign of complaint. Indeed the discomfort throughout the mess deck has been extreme. Everything has been thrown about, water has found its way down in a dozen places. There is no daylight, and air can come only through the small forehatch; the artificial lamplight has given much trouble. The men have been wetted to the skin repeatedly on deck, and have no chance of drying their clothing. All things considered, their cheerful fortitude is little short of wonderful.

In the Pack – 1910/11

Tuesday, December 13. – I was up most of the night. Never have I experienced such rapid and complete changes of prospect. Cheetham in the last dog watch was running the ship through sludgy new ice, making with all sail set four or five knots. Bruce, in the first, took over as we got into heavy ice again; but after a severe tussle got through into better conditions. The ice of yesterday loose with sludgy thin floes between. The middle watch found us making for an open lead, the ice around hard and heavy. We got through and by sticking to the open water and then to some recently frozen pools made good progress. At the end of the middle watch trouble began again, and during this and the first part of the morning we were wrestling with the worst conditions we have met. Heavy hummocked bay ice, the floes standing 7 or 8 feet out of water, and very deep below. It was just such ice as we encountered at King Edward's Land in the *Discovery*. I have never seen anything more formidable. The last part of the morning watch was spent in a long recently-frozen lead or pool, and the ship went well ahead again.

These changes sound tame enough, but they are a great strain on one's nerves – one is for ever wondering whether one has done right in trying to come down so far east, and having regard to coal, what ought to be done under the circumstances.

In the first watch came many alterations of opinion; time and again it looks as though we ought to stop when it seemed futile to be pushing and pushing without result; then would come a stretch of easy going and the impression that all was going very well with us. The fact of the matter is, it is difficult not to imagine the conditions in which one finds oneself to be more extensive than they are. It is wearing to have to face new conditions every hour. This morning we met at breakfast in great spirits; the ship has been boring along well for two hours; then Cheetham suddenly ran her into a belt of the worst and we were held up immediately. We can push back again, I think, but meanwhile we have taken advantage of the conditions to water ship. These big floes are very handy for that purpose at any rate.

We have decided to put fires out and remain here till the conditions change altogether for the better. It is sheer waste of coal to make further attempts to break through as things are at present.

Alfred Cheetham was the Bosun, a professional sailor who had been on Scott's earlier expedition, and was later to go south with Shackleton as Third Officer. He was once described as 'a pirate to his fingertips'.

Anchored to the ice. Dec 11th 1910. The day before the ship had entered the Antarctic Circle. She was now surrounded by ice floes to the horizon, and anchored by a thick cable.

The Terra Nova *held up in the Pack. Dec 13th 1910. Ponting remarked laconically that economy in coal had not proved to be a virtue of the ship's engine, so the fires were put out until she could escape from the ice. They were three days trapped in the pack and only recovered their leeway five days later. 'Time was of vital importance,' said Ponting. The depôts of supplies must be laid before winter set in, and it was exasperating to be drifting north instead of south.*

We have been set to the east during the past days; is it the normal set in the region, or due to the prevalence of westerly winds? Possibly much depends on this as concerns our date of release. It is annoying, but one must contain one's soul in patience and hope for a brighter outlook in a day or two. Meanwhile we shall sound, and do as much biological work as is possible.

Wednesday, December 14. – One realises the awful monotony of a long stay in the pack, such as Nansen and others experienced. One can imagine such days as these lengthening into interminable months and years. For us there is novelty, and every one has work to do or makes work, so that there is no keen sense of impatience.

The current is satisfactory. Both days the observations have been good – it is best that we should go north and west. I had a great fear that we should be drifted east and so away to regions of permanent pack. If we go on in this direction it can only be a question of time before we are freed.

We have all been away on ski on the large floe to which we anchored this morning. Gran is wonderfully good and gives instruction well. It was hot, and garments came off one by one – the Soldier and Atkinson were stripped to the waist eventually, and have been sliding round the floe for some time in that condition. Nearly everyone has been wearing goggles; the glare is very bad. Ponting tried to get a colour picture, but unfortunately the ice colours are too delicate for this.

The Norwegian Tryggve Gran, a great Shackleton fan, wanted to form his own expedition. However, he met Scott, then visiting Nansen, who persuaded Scott to adopt skis and two sticks, and to take Gran on the party as ski instructor. Fate thus dictated that Tryggve should find himself racing unsuccessfully against his fellow-countryman Amundsen. At the beginning of 1911 Gran opened his 'ski school' with enthusiastic support from officers and scientists; most seamen declined to join.

Telephoto. Berg in Pack. Gran and McLeod in ice. Dec 20th 1910. Gran was teaching McLeod to ski while they were trapped in the ice. This was probably the berg that Ponting described as 'immense' and 'remarkably picturesque' because it was 'midway on its journey to decay'. As the area under the water decays, the berg slowly tips and turns over.

Tonight Campbell, E. Evans, and I went out over the floe, and each in turn towed the other two; it was fairly easy work – that is, to pull 310 to 320 lb. One could pull it perhaps more easily on foot, yet it would be impossible to pull such a load on a sledge. What a puzzle this pulling of loads is! If one could think that this captivity was soon to end there would be little reason to regret it; it is giving practice with our deep-sea gear, and has made every one keen to learn the proper use of ski.

Wednesday, December 21. – Wilson went over the floe to capture some penguins and lay flat on the surface. We saw the birds run up to him, then turn within a few feet and rush away again. He says that they came towards him when he was singing, and ran away again when he stopped. They were all one-year birds, and seemed exceptionally shy; they appear to be attracted to the ship by a fearful curiosity.

[**From Dr Wilson's Journal.** Now and again one hears a Penguin cry out in the stillness near at hand or far away, and then perhaps he appears in his dress tail coat and white waistcoat suddenly upon an ice-floe from the water, and catching sight of the ship runs curiously towards her, crying out in his amazement as he comes, from time to time, but only intensifying the wonderful stillness and beauty of the whole fairy-like scene as the glaring sun in the South just touches the horizon and begins again to rise gradually without ever having set at all. We have now broad daylight night and day, but the beauty of the day with its lovely blues and greens amongst the bergs and ice-floes is eclipsed altogether by the marvellous beauty of the midnight when white ice becomes deepest purple and golden rose and the sky is lemon green without a cloud. No scene in the whole world was ever more beautiful than a clear midnight in the pack.

. . . (The penguins) have lost none of their attractiveness, and are most comical and interesting; as curious as ever, they will always come up at a trot when we sing to them, and you may often see a group of explorers on the poop singing 'For she's got bells on her fingers and rings on her toes, elephants to ride upon wherever she goes', and so on at the top of their voices to an admiring group of Adélie penguins. Meares is the greatest attraction; he has a full voice which is musical but always very flat. He declares that 'God save the King' will always send them to the water, and certainly it is often successful.]

No doubt Scott is using hyperbole. There were occasional tensions, as for example with Teddie Evans after Scott took over command of the ship. But generally the established naval hierarchy worked well, and many close friendships were formed.

Friday, December 23. – Very little can happen in the personal affairs of our company in this comparatively dull time, but it is good to see the steady progress that proceeds unconsciously in cementing the happy relationship that exists between the members of the party. Never could there have been a greater freedom from quarrels and trouble of all sorts. I have not heard a harsh word or seen a black look. A spirit of tolerance and good humour pervades the whole community, and it is glorious to realise that men can live under conditions of hardship, monotony, and danger in such bountiful good comradeship.

Preparations are now being made for Christmas festivities. It is curious to think that we have already passed the longest day in the southern year.

Saw a whale this morning – estimated 25 to 30 feet. Wilson thinks a new species. Find Adélie penguins in batches of twenty or so. Do not remember having seen so many together in the pack.

Sunday, December 25, Christmas Day. – The night before last I had bright hopes that this Christmas Day would see us in open water. The scene is altogether too Christmassy. Ice surrounds us, low nimbus clouds intermittently discharging light snow flakes obscure the sky, here and there small pools of open water throw shafts of black shadow on to the cloud – this black predominates in the direction from whence we have come, elsewhere the white haze of ice reflection is pervading.

We are captured. We do practically nothing under sail to push through, and could do little under steam; and the possibility of advance seems to lessen.

The wind, which has persisted from the west for so long, fell light last night, and today comes from the N.E. by N., a steady breeze from 2 to 3 in force. Since one must have hope, ours is pinned to the possible effect of a continuance of easterly wind. Again the call is for patience and again patience. Here at least we seem to enjoy full security. The ice is so thin that it could not hurt by pressure – there are no bergs within reasonable distance – indeed the thinness of the ice is one of the most tantalising conditions. In spite of the unpropitious prospect every one on board is cheerful and one foresees a merry dinner tonight.

The mess is gaily decorated with our various banners. There was full attendance at the Service this morning and a lusty singing of hymns.

Midnight. – A merry evening has just concluded. We had an excellent dinner: tomato soup, penguin breast stewed as an entrée, roast beef, plum pudding and mince pies,

Evening in the pack. Xmas Eve. Dec 24th 1910. Ponting secured several romantic pictures of 'evening in the pack', this one particularly moving as it was taken on Christmas Eve. They had spent 14 days in constant summer daylight 24 hours a day, but the sky had often been overcast. Now 'a shaft of sunlight falling on the uneven surfaces instantly transformed desolation into entrancing beauty', wrote Ponting.

asparagus, champagne, port and liqueurs – a festive menu. Dinner began at 6 and ended at 7. For five hours the company has been sitting round the table singing lustily; we haven't much talent, but every one has contributed more or less, 'and the choruses are deafening. It is rather a surprising circumstance that such an unmusical party should be so keen on singing. On Xmas night it was kept up till 1 a.m., and no work is done without a chanty. I don't know if you have ever heard sea chanties being sung. The merchant sailors have quite a collection of them, and invariably call on it when getting up anchor or hoisting sails. Often as not they are sung in a flat and throaty style, but the effect when a number of men break into the chorus is generally inspiriting.'

Tonight I noticed a skua gull settle on an upturned block of ice at the edge of a floe on which several penguins were preparing for rest. It is a fact that the latter held a noisy confabulation with the skua as subject – then they advanced as a body towards it; within a few paces the foremost penguin halted and turned, and then the others pushed him on towards the skua. One after another they jibbed at being first to approach their enemy, and it was only with much chattering and mutual support that they gradually edged towards him.

They couldn't reach him as he was perched on a block, but when they got quite close the skua, who up to that time had appeared quite unconcerned, flapped away a few yards and settled close on the other side of the group of penguins. The latter turned and repeated their former tactics until the skua finally flapped away altogether. It really was extraordinarily interesting to watch the timorous protesting movements of the pen-

Another example of Scott's scientific interests. Underwater life of all kinds was daily monitored by Edward Nelson, the biologist, working in his 'hole' with his instruments.

Some of the Terra Nova *crew on the Fo'c's'le. Dec 28th 1910. These photographs are not captioned with names, but by 'the crew' Ponting probably meant the 'men' as distinct from the officers and scientists.*

34

A lead opening in the Pack. Dec 28th 1910. As the ship passed out of the ice, Ponting wrote that 'the good old ship had become to me an object of affection, an almost human thing—a symbol of all that is steadfast, sound and true'. Scott felt the same.

guins. The frame of mind producing every action could be so easily imagined and put into human sentiments.

On the other side of the ship part of another group of penguins were quarrelling for the possession of a small pressure block which offered only the most insecure foothold. The scrambling antics to secure the point of vantage, the ousting of the bird in possession, and the incontinent loss of balance and position as each bird reached the summit of his ambition was almost as entertaining as the episode of the skua. Truly these little creatures afford much amusement.

Wednesday, December 28, 1910. – This morning a number of penguins were diving for food around and under the ship. It is the first time they have come so close to the ship in the pack, and there can be little doubt that the absence of motion of the propeller has made them bold. The Adélie penguin on land or ice is almost wholly ludicrous. Whether sleeping, quarrelling, or playing, whether curious, frightened, or angry, its interest is continuously humorous; but in the water it is another thing: as it darts to and fro a fathom or two below the surface, as it leaps porpoise-like into the air or swims skimmingly over the rippling surface of a pool, it excites nothing but admiration. Its speed probably appears greater than it is, but the ability to twist and turn and the general control of movement is both beautiful and wonderful.

As one looks across the barren stretches of the pack, it is sometimes difficult to realise what teeming life exists immediately beneath its surface.

Working the pram through pack to get at penguins for food supply. Dec 1910.

A tow-net is filled with diatoms in a very short space of time, showing that the floating plant life is many times richer than that of temperate or tropic seas. These diatoms mostly consist of three or four well-known species. Feeding on these diatoms are countless thousands of small shrimps; they can be seen swimming at the edge of every floe and washing about on the overturned pieces. In turn they afford food for creatures great and small: the crab-eater or white seal, the penguins, the Antarctic and snowy petrel, and an unknown number of fish.

These fish must be plentiful, as shown by our capture of one on an overturned floe and the report of several seen two days ago by some men leaning over the counter of the ship. These all exclaimed together, and on inquiry all agreed that they had seen half a dozen or more a foot or so in length swimming away under a floe. Seals and penguins capture these fish, as also, doubtless, the skuas and the petrels.

Coming to the larger mammals, one occasionally sees the long lithe sea-leopard, formidably armed with ferocious teeth and doubtless containing a penguin or two and perhaps a young crab-eating seal. The killer whale, unappeasably voracious, devouring or attempting to devour every smaller animal, is less common in the pack but numerous on the coasts. Finally, we have the great browsing whales of various species, from the vast blue whale, the largest mammal of all time, to the smaller and less common bottle-nose and such species as have not yet been named. Great numbers of these huge animals are seen, and one realises what a demand they must make on their food supply and therefore how immense a supply of small sea beasts these seas must contain. Beneath the placid ice floes and under the calm water pools the old universal warfare is raging incessantly in the struggle for existence.

Friday, December 30. – We are out of the pack at length and at last; one breathes again and hopes that it will be possible to carry out the main part of our programme, but the coal will need tender nursing.

At six this morning we were well in the open sea, the sky thick and overcast with occasional patches of fog. We passed one small berg on the starboard hand with a group of antarctic petrels on one side and a group of snow petrels on the other. It is

Scott had finally admitted to himself the disadvantages of a coal-fired engine. Amundsen made much better time with his revolutionary diesel-powered vessel, only the third ever fitted to an ocean-going ship.

evident that these birds rely on sea and swell to cast their food up on ice ledges – only a few find sustenance in the pack where, though food is plentiful, it is not so easily come by. A flight of Antarctic petrel accompanied the ship for some distance, wheeling to and fro about her.

'We hold the record for reaching the northern edge of the pack, whereas three or four times the open Ross Sea has been gained at an earlier date.

'I can imagine few things more trying to the patience than the long wasted days of waiting. Exasperating as it is to see the tons of coal melting away with the smallest mileage to our credit, one has at least the satisfaction of active fighting and the hope of better fortune. To wait idly is the worst of conditions. You can imagine how often and how restlessly we climbed to the crow's nest and studied the outlook. And strangely enough there was generally some change to note. A water lead would mysteriously open up a few miles away or the place where it had been would as mysteriously close. Huge icebergs crept silently towards or past us, and continually we were observing these formidable objects with range-finder and compass to determine the relative movement, sometimes with misgiving as to our ability to clear them. Under steam the change of conditions was even more marked. Sometimes we would enter a lead of open water and proceed for a mile or two without hindrance; sometimes we would come to big sheets of thin ice which broke easily as our iron-shod prow struck them, and sometimes even a thin sheet would resist all our attempts to break it; sometimes we would push big floes with comparative ease and sometimes a small floe would bar our passage with such obstinacy that one would almost believe it possessed of an evil spirit; sometimes we passed through acres of sludgy sodden ice which hissed as it swept along the side, and sometimes the hissing ceased seemingly without rhyme or reason, and we found our screw churning the sea without any effect.

'Thus the steaming days passed away in an ever-changing environment and are remembered as an unceasing struggle.

'The ship behaved splendidly – no other ship, not even the *Discovery*, would have come through so well. Certainly the *Nimrod* would never have reached the south water had she been caught in such pack. As a result I have grown strangely attached to the *Terra Nova*. As she bumped the floes with mighty shocks, crushing and grinding a way through some, twisting and turning to avoid others, she seemed a living thing fighting a great fight. If only she had more economical engines she would be suitable in all respects.

'Once or twice we got among floes which stood 7 or 8 feet above water, with hummocks and pinnacles as high as 25 feet. The ship could have stood no chance had such floes pressed against her, and at first we were a little alarmed in such situations. But familiarity breeds contempt; there never was any pressure in the heavy ice, and I'm inclined to think there never would be.

'The weather changed frequently during our journey through the pack. The wind blew strong from the west and from the east; the sky was often darkly overcast; we had

Mt Terror at 6.30pm. Jan 3rd 1911. The Terra Nova *was heading north-west for the northern point of Ross Island. Mt Terror 'rose, an icy cone of lava, many thousands of feet above the glaciers with which the lower slopes were covered.'*

snowstorms, flaky snow, and even light rain. In all such circumstances we were better placed in the pack than outside of it. The foulest weather could do us little harm. During quite a large percentage of days, however, we had bright sunshine, which, even with the temperature well below freezing, made everything look bright and cheerful. The sun also brought us wonderful cloud effects, marvellously delicate tints of sky, cloud, and ice, such effects as one might travel far to see. In spite of our impatience we would not willingly have missed many of the beautiful scenes which our sojourn in the pack afforded us.

'Scientifically we have been able to do something. We have managed to get a line of soundings on our route showing the raising of the bottom from the ocean depths to the shallow water on the continental shelf, and the nature of the bottom. With these soundings we have obtained many interesting observations of the temperature of different layers of water in the sea.

'Then we have added a great deal to the knowledge of life in the pack from observation of the whales, seals, penguins, birds, and fishes as well as of the pelagic beasts which are caught in tow-nets. Life in one form or another is very plentiful in the pack, and the struggle for existence here as elsewhere is a fascinating subject for study.

'We have made a systematic study of the ice also, both the bergs and sea ice, and have got a good deal of useful information concerning it. Also Pennell has done a little magnetic work.

'But of course this slight list of activity in the cause of science is a very poor showing for the time of our numerous experts; many have had to be idle in regard to their own specialities, though none is idle otherwise. All the scientific people keep night watch when they have no special work to do, and I have never seen a party of men so anxious to be doing work or so cheerful in doing it. When there is anything to be done, such as making or shortening sail, digging ice from floes for the water supply, or heaving up the sounding line, it goes without saying that all the afterguard turn out to do it. There is no hesitation and no distinction. It will be the same when it comes to landing stores or doing any other hard manual labour.

'The spirit of the enterprise is as bright as ever. Every one strives to help every one else, and not a word of complaint or anger has been heard on board. The inner life of our small community is very pleasant to think upon and very wonderful considering the extremely small space in which we are confined.

'The attitude of the men is equally worthy of admiration. In the forecastle as in the wardroom there is a rush to be first when work is to be done, and the same desire to sacrifice selfish consideration to the success of the expedition. It is very good to be able to write in such high praise of one's companions, and I feel that the possession of such support ought to ensure success. Fortune would be in a hard mood indeed if it allowed such a combination of knowledge, experience, ability, and enthusiasm to achieve nothing.'

[**From Dr Wilson's Journal. Off Cape Crozier. Tuesday, January 3.** . . . Here we brought the ship close in and then we lowered a boat in which were Capt. Scott, Campbell, myself, Cherry-Garrard, Titus Oates and Taylor. We were to examine the possibilities of landing, but the swell was so heavy in its break amongst the floating blocks of ice along the actual beach and ice-foot that a landing was out of the question. We should have broken up the boat and have all been in the water together. But I assure you it was tantalising to me, for there, about 6 feet above us, on a small dirty piece of the old bay ice about 10 feet square, one living Emperor Penguin chick was standing disconsolately stranded, and close by it stood one faithful old Emperor Penguin parent asleep. This young Emperor was still in the down, a most interesting fact in the bird's life history, at which we had rightly guessed, but which no one had actually observed before. It was, however, in a stage never yet seen or collected, for the wings were already quite clean of down and feathered as in the adult; also a line down the breast and part of the head was shed of down. This bird would have been a trea-

Harry Pennell, Lieutenant, RN, was a member of the ship's party, specialising in navigation. Much has been made of Scott's separation of the 'men' from the officers and the scientists, but they were almost all Royal Navy in training, and this division of 'ranks' was what they expected and would have been uncomfortable without. Scott had taken care to choose men with a R.N. background. In addition there was a small nucleus of *Discovery* people – Wilson, Crean, Lashly, Edgar Evans and Williamson. There was also, says Huntford, a majority with no polar, or indeed cold-weather, experience. The scientists were mostly from Cambridge. Two men came as paying guests, Cherry-Garrard and Oates. By contrast, Amundsen describes his party as 'a little republic . . . [We] let everybody have the feeling of being independent within his own sphere.'

There were very few sightings of Emperor penguins, and this was a particular disappointment to Ponting, who had been assured by Scott that he would get plenty of footage of wildlife here.

Several pages about the actual landing are deleted here, but Preston summarises as follows: 'The *Terra Nova* now made for the familiar territory of McMurdo Sound and a landing place was found on the northern side of a tongue of land ... It lay some 15 miles north of the *Discovery*'s old winter quarters at Hut Point and was separated from it by two deep bays which, when frozen, could be marched over in a day. The bays themselves were divided by a jutting spur of ice, Glacier Tongue. With characteristic generosity, Scott named their new home Cape Evans in honour of his number two. Amundsen had landed on Ross Island Barrier, which no one had done before for fear of floating out to sea on an iceberg when it broke off from the ice shelf. He chose the Bay of Whales as his base, as he was convinced from his reading that it had remained basically unchanged for 70 years and it was 60 miles nearer the Pole than McMurdo Sound. He proposed to follow the shortest path, having deduced that this would be a "ski race writ large"'.

sure to me, but we couldn't risk life for it, so it had to remain there with its faithful parent asleep. It was a curious fact that with as much clean ice to live on as they could have wished for, these destitute derelicts of a flourishing colony now gone North on floating bay-ice should have preferred to remain standing on the only piece of bay-ice left – a piece about 10 feet square and now pressed up 6 feet above water-level; evidently wondering why it was so long in starting North with the general exodus which must have taken place just a month ago. The whole incident was most interesting and full of suggestion as to the slow working of the brains of these queer people. Another point was most weird to see, namely, that on the *under* surface of this very dirty piece of sea-ice which was about 2 feet thick, and which hung over the water as a sort of cave, we could see the legs and lower halves of dead Emperor chicks hanging through, and in one place even a dead adult. I hope to make a picture of the whole quaint incident, for it was a corner cram full of Imperial history in the light of what we already knew, and it would otherwise have been about as unintelligible as any group of animate and inanimate nature could possibly have been. As it is, it throws more light on the life history of this strangely primitive bird.

Jan 4. . . . These days are with one for all time – they are never to be forgotten – and they are to be found nowhere else in the world but at the poles. The peace of God which passes all understanding reigns here in these days. One only wishes one could bring a glimpse of it away with one with all its unimaginable beauty. . . .]

Disembarking the ponies. Jan 4th 1911. 'The dogs, too, were in high spirits', recorded Ponting. Once on shore tethered to a rope extending from the ship's bow, they were attacked by a company of penguins. Alas, the latter were 'mercilessly slaughtered'.

Land—1911

Wednesday, January 4, 1 a.m.—A group of killer whales was idly diving off the penguin rookery; an old one with a very high straight dorsal fin and several youngsters. We watched a small party of penguins leaping through the water towards their enemies. It seemed impossible that they should have failed to see the sinister fins during their frequent jumps into the air, yet they seemed to take no notice whatever—stranger still, the penguins must have actually crossed the whales, yet there was no commotion whatever, and presently the small birds could be seen leaping away on the other side. One can only suppose the whales are satiated.

Wednesday, January 4, p.m.—This work is full of surprises. After many frowns fortune has treated us to the kindest smile—for twenty-four hours we have had a calm with brilliant sunshine. Such weather in such a place comes nearer to satisfying my ideal of perfection than any condition that I have ever experienced. The warm glow of the sun with the keen invigorating cold of the air forms a combination which is inexpressibly health-giving and satisfying to me, whilst the golden light on this wonderful scene of mountain and ice satisfies every claim of scenic magnificence. No words of mine can

End of The Barrier. Jan 3rd 1911. This is at Cape Crozier, which Scott thought the most desirable part of the Great Ice Barrier on which to establish winter quarters. But no landing place could be found and worse, from Ponting's point of view, there was no time to stop and take photographs of this area where there was the largest Adélie penguin rookery and the breeding ground of the Emperor penguins.

Scott was now taking a much closer interest in Ponting's photographic work, including some instruction in composition.

convey the impressiveness of the wonderful panorama displayed to our eyes. Ponting is enraptured and uses expressions which in any one else and alluding to any other subject might be deemed extravagant.

The Landing: A Week's Work

Whilst we were on shore Campbell was taking the first steps towards landing our stores. Two of the motor sledges were soon hoisted out, and Day with others was quickly unpacking thcm. Our luck stood again. In spite of all the bad weather and the tons of sea water which had washed over them the sledges and all the accessories appeared as fresh and clean as if they had been packed on the previous day – much credit is due to the officers who protected them with tarpaulins and lashings. After the sledges came the turn of the ponies – there was a good deal of difficulty in getting some of them into the horse box, but Oates rose to the occasion and got most in by persuasion, whilst others were simply lifted in by the sailors. Though all are thin and some few looked pulled down, I was agreeably surprised at the evident vitality which they still possessed – some were even skittish. I cannot express the relief when the whole seventeen were safely picketed on the floe. From the moment of getting on the snow they seemed to take a new lease of life, and I haven't a doubt they will pick up very rapidly. It really is a triumph to have got them through safely and as well as they are. Poor brutes, how they must have enjoyed their first roll, and how glad they must be to have

This display of anthropomorphic feeling was typical of Scott, who according to Oates was ignorant about animals. By ascribing to them human emotions, he failed to make proper use of their true qualities.

Getting the ill-fated motor-sledge off the ship. Jan 8th 1911. This was the last of the three 'caterpillar' tractors, and when it was hauled away from the ship, the ice sank under its weight, and the machine disappeared. Frantic efforts were made to save it, and Petty Officer Williamson was dragged into the water up to his armpits. Ponting commented that while considered a grave calamity at the time, later some deemed it a stroke of luck and others went so far as to wish the remaining two had sunk as well.

freedom to scratch themselves! It is evident all have suffered from skin irritation – one can imagine the horror of suffering from such an ill for weeks without being able to get at the part that itched. I note that now they are picketed together they administer kindly offices to each other; one sees them gnawing away at each other's flanks in most amicable and obliging manner.

Meares and the dogs were out early, and have been running to and fro most of the day with light loads. The great trouble with them has been due to the fatuous conduct of the penguins. Groups of these have been constantly leaping on to our floe. From the moment of landing on their feet their whole attitude expressed devouring curiosity and a pig-headed disregard for their own safety. They waddle forward, poking their heads to and fro in their usually absurd way, in spite of a string of howling dogs straining to get at them. 'Hulloa!' they seem to say, 'here's a game – what do all you ridiculous things want?' And they come a few steps nearer. The dogs make a rush as far as their leashes or harness allow. The penguins are not daunted in the least, but their ruffs go up and they squawk with semblance of anger, for all the world as though they were rebuking a rude stranger – their attitude might be imagined to convey 'Oh, that's the sort of animal you are; well, you've come to the wrong place – we aren't going to be bluffed and bounced by you', and then the final fatal steps forward are taken and they come within reach. There is a spring, a squawk, a horrid red patch on the snow, and the incident is closed. Nothing can stop these silly birds. Members of our party rush to head them off, only to be met with evasions – the penguins squawk and duck as much as to say, 'What's it got to do with you, you silly ass? Let us alone.'

With the first spilling of blood the skua gulls assemble and soon, for them at least, there is a gruesome satisfaction to be reaped. Oddly enough, they don't seem to excite the dogs; they simply alight within a few feet and wait for their turn in the drama, clamouring and quarrelling amongst themselves when the spoils accrue. Such incidents were happening constantly today, and seriously demoralising the dog teams. Meares was exasperated again and again.

The motor sledges were running by the afternoon, Day managing one and Nelson the other. In spite of a few minor breakdowns they hauled good loads to the shore. It is early to call them a success, but they are certainly extremely promising.

The next thing to be got out of the ship was the hut, and the large quantity of timber comprising it was got out this afternoon.

And so tonight, with the sun still shining, we look on a very different prospect from that of 48 or even 24 hours ago.

Skua gulls, male and female. Jan 6th 1911. 'There is nothing refined about skua gulls,' observed Ponting, 'both are scamps and malefactors.' Full-grown birds are about four feet from tip to tip and there is little apparent difference between cock and hen. Their plumage is a symphony in browns, and they are remarkably handsome on the wing.

Scott had originally planned that motor sledges and ponies would be his methods of transport. Both failed. By contrast, Amundsen had chosen skis and dogs. Both were a success. When Scott is condemned for his prejudice against dogs and skis, it must be remembered that Sir Clements Markham, President of the Royal Geographical Society until 1905, had always held the same prejudice throughout the many years of their close association. It would have been politically unwise for Scott to have taken a view contrary to that of his sponsor.

Scott told Ponting that a panoramic view with his 'telephotographic' camera of the range of mountains that spread for 50 miles in Victoria Land, as seen from Ross Island across the frozen sea, would be 'of lasting value to geography'. However, the quivering air made this impossible, though one morning in autumn he was able to capture 'the Queen of the range, the Lister, some 70 miles away and 13,000 feet high'. Early in January, he succeeded in finding the right conditions and exposing a double series of 7 x 5 plates photographing the range from end to end, which he developed into '12 beautiful negatives of one of the longest-distance panoramic telephotographs ever secured'.

I have just come back from the shore.

The site for the hut is levelled and the erecting party is living on shore in our large green tent with a supply of food for eight days. Nearly all the timber, etc., of the hut is on shore, the remainder halfway there. The ponies are picketed in a line on a convenient snow slope so that they cannot eat sand. Oates and Anton are sleeping ashore to watch over them. The dogs are tied to a long length of chain stretched on the sand; they are coiled up after a long day, looking fitter already. Meares and Dimitri are sleeping in the green tent to look after them. A supply of food for ponies and dogs as well as for the men has been landed. Two motor sledges in good working order are safely on the beach.

A fine record for our first day's work. All hands start again at 6 a.m. tomorrow.

It's splendid to see at last the effect of all the months of preparation and organisation. There is much snoring about me as I write (2 p.m.) from men tired after a hard

Erebus with Adélie penguins on ice in foreground and open water. Jan 5th 1911. Steaming along from Mt Terror, past Mt Terra Nova, the towering mass of Mt Erebus came into sight, and Ponting secured his first picture of it at 11pm. Two hours later they rounded Cape Bird and then entered McMurdo Sound. 'All that night we steamed leisurely along, and at 5am we were passing through loose pack off Cape Royds, where Shackleton's 1907 Expedition had wintered', and whose little hut Ponting could see through his glass.

Attacked by killer whales. Thurs Jan 5th 1911. Ponting said that the painting here was 'drawn' from his and Scott's descriptions of the incident and from his own photographs of the surrounding landmarks. In addition the artist visited the Natural History Museum in London to study the whales there. Despite his newly-won 'wholesome respect' for the whales, Ponting was anxious for a photograph, but next day, as he leaned over the rail, the lens (his finest) dropped into the sea and no picture was obtained.

day's work and preparing for such another tomorrow. I also must sleep, for I have had none for 48 hours – but it should be to dream happily.

Thursday, January 5. – All hands were up at 5 this morning and at work at 6. Words cannot express the splendid way in which every one works and gradually the work gets organised. I was a little late this morning, and thereby witnessed a most extraordinary scene. Some 6 or 7 killer whales, old and young, were skirting the fast floe edge ahead of the ship; they seemed excited and dived rapidly, almost touching the floe. As we watched, they suddenly appeared astern, raising their snouts out of water. I had heard weird stories of these beasts, but had never associated serious danger with them. Close to the water's edge lay the wire stern rope of the ship, and our two Esquimaux dogs were tethered to this. I did not think of connecting the movements of the whales with this fact, and seeing them so close I shouted to Ponting, who was standing abreast of the ship. He seized his camera and ran towards the floe edge to get a close picture of the beasts, which had momentarily disappeared. The next moment the whole floe under him and the dogs heaved up and split into fragments. One could hear the 'booming' noise as the whales rose under the ice and struck it with their backs. Whale after whale rose under the ice, setting it rocking fiercely; luckily Ponting kept his feet and was able to fly to security. By an extraordinary chance also, the splits had been made around and between the dogs, so that neither of them fell into the water. Then it was clear that the whales shared our astonishment, for one after another their huge hideous heads shot vertically into the air through the cracks which they had made. As they

Penguins and an iceberg. Jan 7th 1911. Ponting referred to these Adélie penguins as 'the comedians of the Antarctic', dressed in swallowtail coats, with an excessive expanse of shirt front. They gazed in comical amazement at the crew through their white-ringed eyes.

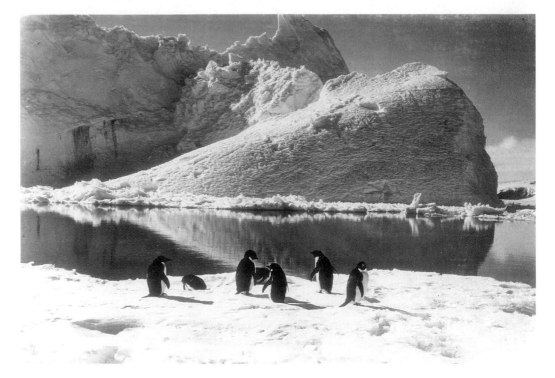

Opposite: Grotto in a berg. Taylor and Wright (interior) Jan 5th 1911. *As he went in, Ponting described it as 'the most wonderful place imaginable. From outside, the interior appeared quite white and colourless, but, once inside, it was a lovely symphony of blue and green.' By incredible luck, the entrance framed a fine view of the* Terra Nova, *a mile away.*

reared them to a height of 6 or 8 feet it was possible to see their tawny head markings, their small glistening eyes, and their terrible array of teeth – by far the largest and most terrifying in the world. There cannot be a doubt that they looked up to see what had happened to Ponting and the dogs.

The latter were horribly frightened and strained to their chains, whining; the head of one killer must certainly have been within 5 feet of one of the dogs.

After this, whether they thought the game insignificant, or whether they missed Ponting, is uncertain, but the terrifying creatures passed on to other hunting grounds, and we were able to rescue the dogs, and what was even more important, our petrol – 5 or 6 tons of which were waiting on a piece of ice which was not split away from the main mass.

Of course, we have known well that killer whales continually skirt the edge of the floes and that they would undoubtedly snap up any one who was unfortunate enough to fall into the water; but the facts that they could display such deliberate cunning, that they were able to break ice of such thickness (at least 2½ feet), and that they could act in unison, were a revelation to us. It is clear that they are endowed with singular intelligence, and in future we shall treat that intelligence with every respect.

Friday, January 6. – Today I walked over our peninsula to see what the southern side was like. Hundreds of skuas were nesting and attacked in the usual manner as I passed. They fly round shrieking wildly until they have gained some altitude. They then swoop

Capt. Oates and some of the ponies.

In the full diary, Scott made three significant admissions here: '(1) I fear the sledges will never draw the loads we expect of them; (2) It is surprising that we never thought of using ski sticks before; (3) Atkinson and Bruce have snow blindness so it's well for people to get experience of the necessity of safeguarding their eyes.'

That is, the two parties moved 7½ tons from ship to shore without the help of dogs or horses. The ponies' excitement was recorded on Ponting's movie film, which shows them rolling in the snow as they were disembarked. The loads included an ice-house full of mutton which they had brought all the way to the Antarctic, even though there were plentiful supplies of fresh seal meat to hand.

down with great impetus directly at one's head, lifting again when within a foot of it. The bolder ones actually beat on one's head with their wings as they pass. At first it is alarming, but experience shows that they never strike except with their wings. A skua is nesting on a rock between the ponies and the dogs. People pass every few minutes within a pace or two, yet the old bird has not deserted its chick. In fact, it seems gradually to be getting confidence, for it no longer attempts to swoop at the intruder. Today Ponting went within a few feet, and by dint of patience managed to get some wonderful cinematograph pictures of its movements in feeding and tending its chick, as well as some photographs of these events at critical times.

Saturday, January 7. – We have done splendidly. Tonight all the provisions except some in bottles are ashore and nearly all the working paraphernalia of the scientific people – no light item. There remains some hut furniture, 2½ tons of carbide, some bottled stuff, and some odds and ends which should occupy only part of tomorrow; then we come to the two last and heaviest items – coal and horse fodder.

If we are not through in the week we shall be very near it. Meanwhile the ship is able to lie at the ice edge without steam; a splendid saving.

There has been a steady stream of cases passing along the shore route all day and transport arrangements are hourly improving.

Two parties of four and three officers made ten journeys each, covering over 25 miles and dragging loads one way which averaged 250 to 300 lbs per man.

The ponies are working well now, but beginning to give some excitement. On the whole they are fairly quiet beasts, but they get restive with their loads, mainly but indirectly owing to the smoothness of the ice. They know perfectly well that the swingle trees and traces are hanging about their hocks and hate it. (I imagine it gives them the nervous feeling that they are going to be carried off their feet.) This makes it hard to start them, and when going they seem to appreciate the fact that the sledges will over-run them should they hesitate or stop. The result is that they are constantly fretful and the more nervous ones tend to become refractory and unmanageable.

Oates is splendid with them – I do not know what we should do without him.

I did seven journeys with ponies and got off with a bump on the head and some scratches.

One pony got away from Debenham close to the ship, and galloped the whole way in with its load behind; the load capsized just off the shore and the animal and sledge dashed into the station. Oates very wisely took this pony straight back for another load.

Two or three ponies got away as they were being harnessed, and careered up the hill again. In fact, there were quite a lot of minor incidents which seemed to endanger life and limb to the animals if not the men, but which all ended safely.

Broken ice, reflections and Terra Nova. Jan 7th 1911. Ponting had been using his camera now for 24 hours, so he took a nap, waking to 'a strange silence'. On deck he found 'the ship was made fast to a great sheet of ice which extended to the shore, 1¹/₂m away'.

View of the deck of Terra Nova *with dogs, taken from the engine room hatch. Jan 3rd 1911. In the gales of early December two dogs had been lost, and one strangled by his chain. However, the natural canine hierarchy reasserted itself once the dogs were on shore. Osman, for example, swept overboard by a wave, survived to become leader of the pack.*

One of Meares' dog teams ran away—one poor dog got turned over at the start and couldn't get up again (Mukàka). He was dragged at a gallop for nearly half a mile; I gave him up as dead, but apparently he was very little hurt.

The ponies are certainly going to keep things lively as time goes on and they get fresher. Even as it is, their condition can't be half as bad as we imagined; the runaway pony wasn't much done even after the extra trip.

The station is beginning to assume the appearance of an orderly camp. We continue to find advantages in the situation; the long level beach has enabled Bowers to arrange his stores in the most systematic manner. Everything will be handy and there will never be a doubt as to the position of a case when it is wanted. The hut is advancing apace—already the matchboarding is being put on. The framework is being clothed. It should be extraordinarily warm and comfortable, for in addition to this double coating of insulation, dry seaweed in quilted sacking, I propose to stack the pony fodder all around it.

I am wondering how we shall stable the ponies in the winter.

The only drawback to the present position is that the ice is getting thin and sludgy in the cracks and on some of the floes. The ponies drop their feet through, but most of them have evidently been accustomed to something of the sort; they make no fuss about it. Everything points to the desirability of the haste which we are making – so we go on tomorrow, Sunday.

A whole host of minor ills besides snow blindness have come upon us. Sore faces and lips, blistered feet, cuts and scratches; there are few without some troublesome ailment, but, of course, such things are 'part of the business'. The soles of my feet are terribly sore.

'Of course the elements are going to be troublesome, but it is good to know them as the only adversary and to feel there is so small a chance of internal friction.'

Ponting had an alarming adventure about this time. Bent on getting artistic photographs with striking objects, such as hummocked floes or reflecting water, in the foreground, he used to depart with his own small sledge laden with cameras and cinematograph to journey along to the grounded icebergs. One morning as he tramped along harnessed to his sledge, his snow glasses clouded with the mist of perspiration, he suddenly felt the ice giving under his feet. He describes the sensation as the worst he ever experienced, and one can well believe it; there was no one near to have lent assistance had he gone through. Instinctively he plunged forward, the ice giving at every step and the sledge dragging through water. Providentially the weak area he had struck was very limited, and in a minute or two he pulled out on a firm surface. He remarked that he was perspiring very freely!

Some critics of Scott have used remarks like this as evidence of his lack of forward planning. His next comment, about minor ills being 'part of the business', is in inverted commas, showing it is a quotation from one of his letters home and not from the journals.

Scott described Jan 8th as 'a day of disaster', when the third motor sledge went through the ice about 200 yards from the ship in an area of sludgy ice, about which Scott had been forewarned. The condition of the ice now worsened, virtually cutting Scott and his party off from the ship's crew on the *Terra Nova*. He found a new place to anchor and continued work on the hut. This was his first night ashore. After the 'disaster', Cherry-Garrard asked Bill Wilson what would happen if Scott did not reach the Pole, and recorded Wilson's answer in his diary: 'We shall probably stop here and have a 2nd go at it – with fewer ponies and dogs but more experience. As Bill said. "Two good failures and we could be forgiven for not succeeding." '

Lunch in the tent. Jan 7th 1911. 'The work of unloading the ship was going on merrily,' said Ponting, 'and there was a clearly defined trail on the ice from ship to shore.' He took his own gear on several lone trips, hauling hundreds of pounds of camera and darkroom equipment on a sledge. 'I fixed up a tent for my sleeping quarters, but so warm was the sun even at midnight that I spread my reindeer skin sleeping bag in the open air.'

Settling in–1911

*Getting camp in order.
Erebus (and Colman's). Jan
23rd 1911. Ponting was
inclined to take photographs
featuring the brand name of
suppliers, and Colman was
one of his favourites.*

Tuesday, January 10.–We have been six days in McMurdo Sound and tonight I can say we are landed. Were it impossible to land another pound we could go on without hitch. Nothing like it has been done before; nothing so expeditious and complete. This morning the main loads were fodder. Sledge after sledge brought the bales, and early in the afternoon the last (except for about a ton stowed with Eastern Party stores) was brought on shore. Some addition to our patent fuel was made in the morning, and later in the afternoon it came in a steady stream. We have more than 12 tons and could make this do if necessity arose.

In addition to this, oddments have been arriving all day–instruments, clothing, and

personal effects. Our camp is becoming so perfect in its appointments that I am almost suspicious of some drawback hidden by the summer weather.

The hut is progressing apace, and all agree that it should be the most perfectly comfortable habitation. 'It amply repays the time and attention given to the planning.' The sides have double boarding inside and outside the frames, with a layer of our excellent quilted seaweed insulation between each pair of boardings. The roof has a single matchboarding inside, but on the outside is a matchboarding, then a layer of 2-ply 'ruberoid', then a layer of quilted seaweed, then a second matchboarding, and finally a cover of 3-ply

Forde and Abbott, building hut. Jan 10th 1911. Both men were Petty Officers, R.N.

'ruberoid'. The first floor is laid, but over this there will be a quilting, a felt layer, a second boarding, and finally linoleum; as the plenteous volcanic sand can be piled well up on every side it is impossible to imagine that draughts can penetrate into the hut from beneath, and it is equally impossible to imagine great loss of heat by contact or radiation in that direction. To add to the wall insulation the south and east sides of the hut are piled high with compressed-forage bales, whilst the north side is being prepared as a winter stable for the ponies. The stable will stand between the wall of the hut and a wall built of forage bales, six bales high and two bales thick. This will be roofed with rafters and tarpaulin, as we cannot find enough boarding. We shall have to take care that too much snow does not collect on the roof, otherwise the place should do excellently well.

Some of the ponies are very troublesome, but all except two have been running today, and until this evening there were no excitements. After tea Oates suggested leading out the two intractable animals behind other sledges; at the same time he brought out the strong, nervous grey pony. I led one of the supposedly safe ponies, and all went well whilst we made our journey; three loads were safely brought in. But whilst one of the sledges was being unpacked the pony tied to it suddenly got scared. Away he dashed with sledge attached; he made straight for the other ponies, but finding the incubus still fast to him he went in wider circles, galloped over hills and boulders, narrowly missing Ponting and his camera, and finally dashed down hill to camp again pretty exhausted—oddly enough, neither sledge nor pony was much damaged. Then we departed again in the same order. Half-way over the floe my rear pony got his foreleg foul of his halter, then got frightened, tugged at his halter, and lifted the unladen sledge to which he was tied—then the halter broke and away he went. But by this time the

Oates wrote to his mother that 'nobody understands severe marching with ponies except myself and Meares . . . Scott and Evans boss the show pretty well and their ignorance about marching with animals is colossal.' Scott had commented that 'the ponies are going to be real good . . . they work with such extraordinary steadiness etc.' Oates had already decided that the dogs were better adapted than horses to polar conditions.

Heinz advertisement.

damage was done. My pony snorted wildly and sprang forward as the sledge banged to the ground. I just managed to hold him till Oates came up, then we started again; but he was thoroughly frightened – all my blandishments failed when he reared and plunged a second time, and I was obliged to let go. He galloped back and the party dejectedly returned. At the camp P.O. Evans got hold of the pony, but in a moment it was off again, knocking Evans off his legs. Finally he was captured and led forth once more between Oates and Anton. He remained fairly well on the outward journey, but on the homeward grew restive again; Evans, who was now leading him, called for Anton, and both tried to hold him, but to no purpose – he dashed off, upset his load, and came back to camp with the sledge. All these troubles arose after he had made three journeys without a hitch and we had come to regard him as a nice, placid, gritty pony. Now I'm afraid it will take a deal of trouble to get him safe again, and we have three very troublesome beasts instead of two. I have written this in some detail to show the unexpected difficulties that arise with these animals, and the impossibility of knowing exactly where one stands. The majority of our animals seem pretty quiet now, but any one of them may break out in this way if things go awry. There is no doubt that the bumping of the sledges close at the heels of the animals is the root of the evil.

The weather has the appearance of breaking. We had a strongish northerly breeze at midday with snow and hail storms, and now the wind has turned to the south and the sky is overcast with threatenings of a blizzard. The floe is cracking and pieces may go

Sledge party having Colman's corn flour. Feb 7th 1911.

out – if so the ship will have to get up steam again. The hail at noon made the surface very bad for some hours; the men and dogs felt it most.

The dogs are going well, but Meares says he thinks that several are suffering from snow blindness. I never knew a dog get it before, but Day says that Shackleton's dogs suffered from it.

Thursday, January 12. – Sledging began as usual this morning; seven ponies and the dog teams were hard at it all the forenoon. I ran six journeys with five dogs, driving them in the Siberian fashion for the first time. It was not difficult, but I kept forgetting the Russian words at critical moments: 'Ki' – 'right'; 'Tchuri' – 'left'; 'Itah' – 'right ahead'; [here is a blank in memory and in Diary] – 'getalong'; 'Paw' – 'stop.' Even my short experience makes me think that we may have to reorganise this driving. I am inclined for smaller teams and the driver behind the sledge. However, it's early days to decide such matters, and we shall learn much on the depôt journey.

Early in the afternoon a message came from the ship to say that all stores had been landed. Nothing remains to be brought but mutton, books and pictures, and the pianola. So at last we really are a self-contained party ready for all emergencies. We are LANDED eight days after our arrival – a very good record.

The hut could be inhabited at this moment, but probably we shall not begin to live in it for a week.

Sunday, January 15. – We had decided to observe this day as a 'day of rest', and so it has been.

At one time or another the majority have employed their spare hours in writing letters.

We rose late, having breakfast at nine. The morning promised well and the day fulfilled the promise: we had bright sunshine and practically no wind.

The day before there had been a blizzard since early morning, but as work on the hut was well ahead, some of the men, sometimes called the 'grotto party', dug 'a spacious apartment' to be the meat store. After lunch the wind dropped and Scott visited the ship; he was glad to see that the ice anchors had held well during the gale.

The ice foot looking to Cape Royds from the Terra Nova, *c. 1911.*

Scott wrote originally that Shackleton's hut had been found filled with snow 'to my chagrin'. The text reads here 'to my annoyance'. In his journals he also had an angry passage describing how 'Boxes full of excrement were found near the provisions and filth of a similar description was thick under the verander [sic] . . . It is horrible to think that people could have lived in such a horrible manner.'

At 10 a.m. the men and officers streamed over from the ship, and we all assembled on the beach and I read Divine Service, our first Service at the camp and impressive in the open air. After Service I told Campbell that I should have to cancel his two ponies and give him two others. He took it like the gentleman he is, thoroughly appreciating the reason.

He had asked me previously to be allowed to go to Cape Royds over the glacier and I had given permission. After our talk we went together to explore the route, which we expected to find much crevassed. I intended to go only a short way, but on reaching the snow above the uncovered hills of our Cape I found the surface so promising and so free from cracks that I went quite a long way. Eventually I turned, leaving Campbell, Gran, and Nelson roped together and on ski to make their way onwards, but not before I felt certain that the route to Cape Royds would be quite easy. As we topped the last rise we saw Taylor and Wright some way ahead on the slope; they had come up by a different route. Evidently they are bound for the same goal.

I returned to camp, and after lunch Meares and I took a sledge and nine dogs over the Cape to the sea ice on the south side and started for Hut Point. We took a little provision and a cooker and our sleeping-bags. Meares had found a way over the Cape which was on snow all the way except about 100 yards. The dogs pulled well, and we went towards the Glacier Tongue at a brisk pace; found much of the ice uncovered. Towards the Glacier Tongue there were some heaps of snow much wind-blown. As we rose the glacier we saw the *Nimrod* depôt some way to the right and made for it. We found a good deal of compressed fodder and boxes of maize, but no grain crusher as expected. The open water was practically up to the Glacier Tongue.

We descended by an easy slope ¼ mile from the end of the Glacier Tongue, but found ourselves cut off by an open crack some 15 feet across and had to get on the glacier again and go some ½ mile farther in. We came to a second crack but avoided it by skirting to the west. From this point we had an easy run without difficulty to Hut Point. There was a small pool of open water and a longish crack off Hut Point. I got my feet very wet crossing the latter. We passed hundreds of seals at the various cracks.

On arrival at the hut, to my annoyance we found it filled with snow. Shackleton reported that the door had been forced by the wind, but that he had made an entrance by the window and found shelter inside – other members of his party used it for shelter. But they actually went away and left the window (which they had forced) open; as a result, nearly the whole of the interior of the hut is filled with hard icy snow, and it is now impossible to find shelter inside.

Meares and I were able to clamber over the snow to some extent and to examine the neat pile of cases in the middle, but they will take much digging out. We got some asbestos sheeting from the magnetic hut and made the best shelter we could to boil our cocoa.

There was something too depressing in finding the old hut in such a desolate condition. I had had so much interest in seeing all the old landmarks and the huts apparently intact. To camp outside and feel that all the old comfort and cheer had departed, was dreadfully heart-rending. I went to bed thoroughly depressed. It seems a fundamental expression of civilised human sentiment that men who come to such places as this should leave what comfort they can to welcome those who follow, and finding that such a simple duty had been neglected by our immediate predecessors oppressed me horribly.

[From Dr Wilson's Journal. January 14. – He (Scott) also told me the plans for our depôt journey on which we shall be starting in about ten days' time. He wants me to

Officers hauling sledges of fodder from the Terra Nova *to Cape Evans. Jan 1911. Fortunately Oates had purchased at his own expense extra supplies of fodder for the ponies he was looking after. They had been housed aboard ship but were now getting exercise on the ice for the first time. Ice was the natural element of these animals, coming as they did from north-eastern Siberia. 'For hours the shaggy little fellows seemed scarcely able to believe their senses and could not stop whinnying and rolling on the ice for joy.'*

Smoke cloud from Erebus. Jan 15th 1911. The right-hand figure in the foreground appears to be carrying a gun; these were initially used for killing seals, but within a few days it was found that they could be clubbed to death. Ponting found that 'blubber as food is a taste that takes a good deal of acquiring; but it makes excellent fuel'.

be a dog driver with himself, Meares and Teddie Evans, and this is what I would have chosen had I had a free choice. . . . The dogs run in two teams and each team wants two men. It means a lot of running as they are being driven now, but it is the fastest and most interesting work of all, and we go ahead of the whole caravan with lighter loads and at a faster rate; moreover, if any traction except ourselves can reach the top of Beardmore Glacier, it will be the dogs, and the dog drivers are therefore the people who will have the best chance of doing the top piece of the ice cap at 10,000 feet to the Pole. May I be there! About this time next year may I be there or thereabouts! With so many young bloods in the heyday of youth and strength beyond my own I feel there will be a most difficult task in making choice towards the end and a most keen competition—and a universal lack of selfishness and self-seeking with a complete absence of any jealous feeling in any single one of the comparatively large number who at present stand a chance of being on the last piece next summer.

It will be an exciting time, and the excitement has already begun in the healthiest possible manner. I have never been thrown in with a more unselfish lot of men – each one doing his utmost fair and square in the most cheery manner possible.]

Tuesday, January 17. – We took up our abode in the hut today and are simply overwhelmed with its comfort. After breakfast this morning I found Bowers making cubicles as I had arranged, but I soon saw these would not fit in, so instructed him to build a bulkhead of cases which shuts off the officers' space from the men's, I am quite sure to the satisfaction of both. The space between my bulkhead and the men's I allotted to five: Bowers, Oates, Atkinson, Meares, and Cherry-Garrard. These five are all special friends and have already made their dormitory very habitable. Simpson and Wright are near the instruments in their corner. Next come Day and Nelson in a space which includes the latter's 'Lab' near the big window; next to this is a space for three – Debenham, Taylor, and Gran; they also have already made their space part dormitory and part workshop.

It is fine to see the way every one sets to work to put things straight; in a day or two the hut will become the most comfortable of houses, and in a week or so the whole station, instruments, routine, men and animals, etc., will be in working order.

It is really wonderful to realise the amount of work which has been got through of late.

It will be a *fortnight tomorrow* since we arrived in McMurdo Sound, and here we are absolutely settled down and ready to start on our depôt journey directly the ponies have had a proper chance to recover from the effects of the voyage. I had no idea we should be so expeditious.

It snowed hard all last night; there were about three or four inches of soft snow over the camp this morning and Simpson tells me some six inches out by the ship. The camp looks very white. During the day it has been blowing very hard from the south, with a great deal of drift. Here in this camp as usual we do not feel it much, but we see the anemometer racing on the hill and the snow clouds sweeping past the ship. The floe is breaking between the point and the ship, though curiously it remains fast on a direct route to the ship. Now the open water runs parallel to our ship road and only a few hundred yards south of it. Yesterday, the whaler was rowed in close to the camp, and if the ship had steam up she could steam round to within a few hundred yards of us. The big wedge of ice to which the ship is holding on the outskirts of the Bay can have very little grip to keep it in and must inevitably go out very soon. I hope this may result in the ship finding a more sheltered and secure position close to us.

A big iceberg sailed past the ship this afternoon. Atkinson declares it was the end of the Cape Barne Glacier. I hope they will know in the ship, as it would be interesting to witness the birth of a glacier in this region.

It is clearing tonight, but still blowing hard. The ponies don't like the wind, but they are all standing the cold wonderfully and all their sores are healed up.

Thursday, January 19. – The hut is becoming the most comfortable dwelling-place imaginable. We have made unto ourselves a truly seductive home, within the walls of which peace, quiet, and comfort reign supreme.

Such a noble dwelling transcends the word 'hut', and we pause to give it a more fitting title only from lack of the appropriate suggestion. What shall we call it?

'The word "hut" is misleading. Our residence is really a house of considerable size, in every respect the finest that has ever been erected in the Polar regions; 50 feet long by 25 wide and 9 feet to the eaves.

'If you can picture our house nestling below this small hill on a long stretch of black sand, with many tons of provision cases ranged in neat blocks in front of it and the sea lapping the ice-foot below, you will have some idea of our immediate vicinity. As for our wider surroundings it would be difficult to describe their beauty in sufficiently glowing terms. Cape Evans is one of the many spurs of Erebus and the one that stands closest under the mountain, so that always towering above us we have the grand snowy peak with its smoking summit. North and south of us are deep bays, beyond which great glaciers come rippling over the lower slopes to thrust high blue-walled snouts into the sea. The sea is blue before us, dotted with shining bergs or ice floes, whilst far over the Sound, yet so bold and magnificent as to appear near, stand the beautiful Western Mountains with their numerous lofty peaks, their deep glacial valley and clear cut scarps, a vision of mountain scenery that can have few rivals.

'Ponting is the most delighted of men; he declares this is the most beautiful spot he has ever seen, and spends all day and most of the night in what he calls "gathering it in" with camera and cinematograph.'

The wind has been boisterous all day, to advantage after the last snow fall, as it has been drifting the loose snow along and hardening the surfaces. The horses don't like it, naturally, but it wouldn't do to pamper them so soon before our journey. I think the hardening process must be good for animals though not for men; nature replies to it in the former by growing a thick coat with wonderful promptitude. It seems to me that the shaggy coats of our ponies are already improving. The dogs seem to feel the

Opposite: The Terra Nova *and a berg at ice-foot. Jan 16th 1911. At this date Ponting had not been on shore as he was too busy at the ship and its surrounding bergs, but today he managed to obtain what he called 'a fresh impression of the old rover'. This came about because 'a small iceberg bore towards her . . . all hanging with icicles from the warmth of the sun, and it composed with the ship to add a treasured page to my now rapidly growing album.'*

Giving whisky to a pony which swam ashore. Feb 8th 1911. Two ponies had been lowered into the sea from the Terra Nova *and had to swim ashore, towed by a boat. Each of the shivering animals had a half-bottle of neat whisky poured down its throat on landing. One of them never recovered – probably Forde's pony, Misery, which was shot a few weeks later.*

Berg aground near Cape Evans. Boat coming off Terra Nova. *Jan 20th 1911. The ship was too close to thick ice, and therefore put out to sea. 'The next afternoon,' noted Ponting, 'as she came up to the ice again, we found that a large tabular berg had borne down upon our old position, and had run aground where the ship had yesterday been berthed. We heard from our friends that this berg had sailed in soon after we departed. Had the ship not steamed out when she did, the berg would probably have wrecked her.'*

cold little so far, but they are not so exposed.

A milder situation might be found for the ponies if only we could picket them off the snow.

Bowers has completed his southern store-room and brought the wing across the porch on the windward side, connecting the roofing with that of the porch. The improvement is enormous and will make the greatest difference to those who dwell near the door.

The carpenter has been setting up standards and roof beams for the stables, which will be completed in a few days.

This morning I overhauled all the fur sleeping-bags and found them in splendid order – on the whole the skins are excellent. Since that I have been trying to work out sledge details, but my head doesn't seem half as clear on the subject as it ought to be.

I have fixed the 25th as the date for our departure. P.O. Evans is to get all the sledges and gear ready whilst Bowers superintends the filling of provision bags.

Griffith Taylor and his companions have been seeking advice as to their Western trip. Wilson, dear chap, has been doing his best to coach them.

Ponting has fitted up his dark-room – doing the carpentering work with extraordinary speed and to everyone's admiration. Tonight he made a window in the dark-room in an hour or so.

Meares has become enamoured of the gramophone. We find we have a splendid selection of records. The pianola is being brought in sections, but I'm not at all sure it will be worth the trouble. Oates goes steadily on with the ponies – he is perfectly excellent and untiring in his devotion to the animals.

Day and Nelson, having given much thought to the proper fitting up of their corner, have now begun work. There seems to be little doubt that these ingenious people will make the most of their space.

I have done quite a lot of thinking over the autumn journeys and much remains to be done, mainly on account of the prospect of being cut off from our winter quarters; for this reason we must have a great deal of food for animals and men.

Friday, January 20. – Our house has assumed great proportions. Bowers' annexe is finished, roof and all thoroughly snow-tight; an excellent place for spare clothing, furs, and ready use stores, and its extension affording complete protection to the entrance porch of the hut. The stables are nearly finished – a thoroughly stout, well-roofed lean-to on the north side. Nelson has a small extension on the east side and Simpson a pre-arranged projection on the S.E. corner, so that on all sides the main building has thrown out limbs. Simpson has almost completed his ice cavern, light-tight lining, niches, floor and all. Wright and Forde have almost completed the absolute hut, a patchwork building for which the framework only was brought – but it will be very well adapted for our needs.

Gran has been putting 'record' on the ski runners. Record is a mixture of vegetable tar, paraffin, soft soap, and linseed oil, with some patent addition which prevents freezing – according to Gran.

P.O. Evans and Crean have been preparing sledges; Evans shows himself wonderfully capable, and I haven't a doubt as to the working of the sledges he has fitted up.

We have been serving out some sledging gear and wintering boots. We are delighted with everything. First the felt boots and felt slippers made by Jaeger and then summer wind clothes and fur mits – nothing could be better than these articles. Finally tonight we have overhauled and served out two pairs of finnesko (fur boots) to each traveller. They are excellent in quality. At first I thought they seemed small, but a stiffness due to cold and dryness misled me – a little stretching and all was well. They are very good indeed. I have an idea to use putties to secure our wind trousers to the finnesko. But indeed the whole time we are thinking of devices to make our travelling work easier.

'We have now tried most of our stores, and so far we have not found a single article that is not perfectly excellent in quality and preservation. We are well repaid for all the trouble which was taken in selecting the food list and the firms from which the various articles could best be obtained, and we are showering blessings on Mr Wyatt's head for so strictly safeguarding our interests in these particulars.

This admission ('I have done quite a lot of thinking . . .') by Scott is surely not, as sometimes suggested, a question of muddle. The fact was that he had counted on his motor sledges backed up by the ponies and both were to some extent seen to be flawed. True, he never seems to have come out with a clear strategy to replace the sledges he had lost, though (see Jan 20th) he had decided 'it won't do to place more reliance on the machines'. Ironically, Amundsen was fretting about the great advantage he thought they gave Scott's party in the polar 'race'.

The period from Saturday, Jan 21st was one of great anxiety, but it has been deleted by the editors. Scott's instincts told him that something was wrong with the ship, and in the middle of the night he walked out of the hut to find 'she was having a bad time … We got out the men and gave some help,' and the ship backed out, narrowly missing a berg. That afternoon, she ran ashore. 'My heart sank,' wrote Scott, who sent Evans off in the whaler to make soundings. 'Visions of the ship failing to return to New Zealand', leaving 60 people stranded, 'arose in my mind with sickening pertinacity.' Ten tons of cargo was shifted aft to enable the *Terra Nova* to get clear. On the following Monday, Scott again rose early to find a channel opening up in the ice. He decided to set off with 12 men, 8 pony sledges and 2 dog sledges now, before winter set in, to lay a series of supply depôts crucial for the polar attempt the following season.

Dimitri and his dog team. This picture was probably taken on Ross Island, a volcanic rock of ice and lava. In the background is Mt Erebus, which might quickly be hidden by a blizzard.

Leaders of the pack.
Top left: *Krisarovitsa.*
Top right: *Tresor.*
Lower left: *Vida.*
Lower right: *Osman.*

'Our clothing is as good as good. In fact, first and last, running through the whole extent of our outfit, I can say with some pride that there is not a single arrangement which I would have had altered.'

The pianola has been erected by Rennick. He is a good fellow. The pianola has been his special care, and it shows well that he should give so much pains in putting it right for us.

Day has been explaining the manner in which he hopes to be able to cope with the motor sledge difficulty. He is hopeful of getting things right, but I fear it won't do to place more reliance on the machines.

Everything looks hopeful for the depôt journey if only we can get our stores and ponies past the Glacier Tongue.

64

We had some seal rissoles today so extraordinarily well cooked that it was impossible to distinguish them from the best beef rissoles. I told two of the party they were beef, and they made no comment till I enlightened them after they had eaten two each. It is the first time I have tasted seal without being aware of its particular flavour. But even its own flavour is acceptable in our cook's hands – he really is excellent.

[**From Dr Wilson's Journal. January 29.** – The seals have been giving a lot of trouble, that is just to Meares and myself with our dogs. The whole teams go absolutely crazy when they sight them or get wind of them, and there are literally hundreds along some of the cracks. Occasionally when one pictures oneself quite away from trouble of that kind, an old seal will pop his head up at a blowhole a few yards ahead of the team, and they are all on top of him before one can say 'Knife!' Then one has to rush in with the whip – and every one of the team of eleven jumps over the harness of the dog next to him and the harnesses become a muddle that takes much patience to unravel, not to mention care lest the whole team should get away with the sledge and its load and leave

Capt Scott (sixth from right) and Southern Party. Erebus in background. Jan 26th 1911.

Capt. Scott. Just before leaving for the Southern Journey. Jan 26th 1911.

On Thursday 26th Scott had all the crew mustered on the deck of the ship, and 'I thanked them for their splendid work. They have behaved like bricks and a finer lot of fellows never sailed in a ship.' The following day he set out for Camp 2, moving fodder. The plan was to march across the Barrier along the polar route depositing supplies. Two days later Oates continued to argue for killing the ponies but met with a blank wall from Scott, whose reply was, 'I have had enough of this cruelty to animals and I am not going to defy my feelings for the sake [of gaining] a few days' march.' Oates said, 'I'm afraid you'll regret it, Sir,' to which Scott answered, 'Regret it or not, my dear Oates, I've made up my mind like a Christian.' They were holed up at Camp 3 until Feb 2nd. In addition to the weather there were problems: Atkinson had an infected foot and eventually had to be left behind after it had been lanced, and Crean stayed with him. Both were distressed, but Scott had little sympathy with the injured man, 'who ought to have reported his trouble long before'. Perhaps people were afraid to report injury, if they knew Scott would be unsympathetic. As the ponies were still proving unsatisfactory, Scott called for snow shoes, only to find that they had been left behind. Gran volunteered to go back for them. Another problem with the ponies was that all their fodder had to be imported to the Antarctic, whereas dogs and men could live off the land.

one behind to follow on foot at leisure. I never did get left the whole of this journey, but I was often very near it and several times had only time to seize a strap or a part of the sledge and be dragged along helter-skelter over everything that came in the way till the team got sick of galloping and one could struggle to one's feet again. One gets very wary and wide awake when one has to manage a team of eleven dogs and a sledge load by oneself, but it was a most interesting experience, and I had a delightful leader, 'Stareek' by name – Russian for 'Old Man', and he was the most wise old man. We have to use Russian terms with all our dogs. 'Ki Ki' means go to the right, 'Chui' means go to the left, 'Esh to' means lie down – and the remainder are mostly swear words which mean everything else which one has to say to a dog team.

Dog driving like this in the orthodox manner is a very different thing to the beastly dog driving we perpetrated in the *Discovery* days. I got to love all my team and they got to know me well, and my old leader even now, six months after I have had anything to do with him, never fails to come and speak to me whenever he sees me, and he knows me and my voice ever so far off. He is quite a ridiculous 'old man' and quite the nicest, quietest, cleverest old dog I have ever come across. He looks in face as if he knew all the wickedness of the world and all its cares and as if he were bored to death by them.]

The Depôt Laying Expedition – 1911

Thursday, February 2. – IMPRESSIONS

The seductive folds of the sleeping-bag.

The hiss of the primus and the fragrant steam of the cooker issuing from the tent ventilator.

The small green tent and the great white road.

The whine of a dog and the neigh of our steeds.

The driving cloud of powdered snow.

The crunch of footsteps which break the surface crust.

The wind-blown furrows.

The blue arch beneath the smoky cloud.

The crisp ring of the ponies' hoofs and the swish of the following sledge.

The droning conversation of the march as driver encourages or chides his horse.

The patter of dog pads.

Nelson, Day and Lashly in Shackleton's hut. Feb 17th 1911. Lashly, Chief Stoker, R.N., soon had a welcome hot meal steaming in the galley. They kept the stove going as the hut was very cold – 'we realised the 1907 Expedition had lived under conditions of discomfort unknown to us in our snug commodious house at Cape Evans.'

The gentle flutter of our canvas shelter.

Its deep booming sound under the full force of a blizzard.

The drift snow like finest flour penetrating every hole and corner – flickering up beneath one's head covering, pricking sharply as a sand blast.

The sun with blurred image peeping shyly through the wreathing drift giving pale shadowless light.

The eternal silence of the great white desert. Cloudy columns of snow drift advancing from the south, pale yellow wraiths, heralding the coming storm, blotting out one by one the sharp-cut lines of the land.

The blizzard – Nature's protest – the crevasse, Nature's pitfall – that grim trap for the unwary – no hunter could conceal his snare so perfectly – the light rippled snow bridge gives no hint or sign of the hidden danger, its position unguessable till man or beast is floundering, clawing and struggling for foothold on the brink.

The vast silence broken only by the mellow sounds of the marching column.

Saturday, February 4. – . . . A dog must be either eating, asleep, or interested. His eagerness to snatch at interest, to chain his attention to something, is almost pathetic. The monotony of marching kills him.

This is the fearfullest difficulty for the dog driver on a snow plain without leading marks or objects in sight. The dog is almost human in its demand for living interest, yet fatally less than human in its inability to foresee.

The dog lives for the day, the hour, even the moment. The human being can live and support discomfort for a future.

This passage is often cited by critics as evidence of Scott's anthropomorphism and contrasted with the practical attitude of Amundsen, or for that matter, of Oates. The Norwegians had no doubts that to reach the Pole they would need to rely on skis, sledges and dogs, but Scott went on debating the matter, and several pages of his journal at this time are filled with the pros and cons. He would, however, suddenly come to earth, as on Feb 3rd, when he wrote at the end of a paragraph of speculation: 'Hunger and fear are the only realities of dog life.' This may have been because two of the dogs had just set on him, and one, Osman, 'my erstwhile friend', had nipped his leg lightly; if it had not been for Meares' intervention, the whole dog team 'would have been at me in a moment'. He noted, 'It is such stern facts that resign one to the sacrifice of animal life in the effort to advance such human projects as this.'

Adventure and peril

The journal entries for the next two months are deleted from this edition, leaving a gap from February 5th, even though they fill up over 40 pages of print in the full transcript. This is a surprising omission, and one wonders why the editors took such a draconian measure. After all, Scott still had plenty to do, yet he found time to commit judgements to the Journals – for example: 'The more I think of our sledging outfit, the more certain I am that we have arrived at something near a perfect equipment for civilised man under such conditions.' This cut by editors who enjoyed the benefit of hindsight is perhaps understandable, but it would be wrong to ignore the high drama of life with Scott in the entries which follow.

It was decided to continue to the next camps by a series of night marches, with the party turning out of their sleeping bags about 9pm and setting off before midnight. The teams would, from time to time, fall on a slippery patch. As they reached the halfway point, Scott would blow his whistle and the pony teams would be 'drawn up in camp formation [in] picket lines'. Tents would go up and the cookers got going. Meanwhile the dog drivers would be catching up and the whole party would rest for an hour to an hour and a half. Final camp was about 8am.

After leaving Corner Camp the amount of ground they covered varied. On February 11th it was 11 miles, on February 12th 12 miles, the next day 9 miles. Sometimes it was down to 7 miles. The difficulty was usually due to the varying performance of the ponies. Scott decided to send the three weakest animals back with Evans, Forde and Keohane. Cherry-Garrard moved into Scott's tent and described the experience thus: '[It was] a comfortable one to live in, and I was always glad when I was told to join it . . . [Scott] was himself extraordinarily quick and no time was ever lost by his party in camping or breaking camp. He was most careful, some said over-careful but I do not think so, that everything should be neat and shipshape . . . And if you went "sledging with the Owner" you had to keep your eyes wide open for the little things which cropped up, and do them quickly, and say nothing about them.'

Scott expected others to be as disciplined as he was himself. Charles Wright later noted that some of the men were so much in awe of their leader that they went outside into the cold to urinate, rather than just using a quiet corner of the tent as was the usual practice.

Having seen the ponies in something of a shambles, Scott was now increasingly impressed by the performance of the dogs, and there were discussions with Meares about their possible performance on the polar plateau. The party had been aiming

Left behind in Victoria Land. Feb 9th 1911. Campbell's party, six in all, were to proceed to King Edward VII Land, some 400 miles east at the other end of the ice barrier. They would be gone for nearly a year. Ponting recalls that they watched the ship disappear 'with mingled feelings'.

Packing a sledge at top of moraine for trip to Shackleton's hut. Feb 11th 1911. Scott had great hopes that they would be able to make good use of this hut, which had been abandoned in 1907.

to reach the 80th parallel, but of the five ponies left only three could go on without difficulty. The men were in trouble too. Bowers had been travelling without a hat and his frostbitten ears needed attention. Oates' nose was giving him great trouble. Scott and Cherry-Garrard were both lightly frostbitten on the cheek. Meares had a toe which caused him a lot of pain. Scott wrote in the journal, 'I have been wondering how I shall stick the summit again, this cold spell gives ideas. I think I shall be alright, but one must be prepared for a pretty good doing.'

The surface had been bad for the dogs and those men travelling by sledge had had to get off and run 'a good part of the time'. On the return now, the dogs went very well and the surface became excellent; on February 14th they did nearly 26 miles. Both dogs and ponies became extremely hungry, despite what in normal circumstances would have been a good allowance of food. Scott noted: 'Both eat their own excrement. With the ponies it does not seem so horrid, as there must be a good deal of grain, etc. which is not fully digested. It is the worst side of dog driving. All the rest is diverting . . . they keep up a steady jog trot for hour after hour . . . their legs seem steel springs. Osman has been restored to leadership.'

The next day they did 29 nautical miles (35 statute miles), but when they stopped Scott still found time to record the scenery. 'We had the most wonderfully beautiful sky-effects on the march with the sun inclining low on the southern horizon. Bright pink clouds hovered overhead on a deep grey-blue background. Gleams of bright sunlight appeared through the stratus . . . Within half an hour all has changed. It seems as though weather is made here rather than dependent on conditions elsewhere. It is all very interesting.'

Adventure and peril

When they reached Safety Camp, they found Evans and the others in excellent health but, alas, with only one pony. Forde's animal had succumbed. The next to go was Evans' Blossom, with only James Pigg remaining. After a few hours' sleep, they set off for Hut Point on February 21st. In an extract from the Journals entitled 'Adventure and Peril', Scott recounts some of the most gripping experiences of the whole expedition. Here they are in full, as originally published.

Tuesday, February 21.—New Camp about 12 miles from Safety Camp. 15½ miles. We made a start as usual about 10 p.m. The light was good at first, but rapidly grew worse till we could see little of the surface. The dogs showed signs of wearying. About an hour and a half after starting we came on mistily-outlined pressure ridges. We were running by the sledges. Suddenly Wilson shouted, 'Hold on to the sledge,' and I saw him slip a leg into a crevasse. I jumped to the sledge, but saw nothing. Five minutes after, as the teams were trotting side by side, the middle dogs of our team disappeared. In a moment the whole team were sinking —two by two we lost sight of them, each pair struggling for foothold. Osman the leader exerted all his great strength and kept a foothold—it was wonderful to see him. The sledge stopped and we leapt aside. The situation was clear in another moment. We had been actually travelling along the bridge of a crevasse, the sledge had stopped on it, whilst the dogs hung in their harness in the abyss, suspended between the sledge and the leading dog. Why the sledge and ourselves didn't follow the dogs we shall never know. I think a fraction of a pound of added weight

Day, Nelson and Lashly probing a crevasse on Barne Glacier. Feb 21st 1911. On one occasion, said Ponting, 'we got into trouble. The ice was badly crevassed in places, and we found ourselves in a maze of dangerous pitfalls—blind chasms bridged over with snow. Some of these bridges were very thin, and I became aware that I was on one when, leading and piloting the sledge, I suddenly broke through to my armpits.'

E. H. Shackleton's hut. Feb 27th 1911. The hut lies in a valley sheltered by black lava hills on the southern side, with a frozen lake and a distant view of the Western Mountains. Stores of food of all descriptions were stacked in and around the building. Ponting said that he entered the simple dwelling-place with a feeling akin to awe, but the interior was all disarranged, showing that the former occupants had left in a hurry.

must have taken us down. As soon as we grasped the position, we hauled the sledge clear of the bridge and anchored it. Then we peered into the depths of the crack. The dogs were howling dismally, suspended in all sorts of fantastic positions and evidently terribly frightened. Two had dropped out of their harness, and we could see them indistinctly on a snow bridge far below. The rope at either end of the chain had bitten deep into the snow at the side of the crevasse, and with the weight below, it was impossible to move it. By this time Wilson and Cherry-Garrard, who had seen the accident, had come to our assistance. At first things looked very bad for our poor team, and I saw little prospect of rescuing them. I had luckily inquired about the Alpine rope before starting the march, and now Cherry-Garrard hurriedly brought this most essential aid. It takes one a little time to make plans under such circumstances, and for some minutes our efforts were rather futile. We could get not an inch on the main trace of the sledge or on the leading rope, which was binding Osman to the snow with a throttling pressure. Then thought became clearer. We unloaded our sledge, putting in safety our sleeping-bags with the tent and cooker. Choking sounds from Osman made it clear that the pressure on him must soon be relieved. I seized the lashing off Meares' sleeping-bag, passed the tent poles across the crevasse, and with Meares managed to get a few inches on the leading line; this freed Osman, whose harness was immediately cut.

Then securing the Alpine rope to the main trace we tried to haul up together. One dog came up and was unlashed, but by this time the rope had cut so far back at the edge that it was useless to attempt to get more of it. But we could now unbend the sledge and do that for which we should have aimed from the first, namely, run the sledge across the gap and work from it. We managed to do this, our fingers constantly numbed. Wilson held on to the anchored trace whilst the rest of us laboured at the leader end. The leading rope was very small and I was fearful of its breaking, so Meares was lowered down a foot or two to secure the Alpine rope to the leading end of the trace; this down, the work of rescue proceeded in better order. Two by two we hauled the animals up to the sledge and one by one cut them out of their harness. Strangely the last dogs were the most difficult, as they were close under the lip of the gap, bound in by the snow-covered rope. Finally, with a gasp we got the last poor creature on to firm snow. We had recovered eleven of the thirteen.

Then I wondered if the last two could not be got, and we paid down the Alpine rope to see if it was long enough to reach the snow bridge on which they were coiled. The rope is 90 feet, and the amount remaining showed that the depth of the bridge was about 65 feet. I made a bowline and the others lowered me down.

The bridge was firm and I got hold of both dogs, which were hauled up in turn to the surface. Then I heard dim shouts and howls above. Some of the rescued animals had wandered to the second sledge, and a big fight was in progress. All my rope-tenders had to leave to separate the combatants; but they soon returned, and with some effort I was hauled to the surface.

All is well that ends well, and certainly this was a most surprisingly happy ending to a very serious episode. We felt we must have refreshment, so camped and had a meal, congratulating ourselves on a really miraculous escape. If the sledge had gone down Meares and I must have been badly injured, if not killed outright. The dogs are wonderful, but have had a terrible shaking—three of them are passing blood and have more or less serious internal injuries. Many were held up by a thin thong round the stomach, writhing madly to get free. One dog better placed in its harness stretched its legs full before and behind and just managed to claw either side of the gap—it had continued attempts to climb throughout, giving vent to terrified howls. Two of those hanging together had been fighting at intervals when they swung into any position which allowed them to bite one another. The

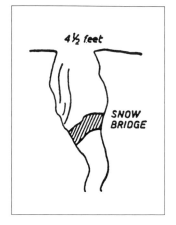

Scott drew this little diagram to show how far they had fallen.

crevasse for the time being was an inferno, and the time must have been all too terribly long for the wretched creatures. It was twenty minutes past three when we had completed the rescue work, and the accident must have happened before one-thirty. Some of the animals must have been dangling for over an hour. I had a good opportunity of examining the crack.

The section seemed such as I have shown. It narrowed towards the east and widened slightly towards the west. In this direction there were curious curved splinters: below the snow bridge on which I stood the opening continued, but narrowing, so that I think one could not have fallen many more feet without being wedged. Twice I have owed safety to a snow bridge, and it seems to me that the chance of finding some obstruction or some saving fault in the crevasse is a good one, but I am far from thinking that such a chance can be relied upon, and it would be an awful situation to fall beyond the limits of the Alpine rope.

We went on after lunch, and very soon got into soft snow and regular surface where crevasses are most unlikely to occur. We have pushed on with difficulty, for the dogs are badly crocked and the surface tries them. We are all pretty done, but luckily the weather favours us. A sharp storm from the south has been succeeded by ideal sunshine which is flooding the tent as I write. It is the calmest, warmest day we have had since we started sledging. We are about 12 miles from Safety Camp, and I trust we shall push on without accident tomorrow, but I am anxious

Western Party crossing the ice to the ship. March 1911. The Western Party were geologists examining the structure of the mountains of Victoria Land. 'Taylor and his merry men were in high spirits with the weather, the scenery and their prospects.' The Terra Nova was returning to pick them up.

about some of the dogs. We shall be lucky indeed if all recover.

On top of this ghastly physical experience ('a very serious episode'), Scott this day suffered a psychological trauma which was recorded in the full edition of the Journals but expurgated from the shorter. He arrived back in camp to be presented with a mailbag which Campbell had brought back on the *Terra Nova* and which Atkinson rushed over to him. 'Every incident pales before [its] startling contents', Scott wrote later.

To understand the gravity of the message, we must turn back in time to the October of the previous year, nearly four months earlier, when the *Terra Nova* had reached Melbourne from the Cape on its outward journey. Scott had then received a cable announcing, for the first time, Amundsen's true intentions – to sail south, not north. (He may not actually have read it until the following day, Friday 13th.) Scott had been secretive about the cable and showed it first privately to Gran, believing that, as a Norwegian, he might be able to explain it. The short message was as follows:

Beg leave to inform you Fram *proceeding Antarctic. Amundsen.*

Scott did not usually take juniors into his confidence, and Huntford suggests that his doing so now then revealed the depth of his perplexity. He continues: 'To neither Scott nor Gran was it immediately apparent that they had received a challenge for the Pole.' Gran noticed that the cable, simply signed 'Amundsen', might have been sent by the explorer's brother, which was indeed the case. He suggested to Scott that they cable Nansen for more information. Huntford quotes from Gran's diary: 'Scott, as always, seemed calm, but made a few remarks which indicated that inwardly he was [irritated]' perhaps even that he suspected something fishy. The circumstances were not exactly suited to put any questions [it was the following day and both men were attending a civil luncheon] but I did so nevertheless . . . I received no reply.'

Huntford continues that Scott now became 'extraordinarily secretive about the cable. Even his officers were kept in the dark.' Gran told Campbell about it, but was met with blank amazement. When the latter reached New Zealand, he found that little was known about it there either, though the Amundsen brothers had assumed that Scott would learn about it through the media, as Leon, Amundsen's brother, had called a press conference at home in Christiania on October 1st. He had also formally told Nansen and King Haakon of his brother's change of plans.

Amundsen himself, in a letter to the press, told the world: 'Alone I have taken this decision; alone I bear the responsibility.' Curiously, the British press, except for *The Daily Telegraph*, did not follow up the story until later. It died a natural death, aided in its demise by such foolish comments as the following from Sir Clements Markham of the Royal Geographical Society, that *Fram* 'has no more sailing qualities than a haystack . . . she is not adapted for very heavy seas, and may turn turtle . . . Scott will be on the ground and settled before Amundsen turns up, if he ever does.'

Huntford emphasises the effect of the cable on Scott's strategies as follows: 'By temperament and character, Scott was unsuited to emergencies; they exacerbated his fluctuating moods and heightened his aleady taut nerves . . . Torn between complacency and fear [he was] convinced that plans were running to perfection, gloomily afraid that something would go wrong. Amundsen's cable knocked him off balance.' Huntford suggests that Scott (still in Australia) could now have taken several courses of action but instead did nothing. Later Cherry-Garrard observed, 'Though we did not appreciate it at the time . . . [in Amundsen] we were up against a very big man.'

Huntford concludes that Scott did not fully realise that the cable was effectively a challenge to race for the Pole until he reached Wellington, New Zealand on October 27th and was interviewed by a local newspaper. Gran reported, 'Scott fell silent. But the interviewer did not give up. Then Scott became angry and brushed the man off by saying, "If, as [your] rumour says, Amundsen wants to try for the South Pole from some part of the coast of the West Antarctica, I can only wish him good luck." ' Huntford comments that until this press interview Scott 'had refused to face the possibility' that Amundsen was to race him. 'He still seemed to shrink from facing the truth, concerned most to hide it from his men.' Eventually, in mid-November, Scott took Gran's advice and cabled Nansen, asking for information about Amundsen's destination. The one-word reply was 'Unknown'.

Scott's reaction, according to Gran, 'Amundsen is acting suspiciously . . . In Norway he avoided me . . . Let me say it right out. Amundsen was too honourable to tell me lies to my face. It's the Pole he's after, all right.' Scott did not believe the report, relayed from London by the Royal Geographical Society, that his rival was going to McMurdo Sound, and he told Nansen so. The picture of confusion and ignorance about the Norwegian intentions can, says Huntford, be blamed on sloppy staff work by Scott's associates in London. Scott tried to put the subject out of his mind and did not want to discuss it. The editors of his journals perhaps thought they too could wipe it off the scene if they failed to quote its relevant passages.

But of course there were others in the know. For example, on November 23rd Oates wrote to his mother: 'What do you think about Amundsen's expedition? If he gets to the Pole first we shall come home with our tail between our legs and no mistake. I must say we have made far too much noise about ourselves all that [publicity] photographing, cheering, steaming through the fleet etc. etc. is rot and if we fail it will look foolish . . . I personally don't see it is underhand to keep your mouth shut [about your intentions] . . . these Norskies are a very tough lot, they have 200 dogs [sic] . . . also they are very good ski-runners while we can only walk [and] if Scott does anything silly like underfeeding his ponies he will be beaten as sure as death.' And the press were also getting more interested in the prospect of a race. When a local journalist asked Scott about his chances of success on November 30th, he replied with a neutral expression: 'No, I don't think I would care to say anything on that subject.' This remained the party line for the next few months, though inevitably the men talked to each other about the impending race.

Now we leap forward again to February 22nd, the day when, wrote Scott, 'every incident pales before the startling contents of the mail bag which Atkinson gave me. One thing only fixes itself in my mind. The proper, as well as the wiser, course for us is to proceed exactly as though this had not happened. To go forward and do our best for the honour of the country without fear or panic.'

What happened that day to cause Scott to panic? What was the startling news? It was simply that, unsuspected by Scott, his Norwegian rival had arrived and had calmly settled *Fram* in an area Scott knew well. Campbell, on his way to Edward VII Land in *Terra Nova*, had steamed into the Bay of Whales, a bight in the Great Ice Barrier near Edward VII Land, and had made the discovery. This was the most southerly point that could be reached by ship, and in 1902 Scott had landed there himself to make a precarious balloon ascent. It was only 400 miles from where Scott was now settled in his winter quarters. Campbell and his men were horrified to find the Norwegian party installed there. It was even worse for Scott—rather like finding a man had installed himself in his wife's bedroom. Emotionally, Scott felt the Bay of Whales was 'his', and he, Campbell and the crew expected to have the whole area to themselves.

His rival had wiped out Scott's lead, having already reached 80°S one week before, whereas Scott had returned to base having failed to reach this target by half a degree. Scott was therefore 30 miles behind. The Norwegians had also been travelling at an average speed twice that of Scott's party, and had marked their track by a more effective method. Also, unknown to Scott, Amundsen's target was to establish a depot at 83°S.

The Norwegian's plan, wrote Scott, 'is a very serious menace to ours. He has a shorter distance to the Pole [from the Bay of Whales] by 60 miles. I never thought he could have got so many dogs safely to the ice. His plan for running them seems excellent. But above and beyond all he can start his journey early in the season—an impossible condition with ponies [because the ice would be too thin]'. No doubt he was more worried than he admitted to his journal. Cherry-Garrard certainly thought so, telling his friend Bernard Shaw later that 'the reaction was fury – he was tempted to rush the *Fram* and have it out with Amundsen. He had never seen Scott so distressed.'

For a more 'gutsy' response than Scott's we have to turn to the reaction of Campbell and the crew on the *Terra Nova* as they calmly sailed into the Bay of Whales and saw, a few hundred yards away, the vessel that those who had read Nansen's books immediately recognised as *Fram*. Huntford quotes Bruce's letter to his sister: 'Curses were heard everywhere', and, in his diary, a judgement on 'the unexpected shock of it all'. 'An eruption of Erebus would fall flat after that.' Campbell, who spoke Norwegian, opened discussion with those on *Fram* (Amundsen was on shore). One of the Norwegians wrote that 'the Englishmen [were] absolutely flabbergasted. No, they had never dreamt that dogs could run in that way before a sledge, and already they felt contempt for their dear ponies.' Campbell, Pennell and Levick, the officers, were invited to breakfast in the hut. They were impressed with it, and more so with *Fram*, which they were invited to inspect. 'When they saw that every man had his own cabin, and everyone [used] a large common saloon, their eyes grew wide with astonishment. No, they had seen nothing like this before.' The British sailors regaled the Norwegians with tales of the squalor of their own quarters. Bruce wrote of the British ship that the 'comfort compared to the *Fram* is nil'. The Norwegians, shown over the *Terra Nova*, responded with, 'I must confess it did not look very inviting.'

Amundsen invited Campbell to camp on land wherever he wanted, but the British demurred, Priestley pointing out 'we cannot according to etiquette [en]trench on their country for winter quarters'. Amundsen and two companions were invited aboard the *Terra Nova* for lunch, and the Norwegian leader was relieved to see that they had no aerial for wireless. They were served a typically luxurious meal, confirming in their minds that the British 'drag many of the luxuries of civilisation with them into the wilderness'. Conversation during the meal was rather strained, suggests Huntford, and due to a misunderstanding the Norwegians were given the impression that Scott's motor sledges, whose value Amundsen over-rated, were already operating and might have reached the Beardmore Glacier. The meal confirmed in the Norwegian's mind that the race was on and the British might have an edge. Amundsen was quite open with the British that he intended to make a dash for the Pole on skis, with the dogs pulling sledges with supplies. It is a strange fact that many of those who should have known better, notably Clements Markham, went on insisting that this was still not a race. Ponting, too, wrote in his book that 'on arrival in London [while Scott was still away] I found a wholly groundless belief that there had been a "race" to the

Pole. I therefore addressed a letter to *The Times'* (published before it was known that there had been a tragedy). His message was: 'Captain Scott has not been racing, nor has he been engaged in a mere "dash to the Pole". He is leading a great scientific expedition—perhaps the greatest sent out from any land—and the reaching of the South Pole was but one part of the extensive programme laid out. To race would have been to jeopardise the success of the main objects of the enterprise, and Captain Scott would not allow the presence of a rival in the field to move him from the course he considered best and wisest.'

Ponting went on to point out that Scott had lost nearly half the ponies on whom he was dependent for transport and that, had any more succumbed, the main objects of the expedition would not have been achieved. Thus he could not start for the Pole until November 1st instead of a month earlier, as the animals would not have survived in the conditions prevalent in October. He concluded his argument: 'That month perhaps lost for Scott the honour of being first at the Pole. But for this delay it is conceivable that the rival explorers might even have met at the goal of their hopes.'

It is stretching credulity to accept that, if the Pole was the goal of Scott's hopes, he was not engaged in a 'race'. He was, and so was Amundsen, as he freely admitted. Another factor was that, psychologically, Scott was also racing against his old enemy Shackleton, though the latter was still in England. Indeed Huntford calls him an 'illusory rival'. Scott carried with him extracts from Shackleton's book, and from time to time he would contrast his own progress favourably with his rival's. Each night in his tent, claims Huntford, Scott was jealously measuring himself against Shackleton. He continued to worry about his past 'luck' compared with Shackleton's, and Huntford finds several such examples. He concludes, however, that 'Shackleton would have the last laugh'.

It has already been noted that over these winter months, while discussion of the 'race' was, according to some unwritten rule, out of order, it inevitably took place. Bruce wrote on 5th February recording the 'heavy arguments in the wardroom about the rights and wrongs of Amundsen's party and the chances of our being able to beat them'. Priestley wrote in his diary that the Norwegians had seemed to be 'good goers and pleasant good-humoured men—all these qualities combine to render them very dangerous rivals.' Oates in turn wrote to his mother that 'Scott having spent too much of his life in an office, he would 50 times sooner stay in the hut seeing how a pair of puttees suited him than come out and look at the ponies' legs.' This may have been unfair, but it underlines the leader's tendency to prefer to be in charge of organisation rather than a 'doer'. So does Oates' later letter, where he compains that 'Scott and Evans boss the show pretty well and their ignorance about marching with animals is colossal'—words which struck home hard now that everyone knew that the outcome of the race would depend on the success of the transport arrangements. Gran recorded in his diary: 'I see the difficulty with complicated transport . . . We will need luck if we are to reach the Pole next year.'

Finally, there are the impressions of those who were sharing quarters with 'the Owner' immediately after he had heard the news about Amundsen's plans. Cherry-Garrard wrote that in the morning, after a bad night, Scott jumped out of his sleeping bag and said, 'By Jove, what a chance we have missed – we might have taken Amundsen and sent him back in the ship . . . Scott argued that there was no law down here & we know Amundsen is acting against the wishes of his King.' Scott now passed into what Cherry-Garrard called 'a state of high excitement bordering on collapse'. According to Huntford he launched into a succession of aimless little marches and counter-marches. This was activity for its own sake. Oates saw the position clearly: 'If it comes to a race Amundsen . . . has been at this kind of game all his life and he has a hard crowd behind him while we are very young.'

On February 28th Scott was 'unbalanced' (Huntford's word) and lost his temper with Wilson, whom he ordered to withdraw over the ice to Hut Point. Scott took command of the ponies, particularly of Weary Willie, who was in a 'pitiable condition' and died in the morning. Meanwhile Wilson and the dogs were having trouble crossing the ice, while Bowers, also caught in its break-up, lost all the ponies under his control, except one. They were making for Hut Point, the old *Discovery* hut which Scott had claimed to be uninhabitable after Shackleton's tenure of it. When they arrived they were not a happy band, and Scott wrote, 'It makes a late start *necessary for next year*. Well, we have done our best and bought our experience at a heavy cost.'

Gran wrote in his diary in even sadder terms. 'Our party is divided, and we are like an army that is defeated, disappointed and inconsolable.' Scott found Gran's attitude unacceptable and gave him a public dressing-down, virtually calling him a lazy malingerer. He filled two pages of journals with complaint about 'the nuisance of his presence', but this too was edited out before publication. When Gran talked the problem over with 'Uncle Bill' Wilson, the latter explained that 'Scott is in a terrible state . . . he thinks that if Amundsen does not have bad luck, he will get to the Pole first and then you know that the expedition will be ruined.' He added, 'You're Norwegian, you can more or less sit down and look into the air, doing nothing, just living in your thoughts. For goodness' sake don't do that. You must never let Scott see you just sitting staring into space. You must do something. If you've nothing else to do, lace your boots and unlace them, two or three times. Just to have something to do.' Huntford believes that Wilson knew what he was talking about as he was in fact 'nursing Scott through a melancholic depression' due to 'the ruin which has assailed our transport'. Scott told him, 'I am losing all faith in the dogs.' Huntford concludes that Scott was at the end of his tether, unwisely insisting on crossing over the young ice to Cape Evans. Depite the risk Scott got through, 'but it was a near thing'.

We now take up the words of the published Journal once more, on April 7th, which the editors entitle 'A Sketch of Life at Hut Point' (the old Discovery hut).

Weathered ice furrows after a blizzard at Cape Evans and crevasses, looking towards Turk's Head. Mar 8th 1911. This was the kind of terrain the party had to deal with when they stepped outside their quarters at Hut Point.

Inside the Hut, Clissold the cook making bread. Mar 26th 1911. He acted as Ponting's model on a number of occasions, but he took risks and came to grief.

A Sketch of Life at Hut Point

April 7th. – We gather around the fire seated on packing-cases, with a hunk of bread and butter and a steaming pannikin of tea, and life is well worth living. After lunch we are out and about again; there is little to tempt a long stay indoors, and exercise keeps us all the fitter.

The failing light and approach of supper drive us home again with good appetites about 5 or 6 o'clock, and then the cooks rival one another in preparing appetising dishes of fried seal liver. A single dish may not seem to offer much opportunity of variation, but a lot can be done with a little flour, a handful of raisins, a spoonful of curry powder, or the addition of a little boiled pea meal. Be this as it may, we never tire of our dish, and exclamations of satisfaction can be heard every night – or nearly every night; for two nights ago (April 4) Wilson, who has proved a genius in the invention of 'plats', almost ruined his reputation. He proposed to fry the seal liver in penguin blubber, suggesting that the latter could be freed from all rankness. The blubber was obtained and melted down with great care, the result appeared as delightfully pure fat free from smell; but appearances were deceptive; the 'fry' proved redolent of penguin, a concentrated essence of that peculiar flavour which faintly lingers in the meat and should not be emphasised. Three heroes got through their pannikins, but the rest of us decided to be contented with cocoa and biscuit after tasting the first mouthful. After supper we have an hour or so of smoking and conversation – a cheering, pleasant hour – in which reminiscences are exchanged by a company which has very literally had world-wide experience. There is scarce a country under the sun which one or another of us has not travelled in, so diverse are our origins and occupations. An hour or so after supper we tail off one by one, spread out our sleeping-bags, take off our shoes and creep into comfort, for our reindeer bags are really warm and comfortable now that they have had a chance of drying, and the hut retains some of the heat generated in it. Thanks to the success of the blubber lamps and to a fair supply of candles, we can muster ample light to read for another hour or two, and so tucked up in our furs we study the social and political questions of the past decade.

We muster no less than sixteen. Seven of us pretty well cover the floor of one wing of the L-shaped enclosure, four sleep in the other wing, which also holds the store, whilst the remaining five occupy the annexe and affect to find the colder temperature more salubrious. Every one can manage eight or nine hours' sleep without a break, and not a few would have little difficulty in sleeping the clock round, which goes to show that our extremely simple life is an exceedingly healthy one, though with faces and hands blackened with smoke, appearances might not lead an outsider to suppose it.

Ponting at work in darkroom. Mar 24th 1911.

Home Impressions—1911

Return of Southern Party. April 13th 1911. This picture must have been taken after they had tidied themselves. (Compare the picture of the bearded Gran with that on p.88.)

On Returning to the Hut, April 13, 1911

After our primitive life at Cape Armitage it was wonderful to enter the precincts of our warm, dry Cape Evans home. The interior space seemed palatial, the light resplendent, and the comfort luxurious. It was very good to eat in civilised fashion, to enjoy the first bath for three months, and have contact with clean, dry clothing. Such fleeting hours of comfort (for custom soon banished their delight) are the treasured remembrance of

every Polar traveller. They throw into sharpest contrast the hardships of the past and the comforts of the present, and for the time he revels in the unaccustomed physical contentment that results.

I was not many hours or even minutes in the hut before I was dragged round to observe in detail the transformation which had taken place during my absence, and in which a very proper pride was taken by those who had wrought it.

Simpson's Corner was the first visited. Here the eye travelled over numerous shelves laden with a profusion of self-recording instruments, electric batteries and switch-boards, whilst the ear caught the ticking of many clocks, the gentle whirr of a motor, and occasionally the trembling note of an electric bell. But such sights and sounds conveyed only an impression of the delicate methodical means by which the daily and hourly variations of our weather conditions were being recorded – a mere glimpse of the intricate arrangements of a first-class meteorological station – the one and only station of that order which has been established in Polar regions. It took me days and even months to realise fully the aims of our meteorologist and the scientific accuracy with which he was achieving them. The first impression, which I am here describing, was more confused; I appreciated only that by going to 'Simpson's Corner' one could ascertain at a glance how hard the wind was blowing and had been blowing, how the barometer was varying, to what degree of cold the thermometer had descended; if one were still more inquisitive he could further inform himself as to the electrical tension of the atmosphere and other matters of like import. That such knowledge could be gleaned without a visit to the open air was an obvious advantage to those who were clothing themselves to face it, whilst the ability to study the variation of a storm without exposure savoured of no light victory of mind over matter.

The dark-room stands next to the parasitologist's side of the bench which flanks Sunny Jim's Corner – an involved sentence. To be more exact, the physicists adjust their instruments and write up books at a bench which projects at right angles to the end wall of the hut; the opposite side of this bench is allotted to Atkinson, who is to write with his back to the dark-room. Atkinson being still absent his corner was unfurnished, and my attention was next claimed by the occupant of the dark-room beyond Atkinson's limit. The art of photography has never been so well housed within the Polar regions and rarely without them. Such a palatial chamber for the development of negatives and prints can only be justified by the quality of the work produced in it, and is only justified in our case by the possession of such an artist as Ponting. He was eager to show me the results of his summer work, and meanwhile my eye took in the neat shelves with their array of cameras, etc., the porcelain sink

They had intended to leave for Cape Evans on April 10th but it snowed all day, so they did not set out until 9am on Thursday, April 13th. The last part of their journey was made in the dark and Scott decided not to continue; they camped overnight, arriving at the Hut at about 10am.

Dr Simpson at work in the magnetic hut. George Simpson was the meteorologist who presided over the physical laboratory, known to the crew as Simpson's Corner, where self-registering instruments told them all about the weather. The most popular was 'The Blizzometer', which registered the wind so that 'Sunny Jim', as its owner was called, could educate the crew with details.

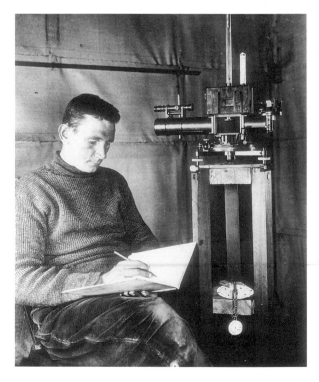

Ponting also mentioned that the photographic firm Lumière had presented him with boxes of Autochrome plates, which produced pictures in natural colours. Although they were now too old to produce satisfactory results, they allowed him to secure an interesting record of afterglow, and some were later printed.

Dr Simpson inflating one of his balloons. April 17th 1911. Ponting went into great detail about the balloons, which Simpson, the meteorologist, had provided to measure upper air currents to a height of five miles. The balloons were carried aloft by small black parachutes and wound on reels ten miles in length. 'Simpson was the wizard of our little community.'

and automatic water tap, the two acetylene gas burners with their shading screens, and the general obviousness of all conveniences of the photographic art. Here, indeed, was encouragement for the best results, and to the photographer be all praise, for it is mainly his hand which has executed the designs which his brain conceived. In this may be clearly seen the advantage of a traveller's experience. Ponting has had to provide for himself under primitive conditions in a new land; the result is a 'handy man' with every form of tool and in any circumstances. Thus, when building operations were to the fore and mechanical labour scarce, Ponting returned to the shell of his apartment with only the raw material for completing it. In the shortest possible space of time shelves and tanks were erected, doors hung and windows framed, and all in a workmanlike manner commanding the admiration of all beholders. It was well that speed could be commanded for such work, since the fleeting hours of the summer season had been altogether too few to be spared from the immediate service of photography. Ponting's nervous temperament allowed no waste of time – for him fine weather meant no sleep; he decided that lost opportunities should be as rare as circumstances would permit.

This attitude was now manifested in the many yards of cinematograph film remaining on hand and yet greater number recorded as having been sent back in the ship, in the boxes of negatives lying on the shelves and a well-filled album of prints.

Of the many admirable points in this work, perhaps the most notable are Ponting's eye for a picture and the mastery he has acquired of ice subjects; the composition of most of his pictures is extraordinarily good, he seems to know by instinct the exact value of foreground and middle distance and of the introduction of 'life', whilst with more technical skill in the manipulation of screens and exposures he emphasises the subtle shadows of the snow and reproduces its wondrously transparent texture. It is good to hear his enthusiasm for results of the past and plans for the future.

Long before I could gaze my fill at the contents of the dark-room I was led to the biologist's cubicle; Nelson and Day had from the first decided to camp together, each having a habit of methodical neatness; both were greatly relieved when the arrangement was approved, and they were freed from the chance of an untidy companion. No attempt had been made to furnish this cubicle before our departure on the autumn journey, but now on my return I found it an example of the best utilisation of space. The prevailing note was neatness; the biologist's microscope stood on a neat bench surrounded by enamel dishes, vessels, and books neatly arranged; behind him, when seated, rose

April 13th 1911 – the date the Southern Party returned to the Hut.

Top left: *Capt. Scott.*

Top right: *The geologist Frank Debenham.*

Lower left: *Lieut. Bowers.*

Lower right: *The geologist Griffith Taylor.*

April 13th 1911 – the date the Southern Party returned to the Hut.

Top left: *The physicist Charles Wright.*

Top right: *Tryggve Gran, the Norwegian ski expert.*

Lower left: *Lieut. Evans.*

Lower right: *Dr E. A. Wilson, a zoologist who was Chief of the Scientific Staff. April 21st 1911. Ponting wrote, 'I was drawn into closer contact with Wilson than with any other of my comrades. He would often submit his sketches to me for advice.'*

two neat bunks with neat, closely curtained drawers for clothing and neat reflecting sconces for candles; overhead was a neat arrangement for drying socks, with several nets, neatly bestowed. The carpentering to produce this effect had been of quite a high order, and was in very marked contrast with that exhibited for the hasty erections in other cubicles. The pillars and boarding of the bunks had carefully finished edges and were stained to mahogany brown. Nelson's bench is situated very conveniently under the largest of the hut windows, and had also an acetylene lamp, so that both in summer and winter he has all conveniences for his indoor work.

Day appeared to have been unceasingly busy during my absence. Everyone paid tribute to his mechanical skill and expressed gratitude for the help he had given in adjusting instruments and generally helping forward the scientific work. He was entirely responsible for the heating, lighting, and ventilating arrangements, and as all these appear satisfactory he deserved much praise. Particulars concerning these arrangements I shall give later; as a first impression it is sufficient to note that the warmth and lighting of the hut seemed as good as could be desired, whilst for our comfort the air seemed fresh and pure. Day had also to report some progress with the motor sledges, but this matter also I leave for future consideration.

My attention was very naturally turned from the heating arrangements to the cooking stove and its custodian, Clissold. I had already heard much of the surpassingly sat-

Meares and Oates at the blubber stove. May 26th 1911. Meares was on the Scientific Staff and in charge of the dogs, so Oates categorised him as a Scientist, but those who did not hold scientific degrees were called Gentlemen.

Capt. Oates and ponies in stable. May 26th 1911. When the ship left New Zealand there were 19 ponies on board, of which 10 survived the first year. Oates looked after Christopher, the strongest and worst-tempered, because he was, in Ponting's words, 'a born master of horses. He never got angry or excited.'

After writing these impressions, Scott had come to the end of a manuscript book, so started a fresh one. This began with some odd jottings, including quotations from Milton and Goethe. He also wrote the following:

'By all means think yourself big but don't think everyone else small.'

───────

'The man who knows everyone's job isn't much good at his own.'

───────

'A man can't be too good, but he can appear too good.'

The period April 17th–22nd was taken up with a sledging excursion, not included here, when Scott discovered that one sledge was much heavier and more difficult to pull than the others and that those hauling it arrived back 'bathed in sweat'. There was almost no quicker way to feel the full effect of the cold than to sweat under one's clothing. This, said Scott, showed the whole trouble of sledging in winter. The reason for the difference in the two sledges was apparently a change in the grain of the wood in the runners.

isfactory meals which his art had produced, and had indeed already a first experience of them. Now I was introduced to the cook's corner with its range and ovens, its pots and pans, its side tables and well-covered shelves. Much was to be gathered therefrom, although a good meal by no means depends only on kitchen conveniences. It was gratifying to learn that the stove had proved itself economical and the patent fuel blocks a most convenient and efficient substitute for coal. Save for the thickness of the furnace cheeks and the size of the oven, Clissold declared himself wholly satisfied. He feared that the oven would prove too small to keep up a constant supply of bread for all hands; nevertheless he introduced me to this oven with an air of pride which I soon found to be fully justified. For connected therewith was a contrivance for which he was entirely responsible, and which in its ingenuity rivalled any of which the hut could boast. The interior of the oven was so arranged that the 'rising' of the bread completed an electric circuit, thereby ringing a bell and switching on a red lamp. Clissold had realised that the continuous ringing of the bell would not be soothing to the nerves of our party, nor the continuous burning of the lamp calculated to prolong its life, and he had therefore added the clockwork mechanism which automatically broke the circuit after a short interval of time; further, this clockwork mechanism could be made to secure the repetition of the same warning signals at intervals of time varied according to the desire of the operator;—thus because, when in bed, he would desire a signal at short periods, but if absent from the hut he would wish to know at a glance what had happened when he returned. Judged by any standard it was a remarkably pretty little device, but when I learnt that it had been made from odds and ends, such as a cog-wheel or spring here and a cell or magnet there, begged from other departments, I began to realise that we had a very exceptional cook. Later, when I found that Clissold was called in to consult on the ailments of Simpson's motor and that he was capable of constructing a dog sledge out of packing cases, I was less surprised, because I knew by this time that he had had considerable training in mechanical work before he turned his attention to pots and pans.

My first impressions include matters to which I was naturally eager to give an early half-hour, namely, the housing of our animals. I found herein that praise was as justly due to our Russian boys as to my fellow Englishmen. Anton, with Lashly's help, had completed the furnishing of the stables. Neat stalls occupied the whole length of the 'lean-to', the sides so boarded that sprawling legs could not be entangled beneath and the front well covered with tin sheet to defeat the 'cribbers'. I could but sigh again to think of the stalls that must now remain empty, whilst appreciating that there was ample room for the safe harbouring of the ten beasts that remained, be the winter never so cold or the winds so wild.

Later we have been able to give double space to all but two or three of our animals, in which they can lie down if they are so inclined.

The ponies looked fairly fit considering the low diet on which they had been kept; their coats were surprisingly long and woolly in contrast with those of the animals I had left at Hut Point. At this time they were being exercised by Lashly, Anton, Dimitri, Hooper, and Clissold, and as a rule were ridden, the sea having only recently frozen. The exercise ground had lain on the boulder-strewn sand of the home beach and extending towards the Skua lake; and across these stretches I soon saw barebacked figures dashing at speed, and not a few amusing incidents in which horse and rider parted with abrupt lack of ceremony. I didn't think this quite the most desirable form of exercise for the beasts, but decided to leave matters as they were till our pony manager returned.

Dimitri had only five or six dogs left in charge, but these looked fairly fit, all things considered, and it was evident the boy was bent on taking every care of them, for he had not only provided shelters, but had built a small 'lean-to' which would serve as a hospital for any animal whose stomach or coat needed nursing.

Such were in broad outline the impressions I received on my first return to our home station; they were almost wholly pleasant and in happy contrast with the fears that had assailed me on the homeward route. As the days went by I was able to fill in the detail in equally pleasant fashion, to watch the development of fresh arrangements and the improvement of old ones. Finally, in this way I was brought to realise what an extensive and intricate but eminently satisfactory organisation I had made myself responsible for.

When they held Divine Service on April 23rd, Scott rather irritably complained that there were only seven hymn books available, the others having gone back to the ship. We must not judge him too harshly – he had grown up in an environment in which a hymn book was a necessary part of life.

In his full journals Scott devoted several pages here to the subject of auroras, which were being watched the whole time by one or other member of the team. Simpson gave an evening lecture on the subject.

The Work and the Workers–1911

Scott had been very depressed for some weeks but now appeared to have returned to his old self. He wrote (a passage cut by the editors): 'Self-assertion is a mask which covers many weaknesses . . . Commonly we accept people on their own evaluation . . . Here the outward show is nothing, it is the inward purpose that counts.'

Tuesday, May 2. – Today have had our first game of football; a harassing southerly wind sprang up, which helped my own side to the extent of three goals.

Friday, May 5. – One sees Wilson busy with pencil and colour box, rapidly and steadily adding to his portfolio of charming sketches and at intervals filling the gaps in his zoological work of *Discovery* times; withal ready and willing to give advice and assistance to others at all times; his sound judgment is appreciated and therefore he is a constant referee.

Simpson, master of his craft, untiringly attentive to the working of his numerous self-recording instruments, observing all changes with scientific discernment, doing the work of two observers at least, and yet ever seeking to extend the scope of his observations. So the current meteorological and magnetic readings are taken as never before by Polar expeditions.

Wright, good-hearted, strong, keen, striving to saturate his mind with the ice problems of this wonderful region. He has taken the electrical work in hand with all its modern interest of association with radio-activity.

Evans, with a clear-minded zeal in his own work, does it with all the success of result which comes from the taking of pains. Therefrom we derive a singularly exact preservation of time – an important consideration to all, but especially necessary for the physical work. Therefrom also, and including more labour, we have an accurate survey of our immediate surroundings and are sure we possess the correctly mapped results of all surveying data obtained. He has Gran for assistant.

Taylor's intellect is omnivorous and versatile – his mind is unceasingly active, his grasp wide. Whatever he writes will be of interest – his pen flows well. Debenham's is clearer. Here we have a well-trained, sturdy worker, with a quiet meaning that carries

The Tenements – bunks in hut of Lieut. Bowers, Mr Cherry-Garrard, Capt. Oates, Mr Meares and Dr Atkinson. This was the least pretentious of the cubicle compartments. It was conspicuous by its lack of any attempt at more than necessary comfort.

conviction; he realises the conceptions of thoroughness and conscientiousness.

To Bowers' practical genius is owed much of the smooth working of our station. He has a natural method in line with which all arrangements fall, so that expenditure is easily and exactly adjusted to supply, and I have the inestimable advantage of knowing the length of time which each of our possessions will last us and the assurance that there can be no waste. Active mind and active body were never more happily blended. It is a restless activity, admitting no idle moments and ever budding into new forms.

So we see the balloon ascending under his guidance and anon he is away over the floe tracking the silk thread which held it. Such a task completed, he is away to exercise his pony, and later out again with the dogs, the last typically self-suggested, because for the moment there is no one else to care for these animals. Now in a similar manner he is spreading thermometer screens to get comparative readings with the home station. He is for the open air, seemingly incapable of realising any discomfort from it, and yet his hours within doors are spent with equal profit. For he is intent on tracking the problems of sledging food and clothing to their innermost bearings and is becoming an authority on past records. This will be no small help to me and one which others never could have given.

Adjacent to the physicists' corner of the hut Atkinson is quietly pursuing the subject of parasites. Already he is in a new world. The laying out of the fish trap was his action and the catches are his field of labour. Constantly he comes to ask if I would like to see some new form, and I am taken to see some protozoa or ascidian isolated on the slide plate of his microscope. The fishes themselves are comparatively new to science; it is strange that their parasites should have been under investigation so soon.

Atkinson's bench with its array of microscopes, test-tubes, spirit lamps, etc., is next the dark-room in which Ponting spends the greater part of his life.

Cherry-Garrard is another of the open-air, self-effacing, quiet workers; his whole heart is in the life, with profound eagerness to help everyone. 'One has caught glimpses of him in tight places; sound all through and pretty hard also.' Indoors he is editing our Polar journal, out of doors he is busy making trial stone huts and blubber stoves, primarily with a view to the winter journey to Cape Crozier, but incidentally these are instructive experiments for any party which may get into difficulty by being cut off from the home station. It is very well to know how best to use the scant resources that Nature provides in these regions. In this connection I have been studying our Arctic library to get details concerning snow-hut building and the implements used for it.

Oates' whole heart is in the ponies. He is really devoted to their care, and I believe will produce them in the best possible form for the sledging season. Opening out the stores, installing a blubber stove, etc., has kept *him* busy, whilst his satellite, Anton, is ever at work in the stables – an excellent little man.

P.O. Evans and Crean are repairing sleeping-bags, covering felt boots, and generally working on sledging kit. In fact, there is no one idle, and no one who has the least prospect of idleness.

The Polar Times was a heavily illustrated publication, of which copies survive, with additional material usually anonymous but fairly easily identified as to authorship by the *cognoscenti*.

Scott was mistaken. Oates had not changed his view that the best that could be done was to shoot the ponies and concentrate on dog-drawn sledges.

It was about this time (end April) that Gran persuaded Ponting to visit some of the caves or 'grottos' he had discovered on his lone skiing foray to the ice cliff in South Bay. 'The glacier face hereabouts was 150 feet sheer and Taylor [the geologist, who went with them] pronounced them to be the exposed ends of crevasses.' He remarked that 'this seems a more sensible way of entering a crevasse than dropping into it'. Ponting noted that there was little colouring, but on cutting pockets with an ice axe, 'the most beautiful blue light imaginable filtered through'. The next day, Ponting took Scott and Wright , 'our ice-investigating physicist', to see them, and the pair were photographed examining them. Wright collected some fine crystals.

Looking to Tent Island, from one of the caves. Capt. Scott and Charles Wright, physicist. April 28th 1911.

The last entry on this page disposes of the suggestion that Scott was invariably over-secretive and did not discuss his plans with the team, in contrast to Shackleton and Amundsen. That is not to say that he always achieved unanimity, even if he thought he had.

On May 13th the party which had remained at Discovery Hut returned, making a total of 25 inhabitants of the so-called 'Hut', though, as Ponting pointed out, 'no such house had been built in the Antarctic [before]'. Scott wrote, 'I am very much impressed with the extraordinary and general cordiality of the relations which exist amongst our people. I do not suppose that a statement of the real truth, namely that there is no friction at all, will be credited ... With me there is no necessity to draw a veil; there is nothing to cover. There are no strained relations in this hut, and nothing is more emphatically evident than the universally amicable spirit which is shown on all occasions.' The only reply to be made to Scott is to draw attention to Gran's remarks in his diary – 'our party is divided' etc.

Sunday, May 7. – Daylight now is very short. Bowers and Cherry-Garrard have set up a thermometer screen containing maximum thermometers and thermographs on the sea floe about ¾' N.W. of the hut. Another smaller one is to go on top of the Ramp. They took the screen out on one of Day's bicycle-wheel carriages and found it ran very easily over the salty ice where the sledges give so much trouble. This vehicle is not easily turned, but may be very useful before there is much snowfall.

Yesterday a balloon was sent up and reached a very good height (probably 2 to 3 miles) before the instrument disengaged; the balloon went almost straight up and the silk fell in festoons over the rocky part of the Cape, affording a very difficult clue to follow; but whilst Bowers was following it, Atkinson observed the instrument fall a few hundred yards out on the Bay – it was recovered and gives the first important record of upper-air temperature.

Atkinson and Crean put out the fish trap in about 3 fathoms of water off the west beach; both yesterday morning and yesterday evening, when the trap was raised it contained over forty fish, whilst this morning and this evening the catches in the same spot have been from twenty to twenty-five. We had fish for breakfast this morning, but an even more satisfactory result of the catches has been revealed by Atkinson's microscope. He has discovered quite a number of new parasites and found work to last quite a long time.

Last night it came to my turn to do night watchman again, so that I shall be glad to have a good sleep tonight.

Yesterday we had a game of football; it is pleasant to mess about, but the light is failing.

Clissold is still producing food novelties; tonight we had galantine of seal – it was *excellent*.

Monday, May 8 – Tuesday, May 9. – As one of the series of lectures I gave an outline of my plans for next season on Monday evening. Everyone was interested, naturally. I could not but hint that in my opinion the problem of reaching the Pole can best be solved by relying on the ponies and man haulage. With this sentiment the whole company appeared to be in sympathy. Everyone seems to distrust the dogs when it comes to glacier and summit. I have asked everyone to give thought to the problem, to freely discuss it, and bring suggestions to my notice. It's going to be a tough job; that is better realised the more one dives into it.

In Winter Quarters: Modern Style – 1911

Sunday, May 21.—Tonight we had a glorious auroral display—quite the most brilliant I have seen. At one time the sky from N.N.W. to S.S.E. as high as the zenith was massed with arches, band, and curtains, always in rapid movement. The waving curtains were especially fascinating—a wave of bright light would start at one end and run along to the other, or a patch of brighter light would spread as if to reinforce the failing light of the curtain.

The auroral light is of a palish green colour, but we now see distinctly a red flush preceding the motion of any bright part.

The green ghostly light seems suddenly to spring to life with rosy blushes. There is infinite suggestion in this phenomenon, and in that lies its charm; the suggestion of life, form, colour, and movement never less than evanescent, mysterious—no reality. It is the language of mystic signs and portents—the inspiration of the gods—wholly spiritual —divine signalling. Remindful of superstition, provocative of imagination. Might not the inhabitants of some other world (Mars) controlling mighty forces thus surround our globe with fiery symbols, a golden writing which we have not the key to decipher?

In a passage excluded from the published account, Scott recorded (May 17th) the death of another dog, commenting 'I am afraid we can place but little reliance on our dog team and reflect ruefully on the misplaced confidence with which I regarded the provision of our transport. Well, one must suffer for errors of judgement.' He might well have gone on to conclude that the only chance now left was human transport. That same night Oates gave 'an excellent little lecture' on the management of horses, though there would not be any left to manage before long.

On May 20th Wilson and Bowers went for a walk in a temperature of –24°F and in consequence got frostbite.

On May 10th Scott wrote: 'It seems more and more certain that a very simple fare is all that is needed – plenty of seal meat, flour and fat, with tea, cocoa and sugar.' This is in marked contrast to the diet they had brought with them on the ship, and to Scott's comments on May 26th. *Scorbutic* means having scurvy.

Friday, May 26. – We are living extraordinarily well. At dinner last night we had come excellent thick seal soup, very much like thick hare soup; this was followed by an equally tasty seal steak and kidney pie and a fruit jelly. The smell of frying greeted us on awaking this morning, and at breakfast each of us had two of our nutty little *Notothenia* fish after our bowl of porridge. These little fish have an extraordinarily sweet taste – bread and butter and marmalade finished the meal. At the midday meal we had bread and butter, cheese, and cake, and tonight I smell mutton in the preparation. Under the circumstances it would be difficult to conceive more appetising repasts or a régime which is less likely to produce scorbutic symptoms. I cannot think we shall get scurvy.

Monday, May 29. – Lecture – Japan. Tonight Ponting gave us a charming lecture on Japan with wonderful illustrations of his own. He is happiest in his descriptions of the artistic side of the people with which he is in fullest sympathy. So he took us to see the flower pageants: the joyful festivals of the cherry blossom, the wistaria, the iris and chrysanthemum, the sombre colours of the beech blossom and the paths about the lotus gardens, where mankind meditated in solemn mood. We had pictures, too, of Nikko and its beauties, of Temples and great Buddhas. Then in more touristy strain of volcanoes and their craters, waterfalls and river gorges, tiny tree-clad islets, that feature of Japan – baths and their bathers, Ainos, and so on. His descriptions were well given and we all of us thoroughly enjoyed our evening.

Wednesday, May 31. – Tonight Wilson has given us a very interesting lecture on sketching. He started by explaining his methods of rough sketch and written colour record, and explained its suitability to this climate as opposed to coloured chalks, etc. – a very practical method for cold fingers and one that becomes more accurate with practice in observation. His theme then became the extreme importance of accuracy, his mode of expression and explanation frankly Ruskinesque. Don't put in meaningless lines – every line should be from observation. So with contrast of light and shade, fine shading, subtle distinction, everything – impossible without care, patience, and trained attention.

He raised a smile by explaining failures in sketches of others of our party which had been brought to him for criticism. He pointed out how much had been put in from preconceived notion. 'He will draw a berg faithfully as it is now and he studies it, but he leaves sea and sky to be put in afterwards, as he thinks they must be like sea and sky everywhere else, and he is content to try and remember how these *should* be done.' Nature's harmonies cannot be guessed at. He quoted much from Ruskin, leading on a little deeper to 'Composition'.

The lecture was delivered in the author's usual modest strain, but unconsciously it was expressive of himself and his whole-hearted thoroughness. He stands very high in the scale of human beings – how high I scarcely knew till the experience of the past few months.

In Winter Quarters: Modern Style – 1911

There is no member of our party so universally esteemed; only tonight I realise how patiently and consistently he has given time and attention to help the efforts of the other sketchers, and so it is all through; he has had a hand in almost every lecture given, and has been consulted in almost every effort which has been made towards the solution of the practical or theoretical problems of our Polar world.

The achievement of a great result by patient work is the best possible object-lesson for struggling humanity, for the results of genius, however admirable, can rarely be instructive. The chief of the Scientific Staff sets an example which is more potent than any other factor in maintaining that bond of good fellowship which is the marked and beneficent characteristic of our community.

Many passages of Scott's journals at this time are filled with information about the scientific work – for example he offered to write a paper for discussion on 'Ice-problems', following Wright's lecture on the subject. However, these were cut from the published text, as was an item on May 27th with details of Bowers' lecture on diet. Nearly three months later Atkinson gave a talk on scurvy.

Once again Scott stressed the value of the Scientific Staff, and also 'the bond of good fellowship' in the party as a whole. Huntford persists in suggesting that the party was split by Scott's weak leadership, though he adds, 'It says a great deal for the character and training of his men that, despite all this, there was little open quarrelling amongst them.'

Angry penguin attacking H. G. Ponting. 1911. Ponting claimed that no Antarctic creature has so endeared itself to explorers as the Adélie penguin, named after the wife of a French explorer. 'We held them in deep affection,' he said, and compared their gait to Charlie Chaplin's. However, he warned that 'if the visitor has the misfortune to give offence in any way, the chances are that the little valiant will go for you; if he does, look out— you will be bruised black and blue.'

To Midwinter Day – 1911

Capt. Scott's birthday dinner. June 6th 1911. An immense birthday cake, presumably made by Thomas Clissold, the cook, had appeared at lunch, but a photograph of this does not seem to have survived.

Tuesday, June 6. – It is my birthday, a fact I might easily have forgotten, but my kind people did not. At lunch an immense birthday cake made its appearance and we were photographed assembling about it. Clissold had decorated its sugared top with various devices in chocolate and crystallised fruit, flags and photographs of myself.

After my walk I discovered that great preparations were in progress for a special dinner, and when the hour for that meal arrived we sat down to a sumptuous spread with our sledge banners hung about us. Clissold's especially excellent seal soup, roast mutton and red currant jelly, fruit salad, asparagus and chocolate – such was our menu. For drink we had cider cup, a mystery not yet fathomed, some sherry and a liqueur.

After this luxurious meal every one was very festive and amiably argumentative. As I write there is a group in the dark-room discussing political progress with large discussions – another at one corner of the dinner table airing its views on the origin of matter and the probability of its ultimate discovery, and yet another debating military problems. The scraps that reach me from the various groups sometimes piece together in ludicrous fashion. Perhaps these arguments are practically unprofitable, but they give a great deal of pleasure to the participants. It's delightful to hear the ring of triumph in some voice when the owner imagines he has delivered himself of a well-rounded period or a clinching statement concerning the point under discussion. They are boys, all of them, but such excellent good-natured ones; there has been no sign of sharpness or anger, no jarring note, in all these wordy contests; all end with a laugh.

Monday, June 19. – A pleasant change to find the air calm and the sky clear – temperature down to −28°. At 1.30 the moon vanished behind the western mountains, after

Hut and Mt Erebus photographed by moonlight. June 13th 1911.

In the fortnight between these two entries, Scott was again preoccupied with diet, following Bowers' lecture (see p.99). On May 30th he recorded that he was busy with his physiological investigations into sledging rations and on June 3rd he was 'digging away at food statistics'.

Oates and Meares on ski. June 4th 1911. Oates was one of the few who had some experience of skiing before he joined the expedition, and Cecil Meares proved a willing pupil of Gran's. One has the impression, reading the full journals, that Scott was spending more time on skis.

One of the most significant contributions to the importance of the expedition might have come about through a change in diet. But though Atkinson lectured on scurvy to the group on Aug 18th, Scott's knowledge was far behind Amundsen's. The British ate seal meat, but not regularly, and they overcooked it. 'It is certain we shall not have [scurvy] here,' wrote Scott, 'but one cannot foresee equally certain avoidance in the [polar] journey to come.' Caused by lack of vitamin C, once acquired untreated scurvy is always fatal. Fresh food is a proven cure.

which, in spite of the clear sky, it was very dark on the floe. Went out on ski across the bay, then round about the cape, and so home, facing a keen northerly wind on return.

Atkinson is making a new fish-trap hole; from one cause and another, the breaking of the trap, and the freezing of the hole, no catch has been made for some time. I don't think we shall get good catches during the dark season, but Atkinson's own requirements are small, and the fish, though nice enough, are not such a luxury as to be greatly missed from our 'menu'.

Our daily routine has possessed a settled regularity for a long time. Clissold is up about 7 a.m. to start the breakfast. At 7.30 Hooper starts sweeping the floor and setting the table. Between 8 and 8.30 the men are out and about, fetching ice for melting, etc. Anton is off to feed the ponies, Dimitri to see the dogs; Hooper bursts on the slumberers with repeated announcements of the time, usually a quarter of an hour ahead of the clock. There is a stretching of limbs and an interchange of morning greetings, garnished with sleepy humour. Wilson and Bowers meet in a state of nature beside a washing basin filled with snow and proceed to rub glistening limbs with this chilling substance. A little later with less hardihood some others may be seen making the most of a meagre allowance of water. Soon after 8.30 I manage to drag myself from a very comfortable bed and make my toilet with a bare pint of water. By about ten minutes to 9 my clothes are on, my bed is made, and I sit down to my bowl of porridge; most of the others are gathered about the table by this time, but there are a few laggards who run the nine o'clock rule very close. The rule is instituted to prevent delay in the day's work, and it has needed a little pressure to keep one or two up to its observance. By 9.20 breakfast is finished, and before the half-hour has struck the table has been cleared. From 9.30 to 1.30 the men are steadily employed on a programme of preparation for sledging, which seems likely to occupy the greater part of the winter. The repair of sleeping-bags and the alteration of tents have already been done, but there are many other tasks uncompleted or not yet begun, such as the manufacture of provision bags, crampons, sealskin soles, pony clothes, etc.

Hooper has another good sweep up the hut after breakfast, washes the mess traps, and generally tidies things. I think it a good thing that in these matters the officers need not wait on themselves; it gives long unbroken days of scientific work and must, therefore, be an economy of brain in the long run.

We meet for our midday meal at 1.30 or 1.45, and spend a very cheerful half-hour over it. Afterwards the ponies are exercised, weather permitting; this employs all the men and a few of the officers for an hour or more – the rest of us generally take exercise in some form at the same time. After this the officers go on steadily with their work, whilst the men do odd jobs to while away the time. The evening meal, our dinner, comes at 6.30, and is finished within the hour. Afterwards people read, write, or play games, or occasionally finish some piece of work. The gramophone is usually started by some kindly disposed person, and on three nights of the week the lectures to which I have referred are given. They still command full audiences and lively discussions.

At 11 p.m. the acetylene lights are put out, and those who wish to remain up or to read in bed must depend on candle-light. The majority of candles are extinguished by midnight, and the night watchman alone remains awake to keep his vigil by the light of an oil lamp.

Day after day passes in this fashion. It is not a very active life perhaps, but certainly not an idle one. Few of us sleep more than eight hours out of the twenty-four. On Saturday afternoon or Sunday morning some extra bathing takes place; chins are shaved, and perhaps clean garments donned. Such signs, with the regular Service on Sunday, mark the passage of the weeks.

Thursday, June 22. – MIDWINTER. The sun reached its maximum depression at about 2.30 p.m. on the 22nd, Greenwich Mean Time: this is 2.30 a.m. on the 23rd according to the local time of the 180th meridian which we are keeping. Dinner tonight

Midwinter Day dinner. June 22nd 1911. Midwinter Day was their 'Christmas', as it was now two months since the sun had deserted them. At teatime Cherry-Garrard produced a colossal cake provided by his family. He then produced the 'South Polar Times', a fifty-page volume beautifully illustrated with watercolour sketches by Wilson (see p.129). Most of the prose was comic, but some of the verses were of a serious nature. Certain of Ponting's photographs were also included. Scott read each one aloud. At dinner the Hut was entirely transformed by Union Jacks, sledging flags, bunting and embroidered silks.

Iceberg. July 10th 1911(?). It was here that Ponting discovered 'one of the finest echoes I have heard in any land'. Here, he said, dwelt the Spirits of the Great White South. The small figure lower left suggests how the photographer must have felt its 'utter desolation and intense and wholly indescribable loneliness'.

is therefore the meal which is nearest the sun's critical change of course, and has been observed with all the festivity customary at Xmas at home.

At tea we broached an enormous Buszard cake, with much gratitude to its provider, Cherry-Garrard. In preparation for the evening our 'Union Jacks' and sledge flags were hung about the large table, which itself was laid with glass and a plentiful supply of champagne bottles instead of the customary mugs and enamel limejuice jugs. At seven o'clock we sat down to an extravagant bill of fare as compared with our usual simple diet.

Beginning on seal soup, by common consent the best liquid refreshment our cook produces, we went on to roast beef with Yorkshire pudding, fried potatoes and Brussels sprouts. Then followed a flaming plum-pudding and excellent mince-pies, and thereafter a dainty savoury of anchovy and cod's roe. A wondrous attractive meal even in so far as judged by our simple lights, but with its garnishments a positive feast, for withal the table was strewn with dishes of burnt almonds, crystallised fruits, chocolates and such toothsome morsels, whilst the unstinted supply of champagne which accompanied the courses was succeeded by a noble array of liqueur bottles from which choice could be made in the drinking of toasts.

I screwed myself up to a little speech which drew attention to the nature of the celebration as a halfway mark not only in our winter but in the plans of the Expedition as originally published. (I fear there are some who don't realise how rapidly time passes and who have barely begun work which by this time ought to be in full swing.)

We had come through a summer season and half a winter, and had before us half a winter and a second summer. We ought to know how we stood in every respect; we did know how we stood in regard to stores and transport, and I especially thanked the officer in charge of stores and the custodians of the animals. I said that as regards the future, chance must play a part, but that

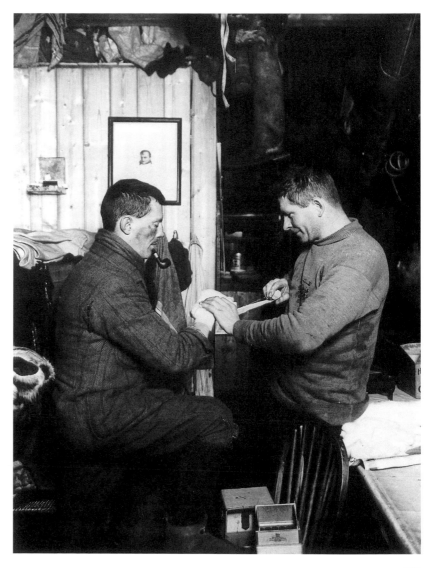

Seaman Evans dressing Dr Atkinson's frostbitten hand. July 6th 1911. Atkinson had got lost on the ice and came back dazed and badly frostbitten, especially on one of his hands. He lay awake writhing with pain all night, and the next morning his fingers were covered with blisters, but with careful treatment he recovered.

experience showed me that it would have been impossible to have chosen people more fitted to support me in the enterprise to the South than those who were to start in that direction in the spring. I thanked them all for having put their shoulders to the wheel and given me this confidence.

We drank to the Success of the Expedition.

Then everyone was called on to speak, starting on my left and working round the table; the result was very characteristic of the various individuals—one seemed to know so well the style of utterance to which each would commit himself.

Needless to say, all were entirely modest and brief; unexpectedly, all had exceedingly kind things to say of me—in fact I was obliged to request the omission of compliments at an early stage. Nevertheless it was gratifying to have a really genuine recognition of my attitude towards the scientific workers of the Expedition, and I felt very warmly towards all these kind, good fellows for expressing it.

If good will and happy fellowship count towards success, very surely shall we deserve to succeed. It was matter for comment, much applauded, that there had not been a single disagreement between any two members of our party from the beginning. By the end of dinner a very cheerful spirit prevailed, and the room was cleared for Ponting and his lantern, whilst the gramophone gave forth its most lively airs.

When the table was up-ended, its legs removed, and chairs arranged in rows, we had quite a roomy lecture hall. Ponting had cleverly chosen this opportunity to display a series of slides made from his own local negatives. I have never so fully realised his work as on seeing these beautiful pictures; they so easily outclass anything of their kind previously taken in these regions. Our audience cheered vociferously.

After this show the table was restored for snap-dragon, and a brew of milk punch was prepared in which we drank the health of Campbell's Party and of our good friends in the *Terra Nova*. Then the table was again removed and a set of lancers formed.

In the midst of the revelry Bowers suddenly appeared, followed by some satellites bearing an enormous Christmas Tree whose branches bore flaming candles, gaudy crackers, and little presents for all. The presents, I learnt, had been prepared with kindly thought by Miss Souper (Mrs Wilson's sister), and the tree had been made by Bowers of pieces of stick and string, with coloured paper to clothe its branches; the whole erection was remarkably creditable and the distribution of the presents caused much amusement.

Whilst revelry was the order of the day within our hut, the elements without seemed desirous of celebrating the occasion with equal emphasis and greater decorum. The eastern sky was massed with swaying auroral light, the most vivid and beautiful display that I had ever seen—fold on fold the arches and curtains of vibrating luminosity rose and spread across the sky, to fade slowly and yet again spring to glowing life.

The brighter light seemed to flow, now to mass itself in wreathing folds in one quarter, from which lustrous streamers shot upward, and anon to run in waves through the system of some dimmer figure as if to infuse new life within it.

The Crozier party left on June 27th, but no mention is made of this epic journey in the truncated text. Fortunately one of the three members of the party, Cherry-Garrard, was a born writer and his account, *The Worst Journey in the World*, remains a classic. The other two members were Wilson and Bowers. Their object was to find the Emperor penguin rookery on Cape Crozier, retrieve some eggs and explore the link between birds and reptiles. Cherry-Garrard and Bowers were, Wilson said, the two best sledgers in the whole expedition; they had to man-haul them because the surface was considered unsuitable for animals. They felt too inexperienced to use skis. The journey took 19 days each way, and was the nearest thing to hell, Cherry-Garrard writing, 'I for one had come to that point of suffering at which I did not really care if only I could die without much pain . . .' It was the darkness that did it (and a temperature that dropped to −47°F, then to −56°, and finally to −77.5°). Scott described the joy when the three men returned on Aug 2nd, after five weeks away. His conclusion (not in Scott's account here) was that the sledging rations were satisfactory, the sleeping bags also, the double tent 'an immense success', and the clothing gear 'excellent', since 'our system of clothing has come through a severer test than ever before'.

It is impossible to witness such a beautiful phenomenon without a sense of awe, and yet this sentiment is not inspired by its brilliancy but rather by its delicacy in light and colour, its transparency, and above all by its tremulous evanescence of form. There is no glittering splendour to dazzle the eye, as has been too often described; rather the appeal is to the imagination by the suggestion of something wholly spiritual, something instinct with a fluttering ethereal life, serenely confident yet restlessly mobile.

One wonders why history does not tell us of 'aurora' worshippers, so easily could the phenomenon be considered the manifestation of 'god' or 'demon'. To the little silent group which stood at gaze before such enchantment it seemed profane to return to the mental and physical atmosphere of our house. Finally, when I stepped within, I was glad to find that there had been a general movement bedwards, and in the next half hour the last of the revellers had succumbed to slumber.

Two or three days later the temperature had fallen to a record −49°F, following the worst gales Scott had 'ever known' in these regions. There were gusts exceeding 70mph – another record. Ten days later, they nearly lost one of the best ponies, Bones, which would have been 'to risk failure'. He survived. On July 16th a second pony, China, went off his food but also survived. But by the 22nd 'all are in good form', although, at the end of the month, one of the best sledge dogs had disappeared (it returned a month later). Incidentally, Scott commented, in a clear reference to 'the race', that it was difficult to see how Amundsen could keep his dogs alive if he met the same temperatures as the Crozier party.

H. G. Ponting at work in darkroom. July 22nd 1911. This was at the far end of the ward-room. He had made it himself during the summer with his own carpenter's tools. It was 8 × 6ft wide, and 8ft high. He covered the walls with ruberoid to keep out the light. On the roof was a 30-gallon iron tank with water for rinsing his plates. Every inch could be used, and his bed folded up in the daytime. 'It was always spotlessly clean and neat,' claimed Ponting.

The Last Months at Cape Evans – 1911

Account of the Winter Journey

Wednesday, August 2. – The Crozier Party returned last night after enduring for five weeks the hardest conditions on record. They looked more weather-worn than anyone I have yet seen. Their faces were scarred and wrinkled, their eyes dull, their hands whitened and creased with the constant exposure to damp and cold, yet the scars of frostbite were very few and this evil had never seriously assailed them. The main part of their afflictions arose, and very obviously arose, from sheer lack of sleep, and today after a night's rest our travellers are very different in appearance and mental capacity.

The story of a very wonderful performance must be told by the actors. It is for me now to give but an outline of the journey, and to note more particularly the effects of the strain which they have imposed on themselves and the lessons which their experiences teach for our future guidance.

Huge ice bastions of the Castle Berg (Clissold). Sept 11th 1911. This berg was originally called Arch Berg, but it partially collapsed and though the arch had gone, the portion that resembled a castle was a perfect medieval fortress. Earlier, in June, Ponting had photographed this magnificent iceberg by flash.

Wilson is very thin, but this morning very much his keen, wiry self – Bowers is quite himself today. Cherry-Garrard is slightly puffy in the face and still looks worn. It is evident that he has suffered most severely – but Wilson tells me that his spirit never wavered for a moment. Bowers has come through best, all things considered, and I believe he is the hardest traveller that ever undertook a Polar journey, as well as one of the most undaunted; more by hint than direct statement I gather his value to the party, his untiring energy and the astonishing physique which enables him to continue to work under conditions which are absolutely paralysing to others. Never was such a sturdy, active, undefeatable little man.

So far as one can gather, the story of this journey in brief is much as follows: the party reached the Barrier two days after leaving C[ape] Evans, still pulling their full load of 250 lbs per man; the snow surface then changed completely and grew worse and worse as they advanced. For one day they struggled on as before, covering 4 miles, but from this onward they were forced to relay, and found the half load heavier than the whole one had been on the sea ice. Meanwhile the temperature had been falling, and now for more than a week the thermometer fell below −60°. On one night the minimum showed −71°, and on the next −77°, 109° of frost. Although in this truly fearful cold the air was comparatively still, every now and again little puffs of wind came eddying across the snow plain with blighting effect. No civilised being has ever encountered such conditions before with only a tent of thin canvas to rely on for shelter.

It took the best part of a fortnight to cross the coldest region, and then rounding C. Mackay they entered the windswept area. Blizzard followed blizzard, the sky was constantly overcast and they staggered on in a light which was little better than complete darkness; sometimes they found themselves high on the slopes of Terror on the left of their track, and sometimes diving into the pressure ridges on the right amidst crevasses and confused ice disturbance. Reaching the foothills near C. Crozier, they ascended 800 feet, then packed their belongings over a moraine ridge and started to build a hut. It took three days to build the stone walls and complete the roof with the canvas brought for the purpose. Then at last they could attend to the object of the journey.

The scant twilight at midday was so short that they must start in the dark and be prepared for the risk of missing their way in returning without light. On the first day in which they set forth under these conditions it took them two hours to reach the pressure ridges, and to clamber over them roped together occupied nearly the same time; finally they reached a place above the rookery where they could hear the birds squawking, but from which they were quite unable to find a way down. The poor light was failing and they returned to camp. Starting again on the following day they wound their way through frightful ice disturbances under the high basalt cliffs; in places the rock overhung, and at one spot they had to creep through a small channel hollowed in the ice. At last they reached the sea ice, but now the light was so far spent they were obliged to rush everything. Instead of the 2,000 or 3,000 nesting birds which had been seen here in *Discovery* days, they could now only count about 100; they hastily killed and skinned three to get blubber for their stove, and collecting six eggs, three of which alone survived, they dashed for camp.

It is possible the birds are deserting this rookery, but it is also possible that this early date found only a small minority of the birds which will be collected at a later one. The eggs, which have not yet been examined, should throw light on this point. Wilson observed yet another proof of the strength of the nursing instinct in these birds. In searching for eggs both he and Bowers picked up rounded pieces of ice which these ridiculous creatures had been cherishing with fond hope.

The light had failed entirely by the time the party were clear of the pressure ridges on their return, and it was only by good luck they regained their camp.

That night a blizzard commenced, increasing in fury from moment to moment. They now found that the place chosen for the hut for shelter was worse than useless. They had far better have built it in the open, for the fierce wind, instead of striking them directly, was deflected on to them in furious whirling gusts. Heavy blocks of snow and rock placed on the roof were whirled away and the canvas ballooned up, tearing and straining at its securings – its disappearance could only be a question of time. They had erected their tent with some valuables inside close to the hut; it had been well spread and more than amply secured with snow and boulders, but one terrific gust tore it up and whirled it away. Inside the hut they waited for the roof to vanish, wondering what they could do if it went, and vainly endeavouring to make it secure. After fourteen hours it went, as they were trying to pin down one corner. The smother of snow was on them and they could only dive for their sleeping-bags with a gasp. Bowers put his head out once and said, 'We're all right,' in as near his ordinary tones as he could compass. The others replied, 'Yes, we're all right,' and all were silent for a night and half a day whilst the wind howled on; the snow entered every chink and crevice of the sleeping-bags, and the occupants shivered and wondered how it would all end.

The wind fell at noon the following day; the forlorn travellers crept from their icy nests, made shift to spread their floorcloth overhead, and lit their primus. They tasted their first food for forty-eight hours and began to plan a means to build a shelter on the homeward route. They decided that they must dig a large pit nightly and cover it as best they could with their floorcloth. But now fortune befriended them; a search to the north revealed the tent lying amongst boulders a quarter of a mile away, and, strange to relate, practically uninjured, a fine testimonial for the material used in its construction. On the following day they started homeward, and immediately another blizzard fell on them, holding them prisoners for two days. By this time the miserable condition of their effects was beyond description. The sleeping-bags were far too stiff to be rolled up, in fact they were so hard frozen that attempts to bend them actually split the skins; the eiderdown bags inside Wilson's and C.-G's reindeer covers served but to fitfully stop the gaps made by such rents. All socks, finnesko, and mitts had long been coated with ice; placed in breast pockets or inside vests at night they did not even show signs of thawing, much less of drying. It sometimes took C.-G. three-quarters of an

Petty Officer Evans at the sewing machine. He was probably overhauling sleeping bags and tents, a job he shared with other P.O.s. They also had to make hundreds of provision bags for the sledging journeys, and there was always footwear to make and patch. Those in charge of dogs and ponies had to repair their harnesses.

hour to get into his sleeping bag, so flat did it freeze and so difficult was it to open. It is scarcely possible to realise the horrible discomforts of the forlorn travellers as they plodded back across the Barrier with the temperature again constantly below −60°. In this fashion they reached Hut Point and on the following night our home quarters.

Wilson is disappointed at seeing so little of the penguins, but to me and to everyone who has remained here the result of this effort is the appeal it makes to our imagination as one of the most gallant stories in Polar History. That men should wander forth in the depth of a Polar night to face the most dismal cold and the fiercest gales in darkness is something new; that they should have persisted in this effort in spite of every adversity for five full weeks is heroic. It makes a tale for our generation which I hope may not be lost in the telling.

Moreover the material results are by no means despicable. We shall know now when that extraordinary bird the Emperor penguin lays its eggs, and under what conditions; but even if our information remains meagre concerning its embryology, our party has shown the nature of the conditions which exist on the Great Barrier in winter. Hitherto we have only imagined their severity; now we have proof, and a positive light is thrown on the local climatology of our Strait.

Preparations for the Southern Journey

Sunday, September 10. – My whole time has been occupied in making plans for the Southern journey. These are finished at last, I am glad to say; every figure has been

The editors deleted a passage of optimism here, where Scott wrote: 'There does not seem to be a single weak spot in the twelve good men and true who are chosen for the Southern advance. All are now experienced sledge travellers, knit together with a bond of friendship which has never been equalled . . . There is not a single detail of our equipment which is not arranged in accordance with the tests of experience.' 'Southern Party' was the term used for the larger party which was to head for the Pole.

Capt. Scott, Dr Simpson, Lieut. Bowers and Evans leaving hut for the west. Going onto sea ice. Sept 15th 1911. This was another of Scott's impromptu expeditions. He said he wanted to look at the Ferrar Glacier and to bring his sledging impressions up to date. He wrote: 'I haven't decided how long we shall stay away or precisely where we shall go; such vague arrangements have an attractive side.' But the temperature had dropped to −35°F.

checked by Bowers, who has been an enormous help to me. If the motors are successful, we shall have no difficulty in getting to the Glacier, and if they fail, we shall still get there with an ordinary degree of good fortune. To work three units of four men from that point onwards requires no small provision, but with the proper provision it should take a good deal to stop the attainment of our object. I have tried to take every reasonable possibility of misfortune into consideration, and to so organise the parties as to be prepared to meet them. I fear to be too sanguine, yet taking everything into consideration I feel that our chances ought to be good. The animals are in splendid form. Day by day the ponies get fitter as their exercise increases, and stronger, harder food toughens their muscles. They are very different animals from those which we took south last year, and with another month of training I feel there is not one of them but will make light of the loads we shall ask them to draw. But we cannot spare any of the ten, and so there must always be anxiety of the disablement of one or more before their work is done.

It is good to have arrived at a point where we can run over facts and figures again and again without detecting a flaw or foreseeing a difficulty.

I do not count on the motors – that is a strong point in our case – but should they work well, our earlier task of reaching the Glacier will be made quite easy. Apart from such help, I am anxious that these machines should enjoy some measure of success and

justify the time, money and thought which have been given to their construction. I am still very confident of the possibility of motor traction, whilst realising that reliance cannot be placed on it in its present untried evolutionary state – it is satisfactory to add that my own view is the most cautious one held in our party. Day is quite convinced he will go a long way, and is prepared to accept much heavier weights than I have given him. Lashly's opinion is perhaps more doubtful, but on the whole hopeful. Clissold is to make the fourth man of the motor party. He has had a great deal of experience with motors, and Day is delighted to have his assistance.

If the Southern journey comes off, nothing, not even priority at the Pole, can prevent the Expedition ranking as one of the most important that ever entered the Polar regions.

Thursday, September 14. – Another interregnum. I have been exceedingly busy finishing up the Southern plans, getting instruction in photographing, and preparing for our jaunt to the west. I held forth on the Southern plans yesterday; every one was enthusiastic, and the feeling is general that our arrangements are calculated to make the best of our resources. Although people have given a good deal of thought to various branches of the subject, there was not a suggestion offered for improvement. The scheme seems to have earned full confidence: it remains to play the game out.

The race

In his introduction to an edition of the *Journals*, Peter Scott, the explorer's son, wrote that when Scott learned that Amundsen had announced that he was heading for the South Pole, 'my father refused to prejudice his scientific programme by making a race of the journey to the Pole and stuck to his original timetable'. It is quite clear that this version of Scott's intentions was mistaken. When Scott himself wrote to his wife from Cape Evans in October 1911 he said, 'I don't know what to think of Amundsen's chances. If he gets to the Pole, it must be before us, as he is bound to travel fast with dogs . . .'.

The word 'chances' gives the game away – of course the Norwegian had forced a race by so arranging things that he set out secretly before Scott and arrived at the winning post a full month before him. In these circumstances Scott had no choice but to 'race' or withdraw from the contest. But no one, so far as is known, ever suggested this.

Then again, Scott repeats what he has claimed before – that he will act exactly as 'if there had been no rival'. But this presupposes that Scott had come to the

Antarctic with a plan from which he would now not deviate. No such plan existed, except in the sense that Scott had given himself several *options*. These were (1) motor sledges (2) ponies (3) dogs (4) skis. If none of these proved available, either singly or in combination, Scott's party was left with the dreadful alternative of man-hauling. Set beside the failure of the options, several other factors – diet, fitness, morale, teamwork, etc. – counted for little, because the latter could not on their own ensure success. The term 'transport' was a weasel word which obscured its fundamental significance. Today, it would be replaced by the term 'logistics'. This would convey the need to move food, forage and fuel to key points along the route in adequate quantities to enable the humans to arrive at their consecutive goals in a timely fashion.

Peter Scott, in the introduction referred to above, claims that his father's 'organisation of rations and equipment had worked out perfectly to plan'. On the contrary, this was Scott's failure – he had no logistics in place to enable him to travel fast enough to beat his opponent, who had these matters all worked out before he left. One by one as Scott's systems failed – first motors, then ponies, then dogs, then skis – he was inexorably set on a course, like a man playing the wrong cards, leading to the ultimate failure of man-hauling. Scott called this bad luck, but he should have given up now, in October.

This was not openly discussed very often. Gran wrote that it was as if there was a notice at Cape Evans: 'Shop Talk not Permitted.' Huntford believes that Debenham probably reflected the general view when he wrote in his diary 'Admundsen's chances . . . are rather better than ours. To begin with they are 60 miles further south than we are and can make south at once, whereas we have to dodge around islands . . . If [Scott] will consult the senior men I think it can be done but if he keeps them in the dark as they were on this depôt trip, things are likely to go wrong.' Debenham wanted to plan a 'very careful organisation'.

As they set out for the Pole, Scott wrote in a letter to his former commanding officer: 'Everything depends on the coming journey.' Huntford's comment is: 'So, in fact, there *was* a race, although Scott, when it suited him, maintained the gentlemanly pretence that there was not.' He goes further when he quotes a letter from Scott to his agent Kinsey. If Amundsen gets to the Pole he is bound to do it with dogs, said Scott, 'But one guesses that success will justify him . . . Anyway he is taking a big risk and perhaps deserves his luck [luck again] if he gets through. But he is not there yet.' The implication, Huntford says, is that using dogs is somehow not 'nice' (Huntford's quotation marks). Scott is trusting to luck to see his opponent defeated in the race by failing to reach the Pole at all.

Curiously, when Amundsen wrote his own book on returning from the Antarctic, he said 'The English expedition was based entirely on scientific research.

The Pole was only a subsidiary matter, while my extended plans made the Pole the first objective.' He added that he 'had to be first past the post; everything had to give way to that'.

The Norwegian never met or spoke to Scott. Although Scott went to Norway to meet his rival, Amundsen avoided him. There is very little about Amundsen in Scott's Journals, though this edition quotes some relevant information from Huntford's book in its marginal notes. Huntford's two books about Amundsen are *The Amundsen Photographs*, which he edited and introduced (Hodder 1987) and his comprehensive biography of the two men *Scott and Amundsen*, first published in 1979.

Amundsen was born in 1872, four years after Scott. His father was a shipowner and merchant skipper, his mother the daughter of a tax collector. He grew up in Oslo (then called Christiana) the capital of Norway. Scott, also middle class, was likewise born and bred by the sea, at Devonport near the Plymouth naval dock-yards. He went to Dartmouth's Britannia Royal Naval College as a cadet at the age of 13. His father was a failed brewer.

There, implies Huntford, the similarity between their upbringing ends. They were, he says, ideal antagonists: on almost every point they stood opposed. Amundsen from a small, poor country with a sparse and scattered population; Scott came from a rich and mighty empire, albeit one in decline.

As soon as he could walk, the Norwegian was put on skis. The period when he grew up is described by Huntford as the Norwegian era of 'Polar exploration that for a short, intense, fertile period was to supplant the British and dominate the field'. It was significant that the heart of this 'school' was the application of skis to Polar travel.

From his very early days Amundsen had ambitions to explore in polar regions. Scott's aims in that direction came about because of his desire to achieve high rank in the Royal Navy, and he was egged on in this respect by Sir Clements Markham, also a navy man with a passion for Polar exploration. Scott first met him when he was a mere midshipman.

Though comparatively unknown to the British, Amundsen had already had a much more successful career in exploration than Scott, having completed the North-West Passage, the legendary route from the Atlantic to the Pacific, which had long eluded explorers. To prepare himself for this he lived with the Eskimos, dressed like them and ate their food.

Huntford lists many other achievements. In 1898 Amundsen had gone to the Arctic and was probably the first man to ski on Arctic *terra firma*. He was on the

When Fram *arrived back in Australia early in Mar 1912, the Norwegians acted with great secrecy because they had a contract with a single newspaper (*The Daily Chronicle *of London*).* When Amundsen went ashore he complained he was 'treated as a tramp' and given 'a miserable little room'. There was no great reception for them, although they were dogged by reporters. In this photograph, taken on the deck, Amundsen sits centre in the bowler hat. Johansen, with whom he quarrelled, and who later shot himself, is seated on the extreme left, same row.*

first sledging expeditions and set up the first Arctic camp. He was also a member of a group which was the first to winter in the Antarctic. He was thus far more experienced than Scott before the latter began his first Antarctic explorations. And, afterwards, he was the first man to circumnavigate the Arctic too.

In terms of character, Huntford draws a sharp distinction between the two men, claiming that the Norwegian was far the more dedicated of the two. One of his team is quoted as saying that 'he was a *man*—the born leader . . . an unusually good human being who was willing to sacrifice everything for those who stood by him in thick and thin'. Huntford adds that Amundsen had the personal magnetism which is the hallmark of great leaders. He also claims that 'intellectually he dwarfs Scott'. He gives many examples of Scott's ineptitude, yet it must be underlined that others who knew Scott praise his high qualities of leadership. It is also pertinent that in September 1911, after his quarrel with Johansen, Amundsen remarked that was 'a sad end to our wonderful unity'. Scott was constantly referring to the 'luck' (good or bad) which dogged his enterprise; Amundsen by contrast wrote in his memoirs: 'Victory awaits those who have everything in order—people call that luck. Defeat is certain for those who have forgotten to take the necessary precautions in time—that is called bad luck.' In so far as Scott failed to make adequate plans, there are in Huntford's account examples of Norwegian failings, too. For example, two of their small party had no experience of driving dogs before joining the expedition. However, in general the case was made that Scott was the less effective organiser.

The crews, too, were quite different. Scott's was large, with several scientists who achieved distinction in their subsequent university careers. There were no Norwegian scientists, and according to Huntford, *Fram*'s crew of 19 included no academics because Amundsen did not trust them.

For more comparative data, read Huntford. There the tragic end of both men is described. Scott's we know. After the polar success Amundsen sailed along the coast of Siberia from Norway to the Bering Strait, thus becoming the second man in recorded history to sail through the North-East Passage. But in the main his life was 'a battle with financial difficulties, relieved by bouts of solvency, with his friends and family trying to save him from himself'. Huntford continues: 'He never married; he ended lonely and unhappy.' He died in 1928 trying to rescue an Italian explorer whose airship had disappeared on a flight to the North Pole. Amundsen's plane disappeared and though some wreckage was found, the bodies of the Norwegian and his crew vanished into the Polar Sea. Huntford writes: "The aircraft was overloaded and too weak for the Arctic . . . [The Italian] was rescued by someone else; Amundsen had thrown away his life. But he would only have been unhappy if he had gone on.'

This comment, in a letter to his wife, that a race would have 'wrecked my plan', lacks logic, as Scott was constantly changing his plan, and the one fact known (if not acknowledged) by all was that everyone was desperate to reach the Pole first.

The character sketches which follow were in a private letter home. According to Preston, Scott 'had spent much of the winter observing his companions and writing shrewd rather than universally flattering pen-portraits, many of which were edited out or toned down in the published version of his diary'. Presumably Scott felt it important to spend time on this character assessment because he still had to pick his team for the final push to the Pole.

October, 1911. – 'I don't know what to think of Amundsen's chances. If he gets to the Pole, it must be before we do, as he is bound to travel fast with dogs and pretty certain to start early. On this account I decided at a very early date to act exactly as I should have done had he not existed. Any attempt to race must have wrecked my plan, besides which it doesn't appear the sort of thing one is out for.

'Possibly you will have heard something before this reaches you. Oh! and there are all sorts of possibilities. In any case you can rely on my not doing or saying anything foolish – only I'm afraid you must be prepared for the chance of finding our venture much belittled.

'After all, it is the work that counts, not the applause that follows.

'Words must always fail me when I talk of Bill Wilson. I believe he really is the finest character I ever met – the closer one gets to him the more there is to admire. Every quality is so solid and dependable; cannot you imagine how that counts down here? Whatever the matter, one knows Bill will be sound, shrewdly practical, intensely loyal and quite unselfish. Add to this a wider knowledge of persons and things than is at first guessable, a quiet vein of humour and really consummate tact, and you have some idea of his values. I think he is the most popular member of the party, and that is saying much.

'Bowers is all and more than I ever expected of him. He is a positive treasure,

Capt. Scott in his den. Oct 7th 1911. In a later edition of the Journals this is captioned: Scott in his 'den' writing up his journal. But there is no evidence that this was not a posed picture, which Scott had taken to emphasise the scientific nature of the enterprise. Ponting said, 'Scott wrote much in his diary and smoked incessantly while doing so. Once, during the winter, I asked him whether he had yet started on his book. He said he would leave that until he got home and his Journal was to be used merely as notes, to be elaborated later into his official account.'

118

Top left: *Ponting on the Matterhorn berg. Oct 8th 1911. Scott may have pressed the button, as he was with Ponting in the morning.*

Top right: *Capt. Scott on ski. Oct 1911.*

Below: *Lieut. T. Gran on ski. Oct 1911.*

absolutely trustworthy and prodigiously energetic. He is about the hardest man amongst us, and that is saying a good deal—nothing seems to hurt his tough little body and certainly no hardship daunts his spirit. I shall have a hundred little tales to tell you of his indefatigable zeal, his unselfishness, and his inextinguishable good humour. He surprises always, for his intelligence is of quite a high order and his memory for details most exceptional. You can imagine him, as he is, an indispensable assistant to me in every detail concerning the management and organisation of our sledging work and a delightful companion on the march.

'One of the greatest successes is Wright. He is very thorough and absolutely ready for anything. Like Bowers he has taken to sledging like a duck to water, and although he hasn't had such severe testing, I believe he would stand it pretty nearly as well. Nothing ever seems to worry him, and I can't imagine he ever complained of anything in his life.

'I don't think I will give such long descriptions of the others, though most of them deserve equally high praise. Taken all round they are a perfectly excellent lot.

'The Soldier is very popular with all—a delightfully humorous cheery old pessimist—striving with the ponies night and day and

The Matterhorn berg, profile and Erebus. Oct 8th 1911. This was the day that Clissold fell from a berg. He was practically insensible and Ponting much distressed.

bringing woeful accounts of their small ailments into the hut.

'The men are equally fine. Edgar Evans has proved a useful member of our party; he looks after our sledges and sledge equipment with a care of management and a fertility of resource which is truly astonishing – on "trek" he is just as sound and hard as ever and has an inexhaustible store of anecdote.

'Crean is perfectly happy, ready to do anything and go anywhere, the harder the work, the better. Evans and Crean are great friends. Lashly is his old self in every respect, hard-working to the limit, quiet, abstemious, and determined. You see altogether I have a good set of people with me, and it will go hard if we don't achieve something.

'The study of individual character is a pleasant pastime in such a mixed community of thoroughly nice people, and the study of relationships and influences is fascinating – men of the most diverse upbringing and experience are really pals with one another, and the subjects which would be delicate ground of discussion between acquaintances are just those which are most freely used for jest. For instance, the Soldier is never tired of jeering at Australia, its people and institutions, and the Australians retaliate by attacking the hide-bound prejudices of the British Army. I have never seen a temper lost in these discussions. So as I sit here I am very satisfied with these things. I think that it would have been difficult to better the organisation of the party – every man has his work and is especially adapted for it; there is no gap and no overlap – it is all that I desired, and the same might be said of the men selected to do the work.'

Friday, October 6. – Today Wilson, Oates, Cherry-Garrard and Crean have gone to Hut Point with their ponies, Oates getting off with Christopher after some difficulty. At 5 o'clock the Hut Point telephone bell suddenly rang (the line was laid by Meares some time ago, but hitherto there has been no communication). In a minute or two we heard a voice, and behold! communication was established. I had quite a talk with Meares and afterwards with Oates. Not a very wonderful fact, perhaps, but it seems wonderful in this primitive land to be talking to one's fellow beings 15 miles away. Oates told me that the ponies had arrived in fine order, Christopher a little done, but carrying the heaviest load. . . .

The photography craze is in full swing. Ponting's mastery is ever more impressive, and his pupils improve day by day; nearly all of us have produced good negatives.

Saturday, October 7. – As though to contradict the suggestion of incompetence, friend 'Jehu' pulled with a will this morning – he covered 3½ miles without a stop, the surface being much worse than it was two days ago. He was not at all distressed when he

Ponting seems to have been universally popular. A descriptive verb, 'to pont', had even been coined in his honour; this was defined by Griffith Taylor, the wit of the party, as 'to spend a deuce of a time posing in an uncomfortable position'. Some negatives by Debenham and others survive at the Scott Polar Research Institute, but on the whole Ponting remains the great master of polar photography. On the other hand he attracted some criticism, as when on Oct 8th Clissold, acting as model, fell and injured himself, and again, towards the end of October, when Debenham hurt his knee while playing football for Ponting's cinematograph. Scott advanced on the photographer saying 'So that's another member of the expedition you've jiggered up!' Debenham, too, probably felt the rough edge of Scott's tongue, because he wrote in a letter to his wife, 'His temper is very uncertain and leads him to absurd lengths even in simple arguments. In crises he acts very peculiarly.'

Harnessing Michael to the sledge. Oct 1911.

The pressure ridges of the ice crack from the Barne Glacier to Inaccessible, looking to Cape Royds (Capt. Scott). Oct 8th 1911. Scott wrote that 'Ponting has been doing some wonderfully fine cinematographic work. My [own] incursion into photography has brought me into close contact with him, and I realise what a very good fellow he is. If he is able to carry out the whole of his programme, we shall have a cinematographic and photographic record which will be absolutely new in expeditionary work.'

stopped. If he goes on like this he comes into practical politics again, and I am arranging to give 10-feet sledges to him and Chinaman instead of 12-feet. Probably they will not do much, but if they go on as at present, we shall get something out of them.

Long and cheerful conversations with Hut Point and of course an opportunity for the exchange of witticisms. . . .

Friday, October 13. – The ponies have been behaving well, with exceptions. Victor is now quite easy to manage, thanks to Bowers' patience. Chinaman goes along very steadily and is not going to be the crock we expected. He has a slow pace which may be troublesome, but when the weather is fine that won't matter if he can get along steadily.

The most troublesome animal is Christopher. He is only a source of amusement as long as there is no accident, but I am always a little anxious that he will kick or bite someone. The curious thing is that he is quiet enough to handle for walking or riding exercise or in the stable, but as soon as a sledge comes into the programme he is seized with a very demon of viciousness, and bites and kicks with every intent to do injury.

The Start of the Motor Sledges

Tuesday, October 24. – Two fine days for a wonder. Yesterday the motors seemed ready to start and we all went out on the floe to give them a 'send off'. But the inevitable little defects cropped up, and the machines only got as far as the Cape. A change made by Day in the working of the petrol engines had caused their internal mechanism to go wrong, so he and Lashly spent the afternoon making good the defects, which they accomplished in a satisfactory manner.

This morning the engines were set going again, and shortly after 10 a.m. a fresh start was made. At first there were a good many stops, but on the whole the engines seemed to be improving all the time. They are not by any means working up to full power yet, and so the pace is very slow. The weights seem to me a good deal heavier than we bargained for. Day sets his motor going, climbs off the car, and walks alongside with an occasional finger on the throttle. Lashly hasn't yet quite got hold of the nice adjustments of his control levers, but I hope will have done so after a day's practice.

The only alarming incident was the slipping of the chains when Day tried to start on some ice very thinly covered with snow. The starting effort on such heavily laden sledges is very heavy, but I thought the grip of the pattens and studs would have been

A few days earlier, Scott wrote: 'I am secretly convinced that we shall not get much help from the [motor sledges], yet nothing has ever happened to them that was unavoidable. A lot more care and foresight would make them splendid allies.' (But Scott had failed to study their fuel requirements thoroughly.) 'The trouble is that if they fail, no one will ever believe this.' Scott forecast that ultimately they would revolutionise polar transport – and of course he was right.

The Motor Party. Lieut. Evans, B. Day, Lashly and Hooper by one of the motors. Oct 1911.

Getting one of the motors on the sea-ice. Oct 1911.

good enough on any surface. Looking at the place afterwards I found that the studs had grooved the ice.

Now as I write at 12.30 the machines are about a mile out in the South Bay; both can be seen still under way, progressing steadily if slowly.

I find myself immensely eager that these tractors should succeed, even though they may not be of great help to our southern advance. A small measure of success will be enough to show their possibilities, their ability to revolutionise Polar transport. Seeing the machines at work today, and remembering that every defect so far shown is purely mechanical, it is impossible not to be convinced of their value. But the trifling mechanical defects and lack of experience show the risk of dispensing with trials. A season of experiment with a small workshop at hand may be all that stands between success and failure.

At any rate before we start we shall certainly know if the worst has happened, or if some measure of success attends this unique effort.

Thursday, October 26. – This morning Simpson has just rung up. He says the motors are in difficulties with the surface. The trouble is just that which I noted as alarming on Monday – the chains slip on the very light snow covering of hard ice. The engines are working well, and all goes well when the machines get on to snow.

I have organised a party of eight men, including myself, and we are just off to see what can be done to help.

Southern Journey: the Barrier Stage – 1911

Friday, November 3. – Camp 1. A keen wind with some drift at Hut Point, but we sailed away in detachments. Atkinson's party, Jehu, Chinaman, and Jimmy Pigg led off at eight. Just before ten Wilson, Cherry-Garrard, and I left. Our ponies marched steadily and well together over the sea ice. The wind dropped a good deal, but the temperature with it, so that the little remaining was very cutting. We found Atkinson at Safety Camp. He had lunched and was just ready to march out again; he reports Chinaman and Jehu tired. Ponting arrived soon after we had camped with Dimitri and a small dog team. The cinematograph was up in time to catch the flying rear-guard which came along in fine form, Snatcher leading and being stopped every now and again – a wonderful little beast. Christopher had given the usual trouble when harnessed, but was evidently subdued by the Barrier Surface. However, it was not thought advisable to halt him, and so the party fled through in the wake of the advance guard.

After lunch we packed up and marched on steadily as before. I don't like these midnight lunches, but for man the march that follows is pleasant when, as today, the wind falls and the sun steadily increases its heat. The two parties in front of us camped 5 miles beyond Safety Camp, and we reached their camp some half or three-quarters of an hour later. All the ponies are tethered in good order, but most of them are tired – Chinaman and Jehu *very tired*. Nearly all are inclined to be off feed, but this is very temporary, I think. We have built walls, but there is no wind and the sun gets warmer every minute.

Mirage. – Very marked waving effect to east. Small objects greatly exaggerated and showing as dark vertical lines.

1 p.m. – Feeding time. Woke the party, and Oates served out the rations – all ponies feeding well. It is a sweltering day, the air breathless, the glare intense – one loses sight of the fact that the temperature is low (+22°) – one's mind seeks comparison in hot sunlit streets and scorching pavements, yet six hours ago my thumb was frostbitten. All the inconveniences of frozen footwear and damp clothes and sleeping-bags have vanished entirely.

Saturday, November 4. – Camp 2. Led march – started in what I think will now become the settled order. Atkinson went at 8, ours at 10,

The Southern Journey – 1,500 miles across a frozen wilderness – was the start of the drive for the Pole, which began on Nov 1st. Before he left Cape Evans, Scott wrote in his diary on Oct 31st (deleted): 'The future is in the lap of the gods. I can think of nothing left undone to deserve success.' Ponting was travelling with the dog team, with what Scott described as 'a great photographic outfit'.

A meal on the march.

Bowers, Oates and Co. at 11.15. Just after starting picked up cheerful note and saw cheerful notices saying all well with motors, both going excellently. Day wrote 'Hope to meet in 80° 30' (Lat.).' Poor chap, within 2 miles he must have had to sing a different tale. It appears they had a bad grind on the morning of the 29th. I suppose the surface was bad and everything seemed to be going wrong. They 'dumped' a good deal of petrol and lubricant. Worse was to follow. Some 4 miles out we met a tin pathetically inscribed, 'Big end Day's motor No. 2 cylinder broken.' Half a mile beyond, as I expected, we found the motor, its tracking sledges and all. Notes from E. Evans and Day told the tale. The only spare [cylinder] had been used for Lashly's machine, and it would have taken a long time to strip Day's engine so that it could run on three cylinders. They had decided to abandon it and push on with the other alone. They had taken the six bags of forage and some odds and ends, besides their petrol and lubricant. So the dream of great help from the machines is at an end! The track of the remaining motor goes steadily forward, but now, of course, I shall expect to see it every hour of the march.

The ponies did pretty well – a cruel soft surface most of the time, but light loads, of course. Jehu is better than I expected to find him, Chinaman not so well. They are bad crocks both of them.

It was pretty cold during the night, –7° when we camped, with a crisp breeze blowing. The ponies don't like it, but now, as I write, the sun is shining through a white haze, the wind has dropped, and the picketing line is comfortable for the poor beasts.

Tuesday, November 7. – Camp 4. A blizzard has continued throughout last night and up to this time of writing, late in the afternoon. Starting mildly, with broken clouds, little snow, and gleams of sunshine, it grew in intensity until this forenoon, when there was heavy snowfall and the sky overspread with low nimbus cloud. In the early afternoon the snow and wind ceased, and the wind is dropping now, but the sky looks very lowering and unsettled.

Last night the sky was so broken that I made certain the end of the blow had come. Towards morning the sky overhead and far to the north was quite clear. More cloud obscured the sun to the south and low heavy banks hung over Ross Island. All seemed hopeful, except that I noted with misgiving that the mantle on the Bluff was beginning to form. Two hours later the whole sky was overcast and the blizzard had fully developed.

This Tuesday evening it remains overcast, but one cannot see that the clouds are travelling fast. The Bluff mantle is a wide low bank of level cloud not particularly windy in appearance; the wind is falling, but the sky still looks lowering to the south, and there is a general appearance of unrest. The temperature has been +10° all day.

The ponies, which had been so comparatively comfortable in the earlier stages, were distressed as usual when the snow began to fall. We have done everything possible to shelter and protect them, but there seems no way of keeping them comfortable when

The dream did not end because Scott had woken up, but because the machines had finally malfunctioned. On Nov 6th Scott noted that 'the engines are not fitted for this climate, but the system of propulsion [i.e. the caterpillar tracks] is altogether satisfactory.'

This is an interesting example of the way the weather in the Antarctic proved so changeable, and difficult to predict even with their sophisticated meteorological equipment.

The previous day he had recorded that the dogs had run over 20 miles in the night in spite of the surface – 'they are working splendidly so far'.

the snow is thick and driving fast. We men are snug and comfortable enough, but it is very evil to lie here and know that the weather is steadily sapping the strength of the beasts on which so much depends. It requires much philosophy to be cheerful on such occasions.

In the midst of the drift this forenoon the dog party came up and camped about a quarter of a mile to leeward. Meares has played too much for safety in catching us so soon, but it is satisfactory to find the dogs will pull the loads and can be driven to face such a wind as we have had. It shows that they ought to be able to help us a good deal.

The tents and sledges are badly drifted up, and the drifts behind the pony walls have been dug out several times. I shall be glad indeed to be on the march again, and oh! for a little sun. The ponies are all quite warm when covered by their rugs. Some of the fine drift snow finds its way under the rugs, and especially under the broad belly straps; this melts and makes the coat wet if allowed to remain. It is not easy to understand at first why the blizzard should have such a withering effect on the poor beasts. I think it is mainly due to the exceeding fineness of the snow particles, which, like finely divided powder, penetrate the hair of the coat and lodge in the inner warmths. Here it melts and, as water, carries off the animal heat. Also, no doubt, it harasses the animals by the bombardment of the fine flying particles on tender places such as nostrils, eyes, and to lesser extent ears. In this way it continually bothers them, preventing rest. Of all things the most important for horses is that conditions should be placid whilst they stand tethered.

Thursday, November 9. – Camp 6. Sticking to programme, we are going a little over the 10 miles (geo.) nightly. Atkinson started his party at 11 and went on for 7 miles to

C. H. Meares and Dimitri with their dog teams ready to start South. Nov 5th 1911. The two dog handlers and their team climbed above the Lower Glacier Depôt, returning on Dec 11th to Cape Evans. When this picture was taken, Scott would have reached Camp 3. Ponting wrote: 'To drive over the frozen sea in the crisp Polar air is one of the most exhilarating experiences imaginable. The yelping of the excited creatures as they are harnessed up; the mad stampede with which they get away, when the driver gives the word to go; the rush of the keen air into one's face; the swish of the sledge runners, and the sound of forty paws pat-a-pat-a-patting on the crackling snow is something that cannot be described.'

Capt. Oates and Snippets. Oct 1911.

Jehu's unhappy days came to an end on Nov 24th, when he was shot and fed to the dogs. Preston says Scott found this event traumatic – Oates described him as having a face 'like a tired sea boot'. However, Scott did not recoil from recording that 'Jehu made four feeds for the dogs. He cut up very well and had quite a lot of fat on him.'

escape a cold little night breeze which quickly dropped. He was some time at his lunch camp, so that starting to join the rear-guard we came in together the last 2 miles. The experience showed that the slow advance guard ponies are forced out of their pace by joining with the others, whilst the fast rear-guard is reduced in speed. Obviously it is not an advantage to be together, yet all the ponies are doing well. An amusing incident happened when Wright left his pony to examine his sledgemeter. Chinaman evidently didn't like being left behind and set off at a canter to rejoin the main body. Wright's long legs barely carried him fast enough to stop this playful stampede, but the ridiculous sight was due to the fact that old Jehu caught the infection and set off at a sprawling canter in Chinaman's wake. As this is the pony we thought scarcely capable of a single march at start, one is agreeably surprised to find him still displaying such commendable spirit. Christopher is troublesome as ever at the start; I fear that signs of tameness will only indicate absence of strength. The dogs followed us so easily over the 10 miles that Meares thought of going on again, but finally decided that the present easy work is best.

Things look hopeful. The weather is beautiful – temp. +12°, with a bright sun. Some stratus cloud about Discovery and over White Island. The sastrugi about here are very various in direction and the surface a good deal ploughed up, showing that the Bluff influences the wind direction even out as far as this camp. The surface is hard; I take it about as good as we shall get.

There is an annoying little southerly wind blowing now, and this serves to show the beauty of our snow walls. The ponies are standing under their lee in the bright sun as comfortable as can possibly be.

Sunday, November 12. – Camp 9. Our marches are uniformly horrid just at present. The surface remains wretched, not quite so heavy as yesterday, perhaps, but very near it at times. Five miles out the advance party came straight and true on our last year's Bluff depôt marked with a flagstaff. Here following I found a note from E. Evans, cheerful in tone, dated 7 a.m. 7th inst. He is, therefore, the best part of five days ahead of us, which is good. Atkinson camped a mile beyond this cairn and had a very gloomy account of Chinaman. Said he couldn't last more than a mile or two. The weather was horrid, overcast, gloomy, snowy. One's spirits became very low. However, the crocks set off again, the rear-guard came up, passed us in camp, and then on the march about 3 miles on, so that they camped about the same time. The Soldier thinks Chinaman will last for a good many days yet, which is an extraordinary confession of hope for him. The rest of the animals are as well as can be expected – Jehu rather better. These weather appearances change every minute. When we camped there was a chill northerly breeze, a black sky and light falling snow. Now the sky is clearing and the sun shining an hour later. The temperature remains about +10° in the daytime.

Wednesday, November 15. – Camp 12. Found our One Ton Camp without any difficulty [130 geographical miles from Cape Evans]. About 7 or 8 miles. After 5½ miles to lunch camp, Chinaman was pretty tired, but went on again in good form after the rest. All the other ponies made nothing of the march, which, however, was over a distinctly better surface. After a discussion we have decided to give the animals a day's rest here, and then to push forward at the rate of 13 geographical miles a day. Oates thinks the ponies will get through, but that they have lost condition quicker than he expected. Considering his usually pessimistic attitude this must be thought a hopeful view. Personally I am much more hopeful. I think that a good many of the beasts are actually in better form than when they started, and that there is no need to be alarmed about the remainder, always excepting the weak ones, which we have always regarded with doubt. Well, we must wait and see how things go.

The atmosphere and the feelings of men on the march are well captured in this poem. It appeared anonymously in the 'South Polar Times' edited by Cherry-Garrard and illustrated by Wilson. Both picture and poem here are generally recognised as the work of Wilson.

THE Silence was deep with a breath like sleep
    As our sledge runners slid on the snow,
And the fate-full fall of our fur-clad feet
    Struck mute like a silent blow
On a questioning "hush", as the settling crust
    Shrank shivering over the floe;
And the sledge in its track sent a whisper back
    Which was lost in a white fog-bow.

AND this was the thought that the Silence wrought
    As it scorched and froze us through,
Though secrets hidden are all forbidden
    Till God means man to know,
We might be the men God meant should know
    The heart of the Barrier snow,
    In the heat of the sun, and the glow
    And the glare from the glistening floe,
As it scorched and froze us through and through
    With the bite of the drifting snow.

Top left: *Seaman Forde. Nov 1911.*

Top right: *Petty Officer Edgar Evans. Nov 1911.*

Lower left: *Seaman Keohane, Petty Officer, R.N. Nov 1911.*

Lower right: *Seaman Crean. Nov 1911.*

Left: Physicist C. S. Wright. Nov 1911.

Right: A. Cherry-Garrard, assistant zoologist. Nov 1911.

Scott recorded that while the next pony to be sacrificed also made four feeds for the dogs, they only had four bags of forage left to be shared between the remaining ponies. In fact, the men were also adding pony meat to their hoosh, and if they had not overcooked it, this would have had the effect of alleviating their scurvy. Christopher was the next pony to be shot, on Dec 1st. Scott remarked, 'less regret goes with him than the others'. One of the remaining ponies, Nobby, tried out some snow shoes, but only made about four miles with them. Scott, however, noted, 'these snow shoes are *the* thing for ponies; had more been able to use them from the beginning' things would have been very different. On Dec 2nd it was Victor's turn to die, Scott commenting, 'He is in excellent condition and will provide 5 feeds for the dogs.' But there was no more forage. Scott admitted, 'We have all taken to horse meat and are so well fed that hunger isn't thought of.' Wilson recalled a supper of 'hoosh with plenty of Victor in it'.

Saturday, November 18. – Camp 14. The ponies are not pulling well. The surface is, if anything, a little worse than yesterday, but I should think about the sort of thing we shall have to expect henceforward. I had a panic that we were carrying too much food and this morning we have discussed the matter and decided we can leave a sack. We have done the usual 13 miles (geo.) with a few hundred yards to make the 15 statute. The temperature was –21° degrees when we camped last night, now it is –3°. The crocks are going on very wonderfully. Oates gives Chinaman at least three days, and Wright says he may go for a week. This is slightly inspiriting, but how much better would it have been to have had ten really reliable beasts! It's touch and go whether we scrape up to the Glacier; meanwhile we get along somehow. At any rate the bright sunshine makes everything *look* more hopeful.

Sunday, November 19. – Camp 15. We have struck a real bad surface, sledges pulling well over it, but ponies sinking very deep. The result is to about finish Jehu. He was terribly done on getting in tonight. He may go another march, but not more, I think. Considering the surface the other ponies did well. The ponies occasionally sink halfway to the hock, little Michael once or twice almost to the hock itself. Luckily the weather now is glorious for resting the animals, which are very placid and quiet in the brilliant sun.

The Penguinry, Cape Royds and Erebus. Nov 27th 1911. This Cape was a major breeding colony for the Adélie penguins where they incubated their eggs for about five weeks. During their last evening together at Discovery Hut, Scott had discussed Ponting's programme of scientific record work, involving several visits to the Adélie colony to record different stages of incubation. His book has a chapter on the subject, and many pictures of the penguins.

Wednesday, November 22. – Camp 18. Everything much the same. The ponies thinner but not much weaker. The crocks still going along. Jehu is now called 'The Barrier Wonder' and Chinaman 'The Thunderbolt'. Two days more and they will be well past the spot at which Shackleton killed his first animal. Nobby keeps his pre-eminence of condition and has now the heaviest load by some 50 lbs; most of the others are under 500 lbs load, and I hope will be eased further yet. The dogs are in good form still, and came up well with their loads this morning (night temp. −1.4°). It looks as though we ought to get through to the Glacier without great difficulty. The weather is glorious and the ponies can make the most of their rest during the warmest hours, but they certainly lose in one way by marching at night. The surface is much easier for the sledges when the sun is warm, and for about three hours before and after midnight the friction noticeably increases. It is just a question whether this extra weight on the loads is compensated by the resting temperature. We are quite steady on the march now, and though not fast yet get through with few stops. The animals seem to be getting accustomed to the steady, heavy plod and take the deep places less fussily. There is rather an increased condition of false crust – that is, a crust which appears firm till the whole weight of the animal is put upon it, when it suddenly gives some three or four inches. This is very trying for the poor beasts. There are also more patches in which the men sink, so that walking is getting more troublesome, but, speaking broadly, the crusts are not comparatively bad and the surface is rather better than it was. If the hot sun continues this should still further improve. One cannot see any reason why the crust should change in the next 100 miles. (Temp. +2°.)

Tuesday, November 28. – Camp 24. The most dismal start imaginable. Thick as a hedge, snow falling and drifting with keen southerly wind. The men pulled out at 3.15 with Chinaman and James Pigg. We followed at 4.20, just catching the party at the lunch camp at 8.30. Things got better half way; the sky showed signs of clearing and the steering improved. Now, at lunch, it is getting thick again. When will the wretched blizzard be over? The walking is better for ponies, worse for men; there is nearly everywhere a hard crust some 3 to 6 inches down. Towards the end of the march we crossed a succession of high hard south-easterly sastrugi, widely dispersed. I don't know what to make of these.

Second march almost as horrid as the first. Wind blowing strong from the south, shifting to S.E. as the snowstorms fell on us, when we could see little or nothing, and the driving snow hit us stingingly in the face. The general impression of all this dirty weather is that it spreads in from the S.E. We started at 4 a.m., and I think I shall stick to that custom for the present. These last few marches have been fought for, but completed without hitch, and, though we camped in a snowstorm, there is a more promising look in the sky, and if only for a time the wind has dropped and the sun shines brightly, dispelling some of the gloomy results of the distressing marching.

Chinaman, 'The Thunderbolt', has been shot tonight. Plucky little chap, he has stuck it out well and leaves the stage but a few days before his fellows. We have only four bags of forage (each one 130 lbs) left, but these should give seven marches with all the remaining animals, and we are less than 90 miles from the Glacier. Bowers tells me that the barometer was phenomenally low during this blizzard and the last. This has certainly been the most unexpected and trying summer blizzard yet experienced in this region. I only trust it is over. There is not much to choose between the remaining ponies. Nobby and Bones are the strongest, Victor and Christopher the weakest, but all should get through. The land doesn't show up yet.

Sunday, December 3. – Camp 29. Our luck in weather is preposterous. I roused the hands at 2.30 a.m., intending to get away at 5. It was thick and snowy, yet we could have got on; but at breakfast the wind increased, and by 4.30 it was blowing a full gale from the south. The Pony wall blew down, huge drifts collected, and the sledges were quickly buried. It was the strongest wind I have known here in summer. At 11 it began to take off. At 12.30 we got up and had lunch and got ready to start. The land appeared, the clouds broke, and by 1.30 we were in bright sunshine. We were off at 2 p.m., the land showing all round, and, but for some cloud to the S.E., everything promising. At 2.15 I saw the south-easterly cloud spreading up; it blotted out the land 30 miles away at 2.30 and was on us before 3. The sun went out, snow fell thickly, and marching conditions became horrible. The wind increased from the S.E., changed to S.W., where it hung for a time, and suddenly shifted to W.N.W. and then N.N.W., from which direction it is now blowing with falling and drifting snow. The changes of conditions are inconceivably rapid, perfectly bewildering. In spite of all these difficul-

Scott wrote that they had almost reached the point when it was daily routine to be 'man-hauling': 'The walking is tiring for the men, one's feet sinking 2 or 3 inches at each step . . . It is always rather dismal work walking over the great snow plain... but it is cheering to be in such good company with everything going on steadily and well.' However, the following day he recorded 'quite the most trying march we have had. The surface very poor . . . the second march even worse . . . the ski becomes hopelessly clogged . . . the surface was unspeakably heavy for pulling.' Because the food for the horses was running low, they had to try to achieve 13 nautical miles daily.

Earlier Scott had noted: 'The changes of conditions are inconceivably rapid, perfectly bewildering.' He was always drawing comparisons with Shackleton's experience, noting for instance that in mid-Dec his rival's party had had splendid weather for a whole month. Scott ascribed a multitude of events to fortune, and at this time suggested that if Amundsen 'has a stroke of luck', he might have found the shorter route to their goal.

ties we have managed to get 11½ miles south and to this camp at 7 p.m. – the conditions of marching simply horrible.

The man-haulers led out 6 miles (geo.) and then camped. I think they had had enough of leading. We passed them, Bowers and I ahead on ski. We steered with compass, the drifting snow across our ski, and occasional glimpse of south-easterly sastrugi under them, till the sun showed dimly for the last hour or so. The whole weather conditions seem thoroughly disturbed, and if they continue so when we are on the Glacier, we shall be very awkwardly placed. It is really time the luck turned in our favour – we have had all too little of it. Every mile seems to have been hardly won under such conditions. The ponies did splendidly and the forage is lasting a little better than expected. Victor was found to have quite a lot of fat on him and the others are pretty certain to have more, so that we should have no difficulty whatever as regards transport if only the weather was kind.

Tuesday, December 5. – Camp 30. Noon. We awoke this morning to a raging, howling blizzard. The gales we have had hitherto have lacked the very fine powdery snow – that especial feature of the blizzard. Today we have it fully developed. After a minute or two in the open one is covered from head to foot. The temperature is high, so that what falls or drives against one sticks. The ponies – heads, tails, legs, and all parts not protected by their rugs – are covered with ice; the animals are standing deep in snow, the sledges are almost covered, and huge drifts above the tents. We have had breakfast, rebuilt the walls, and are now again in our bags. One cannot see the next tent, let alone the land. What on earth does such weather mean at this time of year? It is more than our share of ill-fortune, I think, but the luck may yet turn. I doubt if any party could travel in such weather even with the wind, certainly no one could travel against it.

Is there some widespread atmospheric disturbance which will be felt everywhere in this region as a bad season, or are we merely the victims of exceptional local conditions? If the latter, there is food for thought in picturing our small party struggling against adversity in one place whilst others go smilingly forward in the sunshine. How great may be the element of luck! No foresight – no procedure – could have prepared us for this state of affairs. Had we been ten times as experienced or certain of our aim we should not have expected such rebuffs.

11 p.m. – It has blown hard all day with quite the greatest snowfall I remember. The drifts about the tents are simply huge. The temperature was +27° this forenoon and rose to +31° in the afternoon, at which time the snow melted as it fell on anything but the snow, and, as a consequence, there are pools of water on everything, the tents are wet through, also the wind clothes, night boots, etc.; water drips from the tent poles and door, lies on the floorcloth, soaks the sleeping-bags, and makes everything pretty wretched. If a cold snap follows before we have had time to dry our things, we shall be mighty uncomfortable. Yet after all it would be humorous enough if it were not for

the seriousness of delay – we can't afford that, and it's real hard luck that it should come at such a time. The wind shows signs of easing down, but the temperature does not fall and the snow is as wet as ever – not promising signs of abatement.

Thursday, December 7. – Camp 30. The storm continues and the situation is now serious. One small feed remains for the ponies after today, so that we must either march tomorrow or sacrifice the animals. That is not the worst; with the help of the dogs we could get on, without doubt. The serious part is that we have this morning started our summit rations – that is to say, the food calculated from the Glacier depôt has been begun. The first supporting party can only go on a fortnight from this date and so forth. The storm shows no sign of abatement and its character is as unpleasant as ever. The promise of last night died away about 3 a.m., when the temperature and wind rose again, and things reverted to the old conditions. I can find no sign of an end, and all of us agree that it is utterly impossible to move. Resignation to misfortune is the only attitude, but not an easy one to adopt. It seems undeserved where plans were well laid and so nearly crowned with a first success. I cannot see that any plan would be altered if it were to do again, the margin for bad weather was ample according to all experience, and this stormy December – our finest month – is a thing that the most cautious

Hut, bergs and clouds. Dec 1911. It is surprising to read Ponting's assertion that he found the Antarctic a disappointing region for photography, because the weather so often would 'thwart one'. However shots like this convey the loneliness of the expedition members left behind in Discovery Hut while Scott and the polar team were making their way towards the Pole, all hoping that the Norwegians had not got there first.

organiser might not have been prepared to encounter. It is very evil to lie here in a wet sleeping-bag and think of the pity of it, whilst with no break in the overcast sky things go steadily from bad to worse (T. +32°). Meares has a bad attack of snow blindness in one eye. I hope this rest will help him, but he says it has been painful for a long time. There cannot be good cheer in the camp in such weather, but it is ready to break out again. In the brief spell of hope last night one heard laughter.

Midnight. Little or no improvement. The barometer is rising – perhaps there is hope in that. Surely few situations could be more exasperating than this of forced inactivity when every day and indeed every hour counts. To be here watching the mottled wet green walls of our tent, the glistening wet bamboos, the bedraggled sopping socks and loose articles dangling in the middle, the saddened countenances of my companions – to hear the everlasting patter of the falling snow and the ceaseless rattle of the fluttering canvas – to feel the wet clinging dampness of clothes and everything touched, and to know that without there is but a blank wall of white on every side – these are the physical surroundings. Add the stress of sighted failure of our whole plan, and any one must find the circumstances unenviable. But yet, after all, one can go on striving, endeavouring to find a stimulation in the difficulties that arise.

Friday, December 8. – Camp 30. Hoped against hope for better conditions, to wake to the mournfullest snow and wind as usual. We had breakfast at 10, and at noon the wind dropped. We set about digging out the sledges, no light task. We then shifted our tent sites. All tents had been reduced to the smallest volume by the gradual pressure of snow. The old sites are deep pits with hollowed icy wet centres. The resetting of the tent has at least given us comfort, especially since the wind has dropped. About 4 the sky showed signs of breaking, the sun and a few patches of land could be dimly discerned. The wind shifted in light airs and a little hope revived. Alas! as I write the sun has disappeared and snow is again falling. Our case is growing desperate. Evans and his man-haulers tried to pull a load this afternoon. They managed to move a sledge with four people on it, pulling in ski. Pulling on foot they sank to the knees. The snow all about us is terribly deep. We tried Nobby and he plunged to his belly in it. Wilson thinks the ponies finished, but Oates thinks they will get another march in spite of the surface, *if it comes tomorrow.* If it should not, we must kill the ponies tomorrow and get on as best we can with the men on ski and the dogs. But one wonders what the dogs can do on such a surface. I much fear they also will prove inadequate. Oh! for fine weather, if only to the Glacier. The temperature remains +33°, and everything is disgustingly wet.

11 p.m. – The wind has gone to the north, the sky is really breaking at last, the sun showing less sparingly, and the land appearing out of the haze. The temperature has fallen to +26°, and the water nuisance is already abating. With so fair a promise of improvement it would be too cruel to have to face bad weather tomorrow. There is good cheer in the camp tonight in the prospect of action. The poor ponies look wist-

Bowers' sense of humour was intact – a 'snipe march', he called it. That same day, Amundsen, unknown to the British party, was within 100 miles of the Pole.

fully for the food of which so very little remains, yet they are not hungry, as recent savings have resulted from food left in their nosebags. They look wonderfully fit, all things considered. Everything looks more hopeful tonight, but nothing can recall four lost days.

Saturday, December 9. – Camp 31. I turned out two or three times in the night to find the weather slowly improving; at 5.30 we all got up, and at 8 got away with the ponies – a most painful day. The tremendous snowfall of the late storm had made the surface intolerably soft, and after the first hour there was no glide. We pressed on the poor half-rationed animals, but could get none to lead for more than a few minutes; following, the animals would do fairly well. It looked as if we could never make headway; the man-haulers were pressed into the service to aid matters. Bowers and Cherry-Garrard went ahead with one 10-foot sledge – thus most painfully we made about a mile. The situation was saved by P.O. Evans, who put the last pair of snow-shoes on Snatcher. From this he went on without much pressing, the other ponies followed, and one by one were worn out in the second place. We went on all day without lunch. Three or four miles (T. +23°) found us engulfed in pressures, but free from difficulty except the awful softness of the snow. By 8 p.m. we had reached within a mile or so of the slope ascending to the gap which Shackleton called the Gateway. I had hoped to be through the Gateway with the ponies still in hand at a very much earlier date and, but for the devastating storm, we should have been. It has been a most serious blow to us, but things are not yet desperate, if only the storm has not hopelessly spoilt the surface. The man-haulers are not up yet, in spite of their light load. I think they have stopped for tea, or something, but under ordinary conditions they would have passed us with ease.

At 8 p.m. the ponies were quite done, one and all. They came on painfully slowly a few hundred yards at a time. By this time I was hauling ahead, a ridiculously light load, and yet finding the pulling heavy enough. We camped, and the ponies have been shot. Poor beasts! they have done wonderfully well considering the terrible circumstances under which they worked, but yet it is hard to have to kill them so early. The dogs are going well in spite of the surface, but here again one cannot get the help one would wish. (T. +19°.) I cannot load the animals heavily on such snow. The scenery is most impressive; three huge pillars of granite form the right buttress of the Gateway, and a sharp spur of Mount Hope the left. The land is much more snow-covered than when we saw it before the storm. In spite of some doubt in our outlook, every one is very cheerful tonight and jokes are flying freely around.

Wilson wrote: 'Thank God ... we begin the heavier work ourselves', a sentiment which, as Preston points out, 'Amundsen would have found incomprehensible, particularly as three-quarters of their journey still lay ahead of them. The unsentimental and wholly pragmatic Norwegian had worked out his plans to the last detail: "In my calculations I figured out exactly the precise day on which I planned to kill each dog as its usefulness should end for drawing the diminishing supplies on the sleds and its usefulness should begin as food for the men." '

Ponting wrote a whole chapter of his book about these Weddell seals. They loved nothing better than to lie on the shore and let the incoming waves roll over them. And Wilson described in his earlier book how the team's constant source of amusement was 'to stir up an old bull seal and make him sing in plaintive piping notes which end up exactly on the call note of a bullfinch'.

Seal lying by Church Berg. Dec 9th 1911. No land animals exist in the far South and only three species of mammals visited us during our stay at Cape Evans, recorded Ponting. Of two of these (sea-leopard and crab-eater seals) they saw only a single specimen. But they did see any number of Weddell seals – eight, nine and ten feet long. These are fish-eating mammals and devoid of fear on the ice, but in the sea ever-watchful for killer whales. The seals came up to breathe through blow holes in the ice. Those in this picture might have proved dangerous if Ponting had got closer for his photograph, as he was once seized by the shin and thrown to the ground. Fortunately the bite soon healed.

On the Beardmore Glacier – 1911

Sunday, December 10. – Camp 32. I was very anxious about getting our loads forward over such an appalling surface, and that we had done so is mainly due to the ski. I roused every one at 8, but it was noon before all the readjustments of load had been made and we were ready to start. The dogs carried 600 lbs of our weight besides the depôt (200 lbs). It was greatly to my surprise when we – my own party – with a 'one, two, three together' started our sledge, and we found it running fairly easily behind us. We did the first mile at a rate of about 2 miles an hour, having previously very carefully scraped and dried our runners. The day was gloriously fine and we were soon perspiring. After the first mile we began

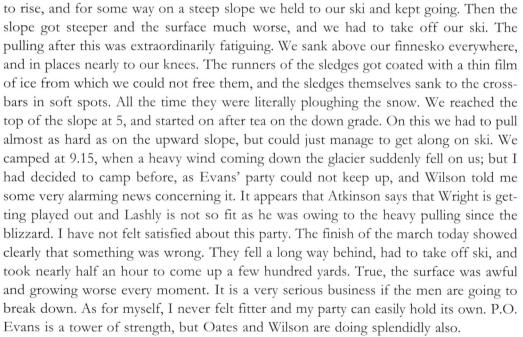

This was the kind of man-hauling on the Beardmore Glacier which eventually killed Scott's party.

to rise, and for some way on a steep slope we held to our ski and kept going. Then the slope got steeper and the surface much worse, and we had to take off our ski. The pulling after this was extraordinarily fatiguing. We sank above our finnesko everywhere, and in places nearly to our knees. The runners of the sledges got coated with a thin film of ice from which we could not free them, and the sledges themselves sank to the cross-bars in soft spots. All the time they were literally ploughing the snow. We reached the top of the slope at 5, and started on after tea on the down grade. On this we had to pull almost as hard as on the upward slope, but could just manage to get along on ski. We camped at 9.15, when a heavy wind coming down the glacier suddenly fell on us; but I had decided to camp before, as Evans' party could not keep up, and Wilson told me some very alarming news concerning it. It appears that Atkinson says that Wright is getting played out and Lashly is not so fit as he was owing to the heavy pulling since the blizzard. I have not felt satisfied about this party. The finish of the march today showed clearly that something was wrong. They fell a long way behind, had to take off ski, and took nearly half an hour to come up a few hundred yards. True, the surface was awful and growing worse every moment. It is a very serious business if the men are going to break down. As for myself, I never felt fitter and my party can easily hold its own. P.O. Evans is a tower of strength, but Oates and Wilson are doing splendidly also.

Here where we are camped the snow is worse than I have ever seen it, but we are in a hollow. Every step here one sinks to the knees and the uneven surface is obviously insufficient to support the sledges. Perhaps this wind is a blessing in disguise; already it seems to be hardening the snow. All this soft snow is an aftermath of our prolonged

Amundsen's team rested on 9th Dec 1911 for the final assault, but it was a dreadful experience as they had to slaughter most of the dogs – the fresh meat was fed to the remainder, and Huntford says that probably saved their lives and 'in consequence that of their masters too'. They reached the Pole on the 14th, planted their flag at the South Pole, and Hanssen took this picture at about 3pm. They celebrated with a little piece of seal meat each. Amundsen is the figure on the right.

Scott, who was extremely fit himself, was not very sympathetic to those who showed physical strain. It had been one of the major causes of his quarrel with Shackleton in 1904 and now he complained as his team, one by one, went under. The last note to his wife which had much chance of reaching her went back with the dogs on Dec 11th and spoke only on this theme: 'I can keep up with the rest.' They were now dependent on human fitness, as motors, ponies and dogs had all gone, and skis were proving of little help. They were doing only two miles an hour, less than walking speed. Scott was measuring himself against Shackleton's crossing of the Beardmore Glacier and assumed 'We are now six days behind.' Priestley, the geologist (and future Chancellor of Birmingham University), wrote later: 'We were working against Shackleton's averages and dates.'

storm. Hereabouts Shackleton found hard blue ice. It seems an extraordinary difference in fortune, and at every step S.'s luck becomes more evident. I take the dogs on for half a day tomorrow, then send them home. We have 200 lbs to add to each sledge load and could easily do it on a reasonable surface, but it looks very much as though we shall be forced to relay if present conditions hold.

'Beardmore Glacier. – Just a tiny note to be taken back by the dogs. Things are not so rosy as they might be, but we keep our spirits up and say the luck must turn. This is only to tell you that I find I can keep up with the rest as well as of old.'

Wednesday, December 13. – Camp 35. A most dismal day. We started at 8 – the pulling terribly bad, the glide good; a new crust in patches, not sufficient to support the ski. Therefore, as the pullers got on the hard patches they slipped back. The sledges plunged into the soft places and stopped dead. Evans' party got away first; we followed, and for some time helped them forward at their stops, but this proved altogether too much for us, so I forged ahead and camped at 1 p.m., as the others were far astern. During lunch I decided to try the 10-feet runners under the crossbars and we spent three hours in securing them. There was no delay on account of the slow progress of the other parties. Evans passed us, and for some time went forward fairly well up a decided slope. The sun was shining on the surface by this time, and the temperature high. Bowers started after Evans, and it was easy to see the really terrible state of affairs with them. They made desperate efforts to get along, but ever got more and more bogged – evidently the glide had vanished. When we got away we soon discovered how awful the surface had become; added to the forenoon difficulties the snow had become wet and sticky. We got our load along, soon passing Bowers, but the toil was simply awful. We were soaked with perspiration and thoroughly breathless with our efforts. Again and again the sledge got one runner on harder snow than the other, fell over on its side, and refused to move. At the top of the rise I found Evans reduced to relay work, and Bowers followed his example soon after. We got our whole load through till 7 p.m., camping time, but only with repeated halts and labour which was altogether too strenuous. The other parties certainly cannot get a full load along on the surface, and I much doubt if we could continue to do so, but we must try again tomorrow.

On the Beardmore Glacier – 1911

I suppose we have advanced a bare 4 miles today and the aspect of things is very little changed. Our height is now about 1,500 feet; I had pinned my faith on getting better conditions as we rose, but it looks as though matters were getting worse instead of better. As far as the Cloudmaker the valley looks like a huge basin for the lodgment of such snow as this. We can but toil on, but it is woefully disheartening. I am not at all hungry, but pretty thirsty. (T. +15°.) I find our summit ration is even too filling for the present. Two skuas came round at lunch time, no doubt attracted by our 'Shambles' camp.

Sunday, December 17. – Camp 39. We got fearfully hot this morning and marched in singlets, which became wringing wet; thus uncovered the sun gets at one's skin, and then the wind, which makes it horribly uncomfortable. Our lips are very sore. We cover them with the soft silk plaster which seems about the best thing for the purpose.

I'm inclined to think that the summit trouble will be mostly due to the chill falling on sunburned skins. Even now one feels the cold strike directly one stops. We get fearfully thirsty and chip up ice on the march, as well as drinking a great deal of water on halting. Our fuel only just does it, but that is all we want, and we have a bit in hand for the summit.

Sledges laid out, hut, glacier and land effect. Dec 19th 1911. The main party waited here, back at base.

Left: *Portrait of Bernard Day on return from the Barrier. Dec 21st 1911.*

Right: *Portrait of Hooper, steward, late R.N., on return from Barrier. Dec 21st 1911.*

Left: *Portrait of Bernard Day on return from the Barrier. Dec 21st 1911.*

Right: *Portrait of Hooper, steward, late R.N., on return from Barrier. Dec 21st 1911.*

Scott was still comparing his progress with Shackleton's. 'If we can keep up the pace, we gain on Shackleton.' This passage was cut, but he repeated the sentiment three days later. Instead of pacing himself against Shackleton, Scott should have remembered that Shackleton had turned back, showing a particular kind of courage that was recognised in England by the award of a knighthood and great public fame. Despite the bad conditions, Scott's party still kept collecting geological samples. On the Tuesday, Scott fell into two cracks and was badly bruised, and on the Thursday most of the party fell into crevasses. Scott wrote again to his wife: 'For your ear also, I am exceedingly fit and can go with the best of them.' At this point, he started a fresh manuscript book and noted on the flyleaf their ages: Self 43, Wilson 39, Evans P.O. 37, Oates 32, Bowers 28, Average 36. It looks from this list as if Scott had already taken the controversial decision to have five, not four, in his team for the assault on the Pole.

The pulling this afternoon was fairly pleasant; at first over hard snow, and then on to pretty rough ice with surface snow-filled cracks, bad for sledges, but ours promised to come through well. We have worn our crampons all day and are delighted with them. P.O. Evans, the inventor of both crampons and ski shoes, is greatly pleased, and certainly we owe him much. The weather is beginning to look dirty again, snow clouds rolling in from the east as usual. I believe it will be overcast tomorrow.

Wednesday, December 20.—Camp 42. 6,500 feet about. Just got off our best half march—10 miles 1150 yards (geo.), over 12 miles stat. With an afternoon to follow we should do well today; the wind has been coming up the valley. Turning this book seems to have brought luck. We marched on till nearly 7 o'clock after a long lunch halt, and covered 19½ geo. miles, nearly 23 (stat.), rising 800 feet. This morning we came over a considerable extent of hard snow, then got to hard ice with patches of snow: a state of affairs which has continued all day. Pulling the sledges in crampons is no difficulty at all. At lunch Wilson and Bowers walked back 2 miles or so to try and find Bowers' broken sledgemeter, without result. During their absence a fog spread about us, carried up the valleys by easterly wind. We started the afternoon march in this fog very unpleasantly, but later it gradually drifted, and tonight it is very fine and warm. As the fog lifted we saw a huge line of pressure ahead; I steered for a place where the slope looked smoother, and we are camped beneath this spot tonight. (Lat. 84° 59' 6".) We must be

P. Keohane on return from Barrier. Dec 21st 1911. This photograph shows Ponting's skill at portraiture. It is a pity that he did not capture the character of Scott, who appears to have fought shy of sitting for this sort of picture.

Edward Nelson's igloo and sledge. Dec 24th 1911. Nelson, the biologist, justified his presence on the expedition as being 'to determine the condition under which organic substances exist in the sea'. His equipment included tow nets and sieves for classifying the life he found on the sea bottom and collected through a hole in the ice, protected by a snow wall. There, he had a telephone connecting him with the Hut, a short distance away.

In the days before Christmas they had some bad times or, as Scott preferred to put it, 'great vicissitudes of fortune'. All of them were constantly falling into crevasses covered with a thin crust of ice and therefore invisible. However, they seemed to have reached the summit of the glacier and Scott wrote, 'I trust this may prove the turning-point in our fortunes for which we have waited so patiently.' Unfortunately on Dec 27th there was a bad accident when Bowers broke the only hypsometer thermometer, which they used to check altitude. (Amundsen, incidentally, carried four in case of accidents.) Scott gave vent to 'an unusual outburst of wrath'. The following day one of the sledges was found to be defective and Scott told the team 'plainly' that they must wrestle with the trouble and get it right for themselves.

ahead of Shackleton's position on the 17th. All day we have been admiring the wonderful banded structure of the rock; tonight it is beautifully clear on Mount Darwin.

I have just told off the people to return tomorrow night: Atkinson, Wright, Cherry-Garrard, and Keohane. All are disappointed–poor Wright rather bitterly, I fear. I dreaded this necessity of choosing–nothing could be more heart-rending. I calculated our programme to start from 85° 10' with 12 units of food and eight men. We ought to be in this position tomorrow night, less one day's food. After all our harassing trouble one cannot but be satisfied with such a prospect.

Thursday, December 21.–Camp 43. 'December 21, 1911. Lat. 85° S. We are struggling on, considering all things, against odds. The weather is a constant anxiety, otherwise arrangements are working exactly as planned.

'For your own ear also, I am exceedingly fit and can go with the best of them.

'It is a pity the luck doesn't come our way, because every detail of equipment is right.

'I write this sitting in our tent waiting for the fog to clear–an exasperating position as we are in the worst crevassed region. Teddie Evans and Atkinson were down to the length of their harness this morning, and we have all been half-way down. As first man I get first chance, and it's decidedly exciting not knowing which step will give way. Still all this is interesting enough if one could only go on.

'Since writing the above I made a dash for it, got out of the valley, out of the fog, and away from crevasses. So here we are practically on the summit and up to date in the provision line. We ought to get through.'

The Summit Journey to the Pole – 1911/12

Monday, December 25, CHRISTMAS. – Lunch. Bar. 21.14. Rise 240 feet. The wind was strong last night and this morning; a light snowfall in the night; a good deal of drift, subsiding when we started, but still about a foot high. I thought it might have spoilt the surface, but for the first hour and a half we went along in fine style. Then we started up a rise, and to our annoyance found ourselves amongst crevasses once more – very hard, smooth névé between high ridges at the edge of crevasses, and therefore very difficult to get foothold to pull the sledges. Got our ski sticks out, which improved matters, but we had to tack a good deal and several of us went half down. After half an hour of this I looked round and found the second sledge halted some way in rear – evidently someone had gone into a crevasse. We saw the rescue work going on, but had to wait half an hour for the party to come up, and got mightily cold. It appears that Lashly went down very suddenly, nearly dragging the crew with him. The sledge ran on and jammed the span so that the Alpine rope had to be got out and used to pull Lashly to the surface again. Lashly says the crevasse was 50 feet deep and 8 feet across, in form U, showing that the word 'unfathomable' can rarely be applied. Lashly is 44 today and as hard as nails.

After topping the crevasse ridge we got on a better surface and came along fairly well, completing over 7 miles (geo.) just before 1 o'clock. We have risen nearly 250 feet this morning; the wind was strong and therefore trying, mainly because it held the sledge; it is a little lighter now.

Night camp No. 47. Bar. 21.18. T. –7°. I am so full up that I can scarcely write. After sundry luxuries, such as chocolate and raisins at lunch, we started off well, but soon got amongst crevasses, huge snow-filled roadways running almost in our direction, and across hidden cracks into which we frequently fell. Passing for two miles or so along between two roadways, we came on a huge pit with raised sides. Is this a submerged mountain peak or a swirl in the stream? Getting clear of crevasses and on a slightly down grade, we came along at a swinging pace – splendid. I marched on till nearly 7.30, when we had covered 15 miles (geo.) (17¼ stat.). I knew that supper was to be a 'tightener', and indeed it has been – so much that I must leave description till the morning.

Dead reckoning, Lat. 85° 50' S.; Long. 159° 8' 2" E. Bar. 21.22.

I must write a word of our supper last night. We had four courses. The first, pemmican, full whack with slices of horse meat flavoured with onion and curry powder and thickened with biscuit; then an arrowroot, cocoa and biscuit hoosh sweetened; then a plum-pudding; then cocoa with raisins, and finally a dessert of caramels and ginger. After the feast it was difficult to move. Wilson and I couldn't finish our share of plum-

'Scott possessed great physical courage and phenomenal stamina', writes Huntford, though this is offset by pages and pages of denigration of Scott's character. He adds: 'He was a man who always raced; against a rival, a friend, and, in the last resort against himself. It was as if he wanted to reassure himself of his physical strength . . . On the march, Scott had an irrational, almost sadistic love of driving his companions to exhaustion.' He takes evidence from Bowers' record of Christmas Day, when Scott 'got fairly wound up and went on and on . . . Our windproofs got oppressively warm and altogether things were pretty rotten. At last he stopped and we found we had done 14¾ miles. He said, "What about fifteen miles for Christmas Day?", so we gladly went on – anything definite is better than indefinite trudgery.'

Pinnacle of Church Berg and icicles with Anton. Dec 29th 1911. Anton, the Russian 'groom', could speak very little English, but Ponting persuaded him to pose on the sunlit side of the berg, and then in the shade. A fringe of icy stalactites descended from the cornices 'and the walls and slopes glistened with the lustre of cut-glass'.

pudding. We have all slept splendidly and feel thoroughly warm – such is the effect of full feeding.

Sunday, December 31. – New Year's Eve. 20.17. Height about 9,126. T. –10°. The second party left in depôt its ski and some other weights equivalent to about 100 lbs. I sent them off first; they marched, but not very fast. We followed and did not catch them before they camped by direction at 1.30. By this time we had covered exactly 7 miles (geo.), and we must have risen a good deal. We rose on one steep incline at the beginning of the march, and topped another at the end, showing a distance of about 5 miles between these wretched slopes which give us the hardest pulling, but as a matter of fact, we have been rising all day.

We had a good full brew of tea and then set to work stripping the sledges. That didn't take long, but the building up the 10-feet sledges is a long job. Evans (P.O.) and Crean are tackling it, and it is a very remarkable piece of work. To build a sledge under these conditions is a fact for special record. Evans (Lieut.) has just found the latitude –86° 56' S., so that we are pretty near the 87th parallel aimed at for tonight. We lose half a day, but I hope to make that up by going forward at much better speed.

This is to be called the '3 Degree Depôt', and it holds a week's provision for both units.

There is extraordinarily little mirage up here and the refraction is very small. Except for the seamen we are all sitting in a double tent – the first time we have put up the inner lining to the tent; it seems to make us much snugger.

10 p.m. – The job of rebuilding is taking longer than I expected, but is now almost done. The 10-feet sledges look very handy. We had an extra drink of tea and are now turned into our bags in the double tent (five of us) as warm as toast, and just enough light to write or work with. Did not get to bed till 2 a.m.

Monday, January 1, 1912. – NEW YEAR'S DAY. Lunch. Bar. 20.04. Roused hands about 7.30 and got away 9.30, Evans' party going ahead on foot. We followed on ski. Very stupidly we had not seen to our ski shoes beforehand, and it took a good half-hour to get them right; Wilson especially had trouble. When we did get away, to our surprise the sledge pulled very easily, and we made fine progress, rapidly gaining on the foot-haulers.

Night camp 54. Bar. 19.98. Risen about 150 feet. Height about 9,600 above Barrier. They camped for lunch at 5½ miles and went on early, completing 11.3 (geo.) by 7.30. We were delayed again at lunch camp, P.O. Evans repairing the tent, and I the cooker. We caught the other party more easily in the afternoon and kept alongside them the last quarter of an hour. It was surprising how easily the sledge pulled; we have scarcely exerted ourselves all day.

We have been rising again all day, but the slopes are less accentuated. I had expected trouble with ski and hard patches, but we found none at all. (T. –14°.) The tempera-

Despite all the food, they were in fact suffering from various dietary problems, and Evans wrote that 'a man trained to watch over men's health ... should have seen something amiss'. Wilson, however, did not notice, or if he did, said nothing. In these low temperatures they needed more vitamin C. They were dehydrated but did not have enough fuel left to melt the ice to make water to drink. Evans and Oates were the first to suffer, the latter giving way to bouts of nostalgia for home. From the Beardmore on, they were all beginning to suffer from food fantasies. Big bars of chocolate in a railway station were Cherry-Garrard's dream, but he always woke up just as he was about to dig his teeth in. They watched Bowers keenly as he cooked up their evening hoosh, but he noted that despite all the food he produced 'we are getting noticeably thinner'.

Huntford believes that at this time, late December, hostility between Scott and Teddie Evans, each pulling a sledge, had grown under the strain of the climb and was now 'poisoning the atmosphere'. Rivalry, he says, was simple and obvious. By a prodigious effort, Scott forced the pace, covering 13 miles a day for 9 or 10 hours, carrying heavy weights. Evans was tiring and was already in the early days of scurvy. A deleted entry in Scott's journals noted that Evans' party were 'not in very high spirits, they have not managed matters well for themselves'. Evans told Wilson that he desperately wanted to go to the Pole – but he could see his chances fading.

Back at base, Meares was keeping up the spirits of the party at the pianola, Jan 1st 1912.

Bowers had been told by Scott to leave his skis behind at the depôt. This saved weight but it increased the difficulty of moving forward uphill on the glacier. Teddie Evans' team could not be expected to be in high spirits when they had just been told that they had be deselected for the Pole, though Bowers was now a member of the Scott team and moved into his tent. Scott wrote: 'We have 5½ units of food – practically over a month's allowance for 5 people – it ought to see us through.' An editor's note here reads: 'Under average conditions, the second return party should easily have fulfilled Scott's expectations. However a blizzard held them up for 3 days and by the time they reached the foot of the glacier, Lieut. Evans had developed symptoms of scurvy. His companions finally brought him in to Corner Camp, in a continuously worsening condition, from where Crean set out on an 18-hour march to bring help from Hut Point.'

A gloomy paragraph has been edited out here. It begins: 'A dreadfully trying day.' Preston, however, suggests that Scott was cheerful now with his own party, writing, 'What castles one builds now hopefully that the Pole is ours.'

ture is steadily falling, but it seems to fall with the wind. We are *very* comfortable in our double tent. Stick of chocolate to celebrate the New Year. The supporting party not in very high spirits, they have not managed matters well for themselves. Prospects seem to get brighter—only 170 miles to go and plenty of food left.

Thursday, January 4.—We were naturally late getting away this morning, the sledge having to be packed and arrangements completed for separation of parties. It is wonderful to see how neatly everything stows on a little sledge, thanks to P.O. Evans. I was anxious to see how we could pull it, and glad to find we went easy enough. Bowers on foot pulls between, but behind, Wilson and myself; he has to keep his own pace and luckily does not throw us out at all.

The second party had followed us in case of accident, but as soon as I was certain we could get along we stopped and said farewell. Teddie Evans is terribly disappointed, but has taken it very well and behaved like a man. Poor old Crean wept and even Lashly was affected. I was glad to find their sledge is a mere nothing to them, and thus, no doubt, they will make a quick journey back. Since leaving them we have marched on till 1.15 and covered 6.2 miles (geo.). With full marching days we ought to have no difficulty in keeping up our average.

Night camp 57. T. −16°. Height 10,280.—We started well on the afternoon march, going a good speed for 1½ hours; then we came on a surface covered with loose sandy snow, and the pulling became very heavy. We managed to get off 12½ miles (geo.) by 7 p.m., but it was very heavy work.

Friday, January 5. – Camp 58. We go little over a mile and a quarter an hour now – it is a big strain as the shadows creep slowly round from our right through ahead to our left. What lots of things we think of on these monotonous marches! What castles one builds now hopefully that the Pole is ours! Bowers took sights today and will take them every third day. We feel the cold very little, the great comfort of our situation is the excellent drying effect of the sun. Our socks and finnesko are almost dry each morning. Cooking for five takes a seriously longer time than cooking for four; perhaps half an hour on the whole day. It is an item I had not considered when reorganising.

Monday, January 8. – Noon. T. –19.8°. Min. for night –25°. Our first summit blizzard. We might just have started after breakfast, but the wind seemed obviously on the increase, and so it has proved. The sun has not been obscured, but snow is evidently falling as well as drifting. The sun seems to be getting a little brighter as the wind increases. The whole phenomenon is very like a Barrier blizzard, only there is much less snow, as one would expect, and at present less wind, which is somewhat of a surprise.

Evans' hand was dressed this morning, and the rest ought to be good for it. I am not sure it will not do us all good as we lie, in our comfortable bags, within our double-walled tent. However, we do not want more than day's delay, both on account of lost time and food and the slow accumulation of ice. (Night T. –13.5°.) It has grown much thicker during the day, from time to time obscuring the sun for the first time. The temperature is low for a blizzard, but the cold snow is not sticky and not easily carried into the tent, so that the sleeping-bags remain in good condition. (T. –3°.) The glass is rising slightly. I hope we shall be able to start in the morning.

It is quite impossible to speak too highly of my companions. Each fulfils his office to the party; Wilson, first as doctor, ever on the look-out to alleviate the small pains and troubles incidental to the work; now as cook, quick, careful and dexterous, ever thinking of some fresh expedient to help the camp life; tough as steel on the traces, never wavering from start to finish.

Evans, a giant worker with a really remarkable headpiece. It is only now I realise how much has been due to him. Our ski shoes and crampons have been absolutely indispensable, and if the original ideas were not his, the details of manufacture and design and the good workmanship are his alone. He is responsible for every sledge, every sledge fitting, tents, sleeping-bags, harness, and when one cannot recall a single expression of dissatisfaction with any one of these items, it shows what an invaluable assistant he has been. Now, besides superintending the putting up of the tent, he thinks out and arranges the packing of the sledge; it is extraordinary how neatly and handily every-

More food required more fuel. Scott had not considered carefully enough the vital implications of the extended polar party. Preston suggests the decision was taken on impulse and says Bowers had not been intended for the Pole, though Scott had increasingly come to admire his great strength, describing him as 'the hardiest traveller that ever undertook a Polar journey, as well as the most undaunted'. He was also, like Wilson, a man of great loyalty to his leader. Scott may, suggests Preston, have needed Bowers' skill as a navigator, since Teddie Evans, who was an experienced navigator, was now discarded as 'played out and incompetent'. The outstanding question remains: Why did Scott choose Oates? The latter, says Preston, did not expect to be selected, and though he did not say so, by this stage he had little desire to go on; he told Teddie Evans that his personal ambition was satisfied once he got to the top of the Beardmore Glacier. Cherry-Garrard recorded in his diary as early as Dec 4th that Atkinson had said Oates 'knew he was done – his face showed him to be, and the way he went along'. This last comment referred to Oates' Boer War wound, which left him with one leg shorter than the other; in these low temperatures old wounds were liable to open up. Perhaps Scott did not notice because, according to Wilson, 'he wanted the Army represented' at the Pole, just as he wanted the 'Lower Deck' represented in the form of P.O. Evans.

Over the next three days they encountered a surface of sastrugi (see Glossary), and Scott abandoned the skis, a mistake as he had to go back to collect them. For the first time on Jan 7th (deleted) he mentioned that P.O. Evans had 'a nasty cut on his hand (sledge making)'. It would not heal, doubtless due to vitamin deficiency. Scott also said: 'I found to my horror we could scarcely move the sledge on ski; the first hour was awful owing to the wretched coating of loose sandy snow. However we persisted, and towards the latter end of our tiring march we began to make better progress, but the work is still awfully heavy. I must stick to the ski after this.' On Jan 9th (also deleted) he began his journal entry with a word in capital letters – 'RECORD'. He had reached the point which Shackleton, with two companions, had reached as their 'Furthest South' three years before, and had then turned back.

'The marching is growing terribly monotonous', wrote Scott, but on Jan 10th they lightened the load by leaving at a cairn a week's supply of food, weighing nearly 100lbs, including 'sundry articles of clothing'. They continued with 18 days' supply of food, but now 'the surface is beyond words', and Scott was uncertain if the food supply would be enough. If he had known that it was the wrong kind of food, and that scurvy was now inevitable, perhaps he would have turned back, but it seems unlikely.

Hair cutting. Anton and Keohane. Jan 1912. Life at base was 'normal'.

thing is stowed, and how much study has been given to preserving the suppleness and good running qualities of the machine. On the Barrier, before the ponies were killed, he was ever roaming round, correcting faults of stowage.

Little Bowers remains a marvel – he is thoroughly enjoying himself. I leave all the provision arrangement in his hands, and at all times he knows exactly how we stand, or how each returning party should fare. It has been a complicated business to redistribute stores at various stages of reorganisation, but not one single mistake has been made. In addition to the stores, he keeps the most thorough and conscientious meteorological record, and to this he now adds the duty of observer and photographer. Nothing comes amiss to him, and no work is too hard. It is a difficulty to get him into the tent; he seems quite oblivious of the cold, and he lies coiled in his bag writing and working out sights long after the others are asleep.

Of these three it is a matter for thought and congratulation that each is specially suited for his own work, but would not be capable of doing that of the others as well as it is done. Each is invaluable. Oates had his invaluable period with the ponies; now he is a foot slogger and goes hard the whole time, does his share of camp work, and stands the hardship as well as any of us. I would not like to be without him either. So our five people are perhaps as happily selected as it is possible to imagine.

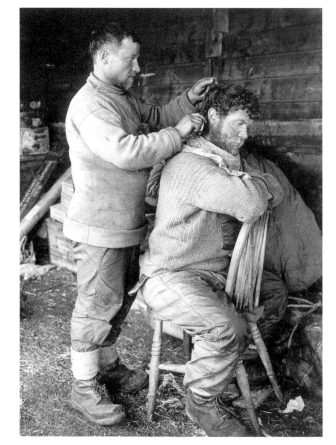

Thursday, January 11. – Night. Height 10,530. Temp. –16.3°. Minimum –25.8°. Another hard grind in the afternoon and five miles added. About 74 miles from the Pole – can we keep this up for seven days? It takes it out of us like anything. None of us ever had such hard work before. Cloud has been coming and going overhead all day, drifting from the S.E., but continually altering shape. Snow crystals falling all the time; a very light S. breeze at start soon dying away. The sun so bright and warm tonight that it is almost impossible to imagine a minus temperature. The snow seems to get softer as we

The Summit Journey to the Pole – 1912

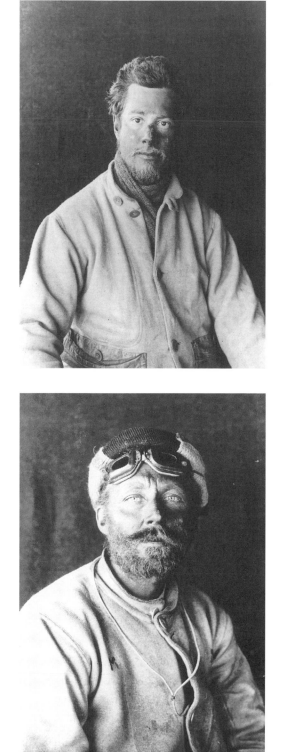

Top left: *A. C. Cherry-Garrard on return from the Barrier. Jan 29th 1912.*

Top right: *C. S. Wright on return from the Barrier. Jan 29th 1912.*

Lower left: *C. H. Meares on return from the Barrier. Jan 1912.*

Lower right: *Dimitri on return from the Barrier. Jan 1912.*

Jan 12th (not recorded here) was another heavy march. 'It is an effort to keep up double figures, but if we can do so for another four marches we ought to get through.' They camped 'only 63 miles from the Pole tonight. We ought to do the trick, but oh! for a better surface.' And the following day, 'We should be in a poor way without our ski, though Bowers manages to struggle through the snow' without.

It was wrong of Scott to claim 'we are all very fit', because Oates was clearly failing and Evans' knuckle had 'a lot of pus in it'.

When on Jan 16th they came across the remains of Amundsen's camp, they were exactly a month behind the Norwegians. Wilson wrote phlegmatically in his diary, 'He has beaten us in so far as he made a race of it. We have done what we came for all the same and as our programme was laid out.' Bowers wrote to his mother on Jan 17th: 'It is sad that we have been forestalled by the Norwegians, but I am glad that we have done it by good British man-hauling. That is the traditional British sledging method and this is the greatest journey done by man since we left our transport at the foot of the Glacier.' To his sister he wrote: 'If ever a journey has been accompanied by honest sweat ours has.' Oates, on the other hand, wrote in his diary: 'The Norskies ... seem to have had a comfortable trip with their dog teams, very different to our wretched man-hauling.'

advance; the sastrugi, though sometimes high and undercut, are not hard—no crusts, except yesterday the surface subsided once, as on the Barrier. Our chance still holds good if we can put the work in, but it's a terribly trying time.

Saturday, January 13. – Only 51 miles from the Pole tonight. If we don't get to it we shall be very close. There is a little southerly breeze tonight; I devoutly hope it may increase in force. The alternation of soft snow and sastrugi seems to suggest that the coastal mountains are not so very far away.

Sunday, January 14. – Camp 66. Lunch T. −18°, Night T. −15°. Sun showing mistily through overcast sky all day. Light southerly wind with very low drift. In consequence the surface was a little better, and we came along very steadily 6.3 miles in the morning and 5.5 in the afternoon, but the steering was awfully difficult and trying; very often I could see nothing, and Bowers in my shadow directed me. Under such circumstances it is an immense help to be pulling on ski. Tonight it is looking very thick. The sun can barely be distinguished, the temperature has risen, and there are serious indications of a blizzard. I trust they will not come to anything; there are practically no signs of heavy wind here, so that even if it blows a little we may be able to march. Meanwhile we are less than 40 miles from the Pole.

Again we noticed the cold; at lunch today (Obs: Lat. 89° 20' 53" S.) all our feet were cold, but this was mainly due to the bald state of our finnesko. I put some grease under the bare skin and found it made all the difference. Oates seems to be feeling the cold and fatigue more than the rest of us, but we are all very fit. It is a critical time, but we ought to pull through. The barometer has fallen considerably. Oh! for a few fine days! So close it seems and only the weather to baulk us.

Night, January 15. – It is wonderful to think that two long marches would land us at the Pole. We left our depôt today with nine days' provisions, so that it ought to be a certain thing now, and the only appalling possibility the sight of the Norwegian flag forestalling ours. Little Bowers continues his indefatigable efforts to get good sights, and it is wonderful how he works them up in his sleeping-bag in our congested tent. (Minimum for night −27.5°.) Only 27 miles from the Pole. We ought to do it now.

Tuesday, January 16. – Camp 68. Height 9,760. T. −23.5°. The worst has happened, or nearly the worst. We marched well in the morning and covered 7½ miles. Noon sight showed us in Lat. 89° 42' S., and we started off in high spirits in the afternoon, feeling that tomorrow would see us at our destination. About the second hour of the march Bowers' sharp eyes detected what he thought was a cairn; he was uneasy about it, but argued that it must be a sastrugus. Half an hour later he detected a black speck ahead. Soon we knew that this could not be a natural snow feature. We marched on, found that it was a black flag tied to a sledge bearer; near by the remains of a camp;

sledge tracks and ski tracks going and coming and the clear trace of dogs' paws – many dogs. This told us the whole story. The Norwegians have forestalled us and are first at the Pole. It is a terrible disappointment, and I am very sorry for my loyal companions. Many thoughts come and much discussion have we had. Tomorrow we must march on to the Pole and then hasten home with all the speed we can compass. All the day-dreams must go; it will be a wearisome return. Certainly we are descending in altitude – certainly also the Norwegians found an easy way up.

Wednesday, January 17. – Camp 69. T. –22° at start. Night –21°. The Pole. Yes, but under very different circumstances from those expected. We have had a horrible day – add to our disappointment a head wind 4 to 5, with a temperature –22°, and companions labouring on with cold feet and hands.

We started at 7.30, none of us having slept much after the shock of our discovery. We followed the Norwegian sledge tracks for some way; as far as we make out there are only two men. In about three miles we passed two small cairns. Then the weather overcast, and the tracks being increasingly drifted up and obviously going too far to the west, we decided to make straight for the Pole according to our calculations. At 12.30 Evans had such cold hands we camped for lunch – an excellent 'week-end' one. We had marched 7.4 miles. Lat. sight gave 89° 53' 37". We started out and did 6½ miles due south. Tonight little Bowers is laying himself out to get sights in terrible difficult circumstances; the wind is blowing hard, T. –21°, and there is that curious damp, cold feeling in the air which chills one to the bone in no time. We have been descending again, I think, but there looks to be a rise ahead; otherwise there is very little that is different from the awful monotony of past days. Great God! this is an awful place and terrible enough for us to have laboured to it without the reward of priority. Well, it is something to have got here, and the wind may be our friend tomorrow. We have had a fat Polar hoosh in spite of our chagrin, and feel comfortable inside – added a small

Huntford points out that Scott wrote, 'Now for the run home and a desperate struggle to get the news through first. I wonder if we can do it,' but for publication this was altered to read 'a desperate struggle. I wonder if we can do it' – a rather different thing. The original suggests Scott 'did not grasp that the return was going to be a fight for survival, although he did understand that there was no time to be lost'. Scott's words, as he read Amundsen's note, were also edited out: 'I am puzzled at the object,' he complained. But, as Huntford says, the Norwegian had left the note as a precaution, in case of an accident to his own party. Scott in turn left a note to say he had been there, in case he, too, did not survive.

Amundsen's tent at the South Pole. The five members of Scott's party were now face to face with the record of the five Norwegians about 1½ miles from the Pole. Photo by Lieut. Bowers.

Western Geological Party. F. Debenham, T. G. Taylor, T. Gran, Forde. This picture was probably taken in Jan 1912 when the Terra Nova returned to pick up the various parties who had wintered in the Hut. The first Supporting Party returned on the 28th, and then went on to the Western Mountains to pick up the geologists under Taylor, who had been searching the valleys for three months. The ship then headed northwards to embark Campbell's party. Their story was an extraordinary one, told elsewhere.

stick of chocolate and the queer taste of a cigarette brought by Wilson. Now for the run home and a desperate struggle. I wonder if we can do it.

Thursday morning, January 18. – Decided after summing up all observations that we were 3.5 miles away from the Pole – one mile beyond it and 3 to the right. More or less in this direction Bowers saw a cairn or tent.

We have just arrived at this tent, 2 miles from our camp, therefore about 1½ miles from the Pole. In the tent we find a record of five Norwegians having been here, as follows:

> *Roald Amundsen*
> *Olav Olavson Bjaaland*
> *Hilmer Hanssen*
> *Sverre H. Hassel*
> *Oscar Wisting.   16 Dec. 1911*

The tent is fine – a small compact affair supported by a single bamboo. A note from Amundsen, which I keep, asks me to forward a letter to King Haakon!

The following articles have been left in the tent: 3 half bags of reindeer [fur] containing a miscellaneous assortment of mitts and sleeping socks, very various in description, a sextant, a Norwegian artificial horizon and a hypsometer without boiling-point thermometers, a sextant and hypsometer of English make.

Left a note to say I had visited the tent with companions; Bowers photographing and Wilson sketching. Since lunch we have marched 6.2 miles S.S.E. by compass (i.e. northwards). Sights at lunch gave us ½ to ¾ of a mile from the Pole, so we call it the Pole Camp. (Temp. Lunch −21°.) We built a cairn, put up our poor slighted Union Jack, and photographed ourselves—cold work all of it—less than ½ a mile south we saw stuck up an old underrunner of a sledge. This we commandeered as a yard for a floor-cloth sail. I imagine it was intended to mark the exact spot of the Pole as near as the Norwegians could fix it. (Height 9,500.) A note attached talked of the tent as being 2 miles from the Pole. Wilson keeps the note. There is no doubt that our predecessors have made thoroughly sure of their mark and fully carried out their programme. I think the Pole is about 9,500 feet in height; this is remarkable, considering that in Lat. 88° we were about 10,500.

We carried the Union Jack about ¾ of a mile north with us and left it on a piece of stick as near as we could fix it. I fancy the Norwegians arrived at the Pole on the 15th Dec. and left on the 17th, ahead of a date quoted by me in London as ideal, viz. Dec. 22. It looks as though the Norwegian party expected colder weather on the summit than they got; it could scarcely be otherwise from Shackleton's account. Well, we have turned our back now on the goal of our ambition and must face our 800 miles of solid dragging—and good-bye to most of the day-dreams!

Huntford claims that Scott's party miscalculated the position of the Pole and 'by their own observations, *they never quite got to the Pole at all*' (his italics).

On the return journey Scott's party at first did well, averaging 14 miles a day to Amundsen's 15 miles. The British leader buoyed himself up by believing that he would beat the Norwegians to the cablehead and send a message to include the words, 'It is satisfactory that the above facts prove that both parties have been at the Pole.' But he came to realise that he had cut fuel and food to the point where he had condemned his men to march and die. They were, says Huntford, now down to half the food they needed. He adds that they were also sledging for up to 12 hours out of 24 at 10,000 feet. 'One can safely do without either food or rest in emergencies, but to deprive onself of both is to ask too much of Nature.' On Jan 25th Bowers recorded, 'We have only three days' food with us and shall be in queer street if we miss the depôt.'

Some of the members of the Norwegian expedition on the ice of the Bay of Whales, where Fram *visited the innermost area to keep her record of having sailed furthest south as well as furthest north. She then spent the winter well away in the South Atlantic to avoid being frozen in. It is interesting to contrast the fur-clad Norwegians with the clothing worn by Scott's party.*

The manly art of man-hauling

Scott had arrived at the Pole having decided, without any sound evidence, that the dogs were unlikely to reach the Beardmore Glacier, though they had shown they could run on ice up to 30 miles a day. So he came to the conclusion that he was 'inclined to chuck them for the last part of the journey'. This left the ponies, Scott said, as the only reliable form of transport, but they could only be taken to the foot of the Glacier—they could not climb it. So for the next 1000 miles and the climb up to the Pole it would be man-hauling all the way.

Bowers wrote to Scott's wife Kathleen on October 27th 1911 that he was delighted at this decision. 'After all, it will be a fine thing to do that plateau with man-haulage in these days of the supposed decadence of the British race.' Another member of the expedition, Simpson, was thinking in a similar vein when he wrote earlier, on hearing of Amundsen's plans, that 'To put it mildly it was not "sporting"'. Now, six months or so later, after he had had time to reflect, he observed in his diary that Scott's decision assumed the best possible conditions. 'It appears', he wrote, 'that with all our resources there is little margin, and a few accidents or a spell of bad weather would not only bring failure but very likely disaster.' Debenham in his diary also suggests that Scott queried whether his men could spend 75 days at an altitude of 10,000 ft on the plateau and said, 'I don't know whether it is possible for men to last out that time. I almost doubt it.'

However, it would have been very difficult for Scott to admit that dogs could do work that men could not do. As long ago as 1905, in his book *Voyage of the 'Discovery'*, he had pontificated: 'No journey ever made with dogs can approach the height of that fine conception which is realised when a party of men go forth to face hardships, dangers and difficulties with their own unaided efforts . . . and succeed in solving some problem of the great unknown.' He concluded this passage with the rallying cry that so many critics feel is typical of the British: 'Surely in this case the conquest is more nobly and splendidly won.'

So perhaps his negative attitude to dogs arose from a preference for man-hauling as the manly alternative. Or perhaps, as Gran believed, there was 'in this question of dogs a certain consolation before Amundsen with his hundred hounds', which presumably meant that Scott could say he was beaten not by men but by a superiority in dogs. Another possible line of thought may have been that Scott knew he not only had too few dogs, but was using animals of the wrong kind. The Eskimo dog was not a horse, but a partner and a companion. Scott's agent had purchased Siberian dogs, whose characteristics were wrong for the job in hand.

Scott is often criticised for this, but even if he had chosen the preferred Greenland dog it is a moot point whether he would have been able to get hold of them. Amundsen had established his prior claim but the government had already, in Huntford's words, ordered that in any case no one else would have been allowed to obtain any more. To deprive your opponent of the best dogs was to beat him in the first round, says Huntford.

Of course this matter of the choice of dogs is not one of scientific determination. Huntford, for instance, claims that the relation between dog and driver in the Antarctic has to be 'between equals'; on the other hand he produces examples of the importance of Amundsen proving his mastery over the (Eskimo) dogs he has chosen and paid for at twice the going rate.

Thus if Scott could not have obtained the right dogs, it is hardly reasonable to blame him for having made such a fundamentally flawed logistical decision. He was forced (had forced himself?) into a course of action where the only solution open to him was manpower. And if man-hauling was to be the chosen course, then the design of the skis and sledges was of paramount importance.

Shackleton admitted on one of his lecture tours, 'Had we taken ski on the Southern journey and understood how to use them, like the Norwegians, we would presumably have reached the Pole.' As we shall see, it was not just a matter of skis, but of the right design of ski used by a trained man. As for Scott, in the four years of preparation he had never learnt to ski or drive dogs. Like Amundsen he had bought skis at Hagen's store in Norway, where he had been taken by Nansen and had met Gran. Gran demonstrated to Scott how skis could work: 'he was the first accomplished skier he had seen in action.' So Scott bought from Gran the skis he had ordered for his own trip—Hagen's was already out of stock. But Huntford explains that the skis bought from Hagen's (by Amundsen as well as Scott) were production models not specially designed for Antarctic work. When Amundsen found that they ran badly, he had his craftsmen re-fashion them, building two pairs for each man, one for running, one in reserve. Huntford also says that Amundsen had a new design of ski made up, rather like the modern cross-country type. In addition he had ski goggles, boots and bindings adapted to his requirements. When the Cape Crozier party went on their winter journey they left their skis behind because none of the three was skilled enough to use them; by contrast, Amundsen's men could not only ski, but several of them were champions.

Scott was much less knowledgeable about skis than about motor sledges. But his Norwegian rival was also, as time went on, concentrating on improvements to his own sledges which, Huntford says, were 'comparatively a failure'. They were unnecessarily heavy for the Barrier, which Amundsen had been misled into supposing was something evil, demanding and treacherous. The fact was that even if Scott had switched at a late date to dogs and sledges as his chosen solution, there were flaws in those available to him which might well have knocked them out of the race, leaving only the men (with their flawed sledges and skis) to try to wrestle leadership from a well-organised and experienced team of Norwegians who had commenced the race well across the starting line.

Clothing was another factor if man-hauling was to be the final solution. Amundsen had lived with the Eskimos, studied their clothing, knew they had solved the problem of perspiration by designing loose-fitting gear, and had acted accordingly. Scott, at the eleventh hour, after the trio had staggered back from the winter journey to Cape Crozier, was too little and too late, observing in his diary: 'One continues to wonder as to the possibilities of fur clothing as made by the Escimaux, with a sneaking feeling that it may outclass our more civilised garb. For us this can only be a matter for speculation, as it would have been quite impossible to obtain such articles.'

The result was that with poor clothing, inadequate skis and boots and sledges which often didn't work, Scott chose the very course which had proved so disastrous to the Cape Crozier men, what Huntford calls 'the dangerous absurdity of man-hauling'. He adds that each Norwegian carried a man-hauling harness against the failure of the dogs, and also to symbolise the penalty of failure. Amundsen reasoned that the daily sight of an instrument of torture rather than a badge of manliness would concentrate the mind wonderfully. Scott, though, did not see it that way. He wrote in his diary: 'The scheme seems to have earned full-confidence: it remains to play the game out.' Man-hauling was, Bowers wrote, 'the most back-breaking work I have ever come up against . . . The starting was worse than [the] pulling, as it required from 10 to 15 desperate jerks on the harness to move the sledge at all. . . . I have never pulled so hard, or so nearly crushed my inside into my backbone by the everlasting jerking with all my strength round my unfortunate tummy.'

At the South Pole. Left to right: Capt. Oates, Lieut. Bowers, Capt. Scott, Dr. Wilson, P.O. Evans. Photo by Lieut. Bowers.

[A cutting from a magazine in the Burberry collection, probably from the *Illustrated London News.* The caption (below) from the magazine contains information not in the Journals, presumably from information supplied after the news reached England that Scott and his party were dead. The film itself was found near Scott's body.]

This camera picture was taken by Lieutenant Bowers, who after placing the camera at a short distance took the photograph by means of a string, which can be seen extending from his fingers. To take the picture he has removed his mitt. Each man is wearing the particular head-dress which he affected as being most perfect for protecting the face from frostbite. Lieutenant Bowers's tufts are quite different from Dr. Wilson's neat-looking helmet. Two of the others have wide-brimmed hats, which have been turned up in order to show the face. All except Lieutenant Oates are wearing mufflers round the neck. The white straps across the shoulders have nothing to do with hauling harness. They are for supporting the heavy fur mitt or glove. The thick fur pre-

vents the fingers from being almost immediately frozen if unprotected in very low temperatures. Captain Scott is distinguished by white fur mitts. Grouped with the party are the special flags made by relatives and friends for this historic moment. The slight breeze is only partially blowing out the Union Jack behind the leader. Here again the sun is shining brightly, but no horizon is visible. The temperature experienced during the stay at the Pole, which includes the moment when this photographic picture was obtained, was 20 deg. below zero, the period corresponding to summer in the temperate latitudes. The surface on which the men are seen grouped was soft, and there was no crust. The party found that this snow when collected from any depth

gave very little water on melting. We presume that this picture was obtained on January 18, for Commander Evans states in his dispatches that "the first day at the Pole was cloudy with a mock sun, but the second day, January 18, was clearer and the sun was visible." Captain Scott while at the Pole took sights with the 4-in. theodolite. The picture gives an excellent idea of Petty-Officer Evans's massive build. It is interesting to remember that his widow received from Captain Scott a personal letter dated October, 1911, in the course of which he stated that "it is possible we may not finish our work this year. Edgar Evans is such an old friend of mine and has done so well on this expedition that he deserves all I could do for him."

The Return from the Pole – 1912

On Saturday 'the surface was terribly bad' and 'pulling really awful'. They reached the Southern depôt and picked up four days' food. From here they estimated seven days with 55 miles to reach Half Degree depôt. Scott said, 'I shall be very pleased when Bowers gets his ski; I'm afraid he must find these long marches very trying with his short legs, but he is an undefeated little sportsman. I think Oates is feeling the cold and fatigue more than most of us.' Scott wanted to return in time to catch the *Terra Nova*.

Friday, January 19. – Lunch 8.1 miles, T. –20.6°. Early in the march we picked up a Norwegian cairn and our outward tracks. We followed these to the ominous black flag which had first apprised us of our predecessors' success. We have picked this flag up, using the staff for our sail, and are now camped about 1½ miles further back on our tracks. So that is the last of the Norwegians for the present. The surface undulates considerably about this latitude; it was more evident today than when we were outward bound.

It is warmer and pleasanter marching with the wind, but I'm not sure we don't feel the cold more when we stop and camp than we did on the outward march. We pick up our cairns easily, and ought to do so right through, I think; but, of course, one will be a bit anxious till the Three Degree Depôt is reached. I'm afraid the return journey is going to be dreadfully tiring and monotonous.

Sunday, January 21. – R. 4: 10,010. Temp. blizzard, –18° to –11°, to –14° now. Awoke to a stiff blizzard; air very thick with snow and sun very dim. We decided not to march owing to likelihood of losing track; expected at least a day of lay up, but whilst at lunch there was a sudden clearance and wind dropped to light breeze. We got ready to march, but gear was so iced up we did not get away till 3.45. Marched till 7.40 – a terribly weary four-hour drag; even with helping wind we only did 5½ miles (6¼ statute). The surface bad, horribly bad on new sastrugi, and decidedly rising again in elevation.

We are going to have a pretty hard time this next 100 miles, I expect. If it was difficult to drag down-hill over this belt, it will probably be a good deal more difficult to drag up. Luckily the tracks are fairly distinct, though we only see our cairns when less than a mile away; 45 miles to the next depôt and 6 days' food in hand – then pick up 7 days' food (T. –22°) and 90 miles to go to the 'Three Degree' Depôt. Once there we ought to be safe, but we ought to have a day or two in hand on arrival and may have difficulty with following the tracks. However, if we can get a rating sight for our watches tomorrow we should be independent of the tracks at a pinch.

Monday, January 22. – 10,000. Temp. –21°. I think about the most tiring march we have had; solid pulling the whole way, in spite of the light sledge and some little helping wind at first. Then in the last part of the afternoon the sun came out, and almost immediately we had the whole surface covered with soft snow.

We got away sharp at 8 and marched a solid 9 hours, and thus we have covered 14.5 miles (geo.) but, by Jove! it has been a grind. We are just about on the 89th parallel.

The Return from the Pole – 1912

Tonight Bowers got a rating sight. We are within 2½ miles of the 64th camp cairn, 30 miles from our depôt, and with 5 days' food in hand. Ski boots are beginning to show signs of wear; I trust we shall have no giving out of ski or boots, since there are yet so many miles to go. I thought we were climbing today, but the barometer gives no change.

Tuesday, January 23. – Lowest Minimum last night –30°, Temp. at start –28°. Lunch height 10,100. Temp. with wind 6 to 7, –19°. Little wind and heavy marching at start. Then wind increased and we did 8.7 miles by lunch, when it was practically blowing a blizzard. The old tracks show so remarkably well that we can follow them without much difficulty – a great piece of luck.

In the afternoon we had to reorganise. Could carry a whole sail. Bowers hung on to the sledge, Evans and Oates had to lengthen out. We came along at a great rate and should have got within an easy march of our depôt had not Wilson suddenly discovered that Evans' nose was frost-bitten – it was white and hard. We thought it best to camp at 6.45. Got the tent up with some difficulty, and now pretty cosy after good hoosh.

There is no doubt Evans is a good deal run down – his fingers are badly blistered and his nose is rather seriously congested with frequent frost-bites. He is very much annoyed with himself, which is not a good sign. I think Wilson, Bowers and I are as fit as possible under the circumstances. Oates gets cold feet. One way and another, I shall be glad to get off the summit! We are only about 13 miles from our 'Degree and half' Depôt, and should get there tomorrow. The weather seems to be breaking up. Pray God we have something of a track to follow to the Three Degree Depôt – once we pick that up we ought to be right.

Thursday, January 25. – Temp. Lunch –11°, Temp. night –16°. Thank God we found our Half Degree Depôt. After lying in our bags yesterday afternoon and all night, we debated breakfast; decided to have it later and go without lunch. At the time the gale seemed as bad as ever, but during breakfast the sun showed and there was light enough to see the old track. It was a long and terribly cold job digging out our sledge and breaking camp, but we got through and on the march without sail, all pulling. This was about 11, and at about 2.30, to our joy, we saw the red depôt flag. We had lunch and left with 9½ days' provisions, still following the track – marched till 8 and covered over 5 miles, over 12 in the day. Only 89 miles (geogr.) to the next depôt, but it's time we cleared off this plateau. We are not without ailments: Oates suffers from a very cold foot; Evans' fingers and nose are in a bad state, and tonight Wilson is suffering tortures from his eyes. Bowers and I are the only members of the party without troubles just at present. The weather still looks unsettled, and I fear a succession of blizzards at this time of year; the wind is strong from the south, and this afternoon has been very helpful with the full sail. Needless to say I shall sleep much better with our provision

Wednesday's entry in the diary begins: 'Things beginning to look a little serious.' They were following their return tracks into a strong wind which developed into a full blizzard by lunch. 'This is the second full gale since we left the Pole. I don't like the look of it. Is the weather breaking up? If so, God help us, with the tremendous summit journey and scant food. Wilson and Bowers are my standby. I don't like the easy way in which Oates and Evans get frostbitten.'

In the full transcript, this day ends with the observation that Bowers was using Wilson's skis whilst 'Old Bill' walked by the sledge or pulled ahead of it. The following day, Friday, they started late, although Scott had 'called the hands rather early'. Alas, they lost their way, but steering right 'by a stroke of fortune' they regained signs of the track. Saturday's entry is given in full, but Sunday begins with a paragraph edited out. It reads as follows: 'Little wind and heavy going in forenoon. We just ran out eight miles in five hours and added another eight in three hours 40 mins in the afternoon with a good wind and better surface. It is very difficult to know if we are going up or down hill; the barometer is quite different from outward readings. We are 43 miles from the depôt with six days' food in hand. We are camped opposite our lunch cairn of the 4th, only half a day's march from the point at which the supporting party left us.'

bag full again. The only real anxiety now is the finding of the Three Degree Depôt. The tracks seem as good as ever so far; sometimes for 30 or 40 yards we lose them under drifts, but then they reappear quite clearly raised above the surface. If the light is good there is not the least difficulty in following. Blizzards are our bugbear, not only stopping our marches, but the cold damp air takes it out of us. Bowers got another rating sight tonight – it was wonderful how he managed to observe in such a horribly cold wind.

Saturday, January 27. – R. 10. Temp. –16° (lunch), –14.3° (evening). Minimum –19°. Height 9,900. Barometer low? Called the hands half an hour late, but we got away in good time. The forenoon march was over the belt of storm-tossed sastrugi; it looked like a rough sea. Wilson and I pulled in front on ski, the remainder on foot. It was very tricky work following the track, which pretty constantly disappeared, and in fact only showed itself by faint signs anywhere – a foot or two of raised sledge-track, a dozen yards of the trail of the sledgemeter wheel, or a spatter of hard snow-flicks where feet had trodden. Sometimes none of these were distinct, but one got an impression of lines which guided. The trouble was that on the outward track one had to shape course constantly to avoid the heaviest mounds, and consequently there were many zigzags. We lost a good deal over a mile by these halts, in which we unharnessed and went on the search for signs. However, by hook or by crook, we managed to stick on the old track. Came on the cairn quite suddenly, marched past it, and camped for lunch at 7 miles. In the afternoon the sastrugi gradually diminished in size and now we are on fairly level ground today, the obstruction practically at an end, and, to our joy, the tracks showing up much plainer again. For the last two hours we had no difficulty at all in following them. There has been a nice helpful southerly breeze all day, a clear sky and comparatively warm temperature. The air is dry again, so that tents and equipment are gradually losing their icy condition.

Our sleeping-bags are slowly but surely getting wetter and I'm afraid it will take a lot of this weather to put them right. However, we all sleep well enough in them, the hours allowed being now on the short side. We are slowly getting more hungry, and it would be an advantage to have a little more food, especially for lunch. If we get to the next depôt in a few marches (it is now less than 60 miles and we have a full week's food) we ought to be able to open out a little, but we can't look for a real feed till we get to the pony food depôt. A long way to go, and, by Jove, this is tremendous labour.

Sunday, January 28. – Three articles were dropped on our outward march – Oates' pipe, Bowers' fur mitts, and Evans' night boots. We picked up the boots and mitts on the track, and tonight we found the pipe lying placidly in sight on the snow. The sledge tracks were very easy to follow today; they are becoming more and more raised, giving a good line shadow often visible half a mile ahead. If this goes on and the weather holds we shall get our depôt without trouble. I shall indeed be glad to get it on the sledge. We are getting more hungry, there is no doubt. The lunch meal is beginning to seem inadequate. We are pretty thin, especially Evans, but none of us are feeling worked out. I doubt if we could drag heavy loads, but we can keep going well with our light one. We talk of food a good deal more, and shall be glad to open out on it.

Monday, January 29. — R. 12. Lunch Temp. −23°. Supper Temp. −25°. Height 10,000. Excellent march of 19½ miles, 10.5 before lunch. Wind helping greatly; considerable drift; tracks for the most part very plain. Some time before lunch we picked up the return track of the supporting party, so that there are now three distinct sledge impressions. We are only 24 miles from our depôt—an easy day and a half. Given a fine day tomorrow we ought to get it without difficulty. The wind and sastrugi are S.S.E. and S.E. If the weather holds we ought to do the rest of the inland ice journey in little over a week. The surface is very much altered since we passed out. The loose snow has been swept into heaps, hard and wind-tossed. The rest has a glazed appearance, the loose drifting snow no doubt acting on it, polishing it like a sand blast. The sledge with our good wind behind runs splendidly on it; it is all soft and sandy beneath the glaze. We are certainly getting hungrier every day. The day after tomorrow we should be able to increase allowances. It is monotonous work, but, thank God, the miles are coming fast at last. We ought not to be delayed much now with the down-grade in front of us.

Tuesday, January 30. — R. 13. 9,860. Lunch Temp. −25°, Supper Temp. −24.5°. Thank the Lord, another fine march—19 miles. We have passed the last cairn before the depôt, the track is clear ahead, the weather fair, the wind helpful, the gradient down—with any luck we should pick up our depôt in the middle of the morning march. This is the bright side; the reverse of the medal is serious. Wilson has strained a tendon in his leg; it has given pain all day and is swollen tonight. Of course, he is full of pluck over it, but I don't like the idea of such an accident here. To add to the trouble Evans has dislodged two fingernails tonight; his hands are really bad, and to my surprise he shows signs of losing heart over it. He hasn't been cheerful since the accident. The wind shifted from S.E. to S. and back again all day, but luckily it keeps strong. We can get along with bad fingers, but it [will be] a mighty serious thing if Wilson's leg doesn't improve.

Sunday, February 4. — R. 18. 8,620 feet. Temp.: Lunch −22°; Supper −23°. Pulled on foot in the morning over good hard surface and covered 9.7 miles. Just before lunch unexpectedly fell into crevasses, Evans and I together—a second fall for Evans—and I camped. After lunch saw disturbance ahead, and what I took for disturbance (land) to the right. We went on ski over hard shiny descending surface. Did very well, especially towards end of march, covering in all 18.1. We have come down some hundreds of feet. Half way in the march the land showed up splendidly, and I decided to make straight for Mt. Darwin, which we are rounding. Every sign points to getting away off

The entries for Wednesday, Jan 31st to the Saturday following have been edited out. They begin with more details about Wilson's problem. He 'rested his leg as much as possible by walking quietly beside the sledge; the result has been good and tonight there is much less inflammation. I hope he will be all right again soon, but it is trying to have an injured limb in the party.' In the afternoon they picked up Bowers' skis, left behind at Scott's instructions on Dec 31st. But in the afternoon the surface became 'fearfully bad . . . ill-luck that this should happen just when we have only four men to pull.' On the Thursday, Feb 1st, it was 'heavy collar work' most of the day, which was 'very heavy pulling'. Scott records that they have eight days' food in hand; Wilson's leg is much better, but 'Evans' fingers now very bad, two nails coming off, blisters burst'. The following day, Friday, started well, and they 'reeled off 9 miles' by lunch at 1.30pm. Unfortunately in the afternoon Scott, on a 'very slippery surface, came an awful "purler" on my shoulder. He concluded: 'Our bags are getting very wet and we ought to have more sleep.' Saturday was a difficult day, with a sail fixed to the sledge to help them up a steep slope. 'Vexatious delays' occurred as they tried to follow their earlier tracks. 'Decided it is a waste of time looking for tracks and cairn, and shall gently push on due north as fast as we can . . . Evans' fingers are going on as well as can be expected, but it will be long before he will be able to help properly with the work. Wilson's leg *much* better, and my shoulder also, though it gives bad twinges.'

The Return from the Pole—1912

Earlier, Scott wrote,' It is horribly sore tonight and another sick person is added to our tent—three out of five injured, and the most troublesome surface yet to come. We shall be lucky if we get through without serious injury.' They were eating extra food but nevertheless were getting 'pretty hungry'. Monday, Feb 5th is also edited out. The morning was good, with few crevasses, but an hour after starting in the afternoon they came across great 'street' crevasses partly open. It was difficult manoeuvring amongst these, and Scott admitted, 'I should not like to do it without ski.' On the favourable side, their camp was 'comfortable for the first time for many weeks'. However, 'Our faces are much cut up by all the winds we have had, mine least of all; the others tell me they feel their noses more going with, than against, the wind. Evans' nose is almost as bad as his fingers. He is a good deal crocked up.'

this plateau. The temperature is 20° lower than when we were here before; the party is not improving in condition, especially Evans, who is becoming rather dull and incapable. Thank the Lord, we have good food at each meal, but we get hungrier in spite of it. Bowers is splendid, full of energy and bustle all the time. I hope we are not going to have trouble with ice-falls.

Tuesday, February 6.—Lunch 7,900; Supper 7,210. Temp. −15° [R. 20]. We've had a horrid day and not covered good mileage. On turning out found sky overcast; a beastly position amidst crevasses. Luckily it cleared just before we started. We went straight for Mt. Darwin, but in half an hour found ourselves amongst huge open chasms, unbridged, but not very deep, I think. We turned to the north between two, but to our chagrin they converged into chaotic disturbance. We had to retrace our steps for a mile or so, then struck to the west and got on to a confused sea of sastrugi, pulling very hard; we put up the sail, Evans' nose suffered, Wilson very cold, everything horrid. Camped for lunch in the sastrugi; the only comfort, things looked clearer to the west and we were obviously going downhill. In the afternoon we struggled on, got out of sastrugi and turned over on glazed surface, crossing many crevasses—very easy work on ski. Towards the end of the march we realised the certainty of maintaining a more or less straight course to the depôt, and estimate distance 10 to 15 miles.

Food is low and weather uncertain, so that many hours of the day were anxious; but this evening, though we are not as far advanced as I expected, the outlook is much more promising. Evans is the chief anxiety now; his cuts and wounds suppurate, his nose looks very bad, and altogether he shows considerable signs of being played out. Things may mend for him on the glacier, and his wounds get some respite under warmer conditions. I am indeed glad to think we shall so soon have done with plateau conditions. It took us 27 days to reach the Pole and 21 days back—in all 48 days—nearly 7 weeks in low temperature with almost incessant wind.

End of the Summit Journey

As they descended the Beardmore on Feb 7th, they had five days' food, but it was five days' march to the next depôt—so there was no safety margin. Scott, with what Huntford calls 'grotesque mismanagement', stopped 'in good weather for the afternoon to collect [these] geological samples and henceforth carried 30 pounds of stones on the sledge. Geology cost him six or seven miles . . . when time was against him.'

Wednesday, February 7.—Mount Darwin [or Upper Glacier] Depôt, R. 21. Height 7,100. Lunch Temp. −9°; Supper Temp. [a blank here]. A wretched day with satisfactory ending. First panic, certainty that biscuit-box was short. Great doubt as to how this has come about, as we certainly haven't over-issued allowances. Bowers is dreadfully disturbed about it. The shortage is a full day's allowance. We started our march at 8.30, and travelled down slopes and over terraces covered with hard sastrugi—very tiresome work—and the land didn't seem to come any nearer. At lunch the wind increased, and what with hot tea and good food, we started the afternoon in a better frame of mind, and it soon became obvious we were nearing our mark. Soon after 6.30 we saw our depôt easily and camped next it at 7.30.

Found note from E. Evans to say the second return party passed through safely at

164

2.30 on January 14 – half a day longer between depôts than we have been. The temperature is higher, but there is a cold wind tonight.

Well, we have come through our 7 weeks' ice camp journey and most of us are fit, but I think another week might have had a very bad effect on P.O. Evans, who is going steadily downhill.

It is satisfactory to recall that these facts give absolute proof of both expeditions having reached the Pole and placed the question of priority beyond discussion.

It is not clear what Scott means here by 'priority'.

Return from First Summit Depôt

Thursday, February 8. – R. 22. Height 6,260. Start Temp. –11°; Lunch Temp. –5°; Supper, zero. 9.2 miles. Started from the depôt rather late owing to weighing biscuit, etc., and rearranging matters. Had a beastly morning. Wind very strong and cold. Steered in for Mt. Darwin to visit rock. Sent Bowers on, on ski, as Wilson can't wear his at present. He obtained several specimens, all of much the same type, a close-grained granite rock which weathers red. Hence the pink limestone. After he rejoined we skidded downhill pretty fast, leaders on ski, Oates and Wilson on foot alongside sledge – Evans detached. We lunched at 2 well down towards Mt. Buckley, the wind half a gale and everybody very cold and cheerless. However, better things were to follow. We decided to steer for the moraine under Mt. Buckley and, pulling with crampons, we crossed some very irregular steep slopes with big crevasses and slid down towards the rocks. The moraine was obviously so interesting that when we had advanced some miles and got out of the wind, I decided to camp and spend the rest of the day geologising. It has been extremely interesting. We found ourselves under perpendicular cliffs of Beacon sandstone, weathering rapidly and carrying veritable coal seams. From the last, Wilson, with his sharp eyes, has picked several plant impressions, the last a piece of coal with beautifully traced leaves in layers, also some excellently preserved impressions of thick stems, showing cellular structure. In one place we saw the cast of small waves in the sand. Tonight Bill has got a specimen of limestone with archeocyathus – the trouble is one cannot imagine where the stone comes from; it is evidently rare, as few specimens occur in the moraine. There is a good deal of pure white quartz. Altogether we have had a most interesting afternoon, and the relief of being out of the wind and in a warmer temperature is inexpressible. I hope and trust we shall all buck up again now that the conditions are more favourable. We have been in shadow all the afternoon, but the sun has just reached us, a little obscured by night haze. A lot could be written on the delight of setting foot on rock after 14 weeks of snow and ice and nearly 7 out of sight of aught else. It is like going ashore after a sea voyage. We deserve a little good bright weather after all our trials, and hope to get a chance to dry our sleeping-bags and generally make our gear more comfortable.

Saturday, February 10. – R. 24. Lunch Temp. +12°; Supper Temp. +10°. Got off a

Friday 9th is edited out. It seems almost incredible that despite their pitiable condition they 'stopped and geologised'. Wilson got 'a great find' of a vegetable impression in a piece of limestone, though Scott was 'too tired to write geological notes'. When they continued, they had to come down over an ice-fall where the crevasses were much firmer than expected. They found their night camp of Dec 20th and lunched an hour later. 'Did pretty well in the afternoon, marching 3¾ hours.' The night was wonderfully calm and warm, and Scott recorded 'it is remarkable to be able to stand outside the tent and sun oneself'. They now faced another dilemma, however: they desperately needed rest, yet had to march on if they were to find their full rations.

good morning march in spite of keeping too far east and getting in rough, cracked ice. Had a splendid night's sleep, showing great change in all faces, so didn't get away till 10 a.m. Lunched just before 3. After lunch the land began to be obscured. We held a course for 2½ hours with difficulty, then the sun disappeared, and snow drove in our faces with northerly wind—very warm and impossible to steer, so camped. After supper, still very thick all round, but sun showing and less snow falling. The fallen snow crystals are quite feathery like thistledown. We have two full days' food left, and though our position is uncertain, we are certainly within two outward marches from the middle glacier depôt. However, if the weather doesn't clear by tomorrow, we must either march blindly on or reduce food. It is very trying. Another night to make up arrears of sleep. The ice crystals that first fell this afternoon were very large. Now the sky is clearer overhead, the temperature has fallen slightly, and the crystals are minute.

Sunday, February 11.—R. 25. Lunch Temp. +6.5°; Supper +3.5°. The worst day we have had during the trip and greatly owing to our own fault. We started on a wretched surface with light S.W. wind, sail set, and pulling on ski—in a horrible light, which made everything look fantastic. As we went on the light got worse, and suddenly we found ourselves in pressure. Then came the fatal decision to steer east. We went on for 6 hours, hoping to do a good distance, which in fact I suppose we did, but for the last hour or two we pressed on into a regular trap. Getting on to a good surface we did not reduce our lunch meal, and thought all going well, but half an hour after lunch we got into the worst ice mess I have ever been in. For three hours we plunged on on ski, first thinking we were too much to the right, then too much to the left; meanwhile the disturbance got worse and my spirits received a very rude shock. There were times when it seemed almost impossible to find a way out of the awful turmoil in which we found ourselves. At length, arguing that there must be a way on our left, we plunged in that direction. It got worse, harder, more icy and crevassed. We could not manage our ski and pulled on foot, falling into crevasses every minute—most luckily with no bad accident. At length we saw a smoother slope towards the land, pushed for it, but knew it was a woefully long way from us. The turmoil changed in character, irregular crevassed surface giving way to huge chasms, closely packed and most difficult to cross. It was very heavy work, but we had grown desperate. We won through at 10 p.m. and I write after 12 hours on the march. I think we are on or about the right track now, but we are

'[The slide below] was prepared by Amundsen for explaining his system of transverse marking to his English-speaking audiences. On either side of the depôt were ten flags at one mile intervals, each numbered as indicated. This meant that in the thickest weather, a single flag was enough to point the way. Since the flags stretched ten miles on either side, the chances of missing one were remote. The conical shapes placed along the line of march are snow cairns seven miles apart, also numbered, to help in finding the depôt.' Huntford makes this point to contrast with Scott's inadequate system.

still a good number of miles from the depôt, so we reduced rations tonight. We had three pemmican meals left and decided to make them into four. Tomorrow's lunch must serve for two if we do not make big progress. It was a test of our endurance on the march and our fitness with small supper. We have come through well. A good wind has come down the glacier which is clearing the sky and surface. Pray God the wind holds tomorrow. Short sleep tonight and off first thing, I hope.

Monday, February 12. – R. 26. In a very critical situation. All went well in the forenoon, and we did a good long march over a fair surface. Two hours before lunch we were cheered by the sight of our night camp of the 18th December, the day after we made our depôt – this showed we were on the right track. In the afternoon, refreshed by tea, we went forward, confident of covering the remaining distance, but by a fatal chance we kept too far to the left, and then we struck uphill and, tired and despondent, arrived in a horrid maze of crevasses and fissures. Divided counsels caused our course to be erratic after this, and finally, at 9 p.m., we landed in the worst place of all. After discussion we decided to camp, and here we are, after a very short supper and one meal only remaining in the food-bag; the depôt doubtful in locality. We *must* get there tomorrow. Meanwhile we are cheerful with an effort. It's a tight place, but luckily we've been well fed up to the present. Pray God we have fine weather tomorrow.

Wednesday, February 14. – There is no getting away from the fact that we are not pulling strong: probably none of us. Wilson's leg still troubles him and he doesn't like to trust himself on ski; but the worst case is Evans, who is giving us serious anxiety. This morning he suddenly disclosed a huge blister on his foot. It delayed us on the march, when he had to have his crampon readjusted. Sometimes I fear he is going from bad to worse, but I trust he will pick up again when we come to steady work on ski like this afternoon. He is hungry and so is Wilson. We can't risk opening out our food again, and as cook at present I am serving something under full allowance. We are inclined to get slack and slow with our camping arrangements, and small delays increase. I have talked of the matter tonight and hope for improvement. We cannot do distance without the hours. The next depôt some 30 miles away and nearly 3 days' food in hand.

Friday, February 16. – 12.5 m. Lunch Temp. +6.1°; Supper Temp. +7°. A rather trying position. Evans has nearly broken down in brain, we think. He is absolutely changed from his normal self-reliant self. This morning and this afternoon he stopped the march on some trivial excuse. We are on short rations, but not very short, food spins out till tomorrow night. We cannot be more than 10 or 12 miles from the depôt, but the weather is all against us. After lunch we were enveloped in a snow sheet, land just looming. Memory should hold the events of a very troublesome march with more

When on Monday 12th Scott lost his way, an awful day followed (not recorded here) until Wilson saw a depôt flag. At that point all they had left was a little bit of pemmican and some tea. The following entry is edited out: 'The worst experience of the trip and gave us a horrid feeling of insecurity … In future food must be worked out so that we do not run so short if the weather fails us. We mustn't get into a hole like this again.' It was too late for Scott to think in these terms.

The journal entry for Tuesday 13th notes that they all slept well despite their grave anxieties of the night before. Scott woke up several times in the night and, going out of the tent, found it was overcast and snowing. They did not get up until 9am and took only a short breakfast, leaving the scant meal remaining for 'eventualities'. More than half the team were incapable of pulling their full weight, and Oates, whom he does not mention, must have been a bad case. His words are as follows: 'Bowers has had a very bad attack of snow blindness, and Wilson another almost as bad. Evans has no power to assist with camping work.' There is also a paragraph missing from the start of the Wednesday entry. They were now well on the glacier and were on crampons and soon hoisted sail.

However, they had to scrape and sandpaper the sledge runners in order to get up any speed. Scott goes on to explain that this was not the equipment which was at fault – there was 'no getting away from the fact that we are not pulling strong. Wilson's leg still troubles him and he doesn't like to trust himself on ski; but the worst case is Evans'. But yet worse was in fact to come. Oates had written in his diary on the 12th: 'It's an extraordinary thing about Evans, he's lost his guts and behaves like an old woman or worse. He's quite worn out with the work, and how he's going to do the 400 odd miles we've still got to do, I don't know.'

Another entry missing on Wednesday 14th recorded: 'We are running short of provisions', at a distance, they calculate, 20 miles from the depôt. Scott wrote: 'as cook at present I am serving something under full allowance', as they only had three days' food in hand. By the afternoon they had reduced their food allowance and their period of sleep. Inevitably they were 'feeling rather done' but hoped that 1½ or 2 days would see them at the depôt.

troubles ahead. Perhaps all will be well if we can get to our depôt tomorrow fairly early, but it is anxious work with the sick man. But it's no use meeting troubles halfway, and our sleep is all too short to write more.

Saturday, February 17. – A very terrible day. Evans looked a little better after a good sleep, and declared, as he always did, that he was quite well. He started in his place on the traces, but half an hour later worked his ski shoes adrift, and had to leave the sledge. The surface was awful, the soft recently fallen snow clogging the ski and runners at every step, the sledge groaning, the sky overcast, and the land hazy. We stopped after about one hour, and Evans came up again, but very slowly. Half an hour later he dropped out again on the same plea. He asked Bowers to lend him a piece of string. I cautioned him to come on as quickly as he could and he answered cheerfully as I thought. We had to push on, and the remainder of us were forced to pull very hard, sweating heavily. Abreast the Monument Rock we stopped, and seeing Evans a long way astern, I camped for lunch. There was no alarm at first, and we prepared tea and our own meal, consuming the latter. After lunch, and Evans still not appearing, we looked out, to see him still afar off. By this time we were alarmed, and all four started back on ski. I was first to reach the poor man and shocked at his appearance; he was on his knees with clothing disarranged, hands uncovered and frost-bitten, and a wild look in his eyes. Asked what was the matter, he replied with a slow speech that he didn't know, but thought he must have fainted. We got him on his feet, but after two or three steps he sank down again. He showed every sign of complete collapse. Wilson, Bowers, and I went back for the sledge, whilst Oates remained with him. When we returned he was practically unconscious, and when we got him into the tent quite comatose. He died quietly at 12.30 a.m. On discussing the symptoms we think he began to get weaker just before we reached the Pole, and that his downward path was accelerated first by the shock of his frost-bitten fingers, and later by falls during rough travelling on the glacier, further by his loss of all confidence in himself. Wilson thinks it certain he must have injured his brain by a fall. It is a terrible thing to lose a companion in this way, but calm reflection shows that there could not have been a better ending to the terrible anxieties of the past week. Discussion of the situation at lunch yesterday shows us what a desperate pass we were in with a sick man on our hands so far from home.

At 1 a.m. we packed up and came down over the pressure ridges, finding our depôt easily.

The Last March – 1912

Monday, February 19. – R. 33. Temp. –17°. We have struggled out 4.6 miles in a short day over a really terrible surface – it has been like pulling over desert sand, without the least glide in the world. If this goes on we shall have a bad time, but I sincerely trust it is only the result of the windless area close to the coast and that, as we are making steadily outwards, we shall shortly escape it. It is perhaps premature to be anxious about covering distance. In all other respects things are improving. We have our sleeping-bags spread on the sledge and they are drying, but, above all, we have our full measure of food again. Tonight we had a sort of stew fry of pemmican and horse-flesh, and voted it the best hoosh we had ever had on a sledge journey. The absence of poor Evans is a help to the commissariat, but if he had been here in a fit state we might have got along faster. I wonder what is in store for us, with some little alarm at the lateness of the season.

Friday, March 2. – Lunch. Misfortunes rarely come singly. We marched to the [Middle Barrier] depôt fairly easily yesterday afternoon, and since that have suffered three distinct blows which have placed us in a bad position. First we found a shortage of oil; with most rigid economy it can scarce carry us to the next depôt on this surface [71 miles away]. Second, Titus Oates disclosed his feet, the toes showing very bad indeed, evidently bitten by the late temperatures. The third blow came in the night, when the wind, which we had hailed with some joy, brought dark overcast weather. It fell below –40° in the night, and this morning it took 1½ hours to get our foot-gear on, but we got away before eight. We lost cairn and tracks together and made as steady as we could N. by W., but have seen nothing. Worse was to come – the surface is simply awful. In spite of strong wind and full sail we have only done 5½ miles. We are in a very queer street, since there is no doubt we cannot do the extra marches and feel the cold horribly.

Sunday, March 4. – Lunch. Things looking *very* black indeed. As usual we forgot our trouble last night, got into our bags, slept splendidly on good hoosh, woke and had another, and started marching. Sun shining brightly, tracks clear, but surface covered with sandy frost-rime. All the morning we had to pull with all our strength, and in 4½ hours we covered 3½ miles. Last night it was overcast and thick, surface bad; this morning sun shining and surface as bad as ever. Under the immediate surface crystals is a hard sastrugi surface, which must have been excellent for pulling a week or two ago. We are about 42 miles from the next depôt and have a week's food, but only about 3 to 4 days' fuel – we are as economical of the latter as one can possibly be, and we cannot afford to save food and pull as we are pulling. We are in a very tight place

The entry for Feb 24th (edited out) contained the dreaded note that when they reached Southern Barrier Depôt they found a shortage of fuel – 'Wish we had more fuel'; 'Fuel shortage is still an anxiety'; and 'Fuel is woefully short' – which Huntford calls the 'litany of remorse'. They still hoped to meet Meares and the dogs bringing supplies, but 'there is a horrid element of doubt'. At the next depôt, reached on Mar 1st, they found hardly a quarter of a gallon of fuel. The shortage was exacerbated by paraffin 'creep', which caused the liquid to evaporate through screwed bungs seated on leather washers. Amundsen had solved the problem with hermetically sealed tins, which were found intact after 50 years. Scott's had gone after 90 days.

Preceding this in the full journals is the entry for Saturday, Mar 3rd, which began, 'Did close on 10 miles and things looked a trifle better [but] then the surface grew awful beyond words … After 4½ hours things so bad that we camped, having covered 4½ miles.' The surface was coated with a thin layer of woolly crystals too firmly fixed to be removed by the wind, and causing impossible friction on the runners. 'God help us,' wrote Scott. 'We can't keep up this pulling, that is certain. Amongst ourselves we are unendingly cheerful, but what each man feels in his heart I can only guess. Putting on footgear in the morning is getting slower and slower, and therefore every day more dangerous.'

indeed, but none of us despondent *yet*, or at least we preserve every semblance of good cheer, but one's heart sinks as the sledge stops dead at some sastrugi behind which the surface sand lies thickly heaped. For the moment the temperature is in the −20°, an improvement which makes us much more comfortable, but a colder snap is bound to come again soon. I fear that Oates at least will weather such an event very poorly. Providence to our aid! We can expect little from man now except the possibility of extra food at the next depôt. It will be real bad if we get there and find the same shortage of oil. Shall we get there? Such a short distance it would have appeared to us on the summit! I don't know what I should do if Wilson and Bowers weren't so determinedly cheerful over things.

Monday, March 5. – Lunch. Regret to say going from bad to worse. We got a slant of wind yesterday afternoon, and going on 5 hours we converted our wretched morning run of 3½ miles into something over 9. We went to bed on a cup of cocoa and pemmican solid with the chill off. (R. 47.) The result is telling on all, but mainly on Oates, whose feet are in a wretched condition. One swelled up tremendously last night and he is very lame this morning. We started march on tea and pemmican as last night – we pretend to prefer the pemmican this way. Marched for 5 hours this morning over a slightly better surface covered with high moundy sastrugi. Sledge capsized twice; we pulled on foot, covering about 5½ miles. We are two pony marches and 4 miles about from our depôt. Our fuel dreadfully low and the poor Soldier nearly done. It is pathetic enough because we can do nothing for him; more hot food might do a little, but only a little, I fear. We none of us expected these terribly low temperatures, and of the rest of us Wilson is feeling them most; mainly, I fear, from his self-sacrificing devotion in doctoring Oates' feet. We cannot help each other, each has enough to do to take care of himself. We get cold on the march when the trudging is heavy, and the wind pierces our worn garments. The others, all of them, are unendingly cheerful when in the tent. We mean to see the game through with a proper spirit, but it's tough work to be pulling harder than we ever pulled in our lives for long hours, and to feel that the progress is so slow. One can only say 'God help us!' and plod on our weary way, cold and very miserable, though outwardly cheerful. We talk of all sorts of subjects in the tent, not much of food now, since we decided to take the risk of running a full ration. We simply couldn't go hungry at this time.

Wednesday, March 7. – A little worse, I fear. One of Oates' feet *very* bad this morning; he is wonderfully brave. We still talk of what we will do together at home.

We only made 6½ miles yesterday. This morning in 4½ hours we did just over 4 miles. We are 16 from our depôt. If we only find the correct proportion of food there and this surface continues, we may get to the next depôt [Mt. Hooper, 72 miles farther] but not to One Ton Camp. We hope against hope that the dogs have been to Mt. Hooper; then we might pull through. If there is a shortage of oil again we can have lit-

The morning entry for Tues 6th said: 'Things have been awful', as 'pulling with all our might (for our lives) we could scarcely advance at a rate of a mile an hour.' Their total achievement was a mere 3½ miles. 'Poor Oates is unable to pull, sits on the sledge when we are track-searching – he is wonderfully plucky, as his feet must be giving him great pain. He makes no complaint, but his spirits only come in spurts now, and he grows more silent in the tent.' Scott comments that the sledge became 'as heavy as lead'. This is the point at which Scott appears to have decided that they would be unable to complete the journey.

tle hope. One feels that for poor Oates the crisis is near, but none of us are improving, though we are wonderfully fit considering the really excessive work we are doing. We are only kept going by good food. No wind this morning till a chill northerly air came ahead. Sun bright and cairns showing up well. I should like to keep the track to the end.

Thursday, March 8. – Lunch. Worse and worse in morning; poor Oates' left foot can never last out, and time over foot-gear something awful. Have to wait in night foot-gear for nearly an hour before I start changing, and then am generally first to be ready. Wilson's feet giving trouble now. We did 4½ miles this morning and are now 8½ miles from the depôt – a ridiculously small distance to feel in difficulties, yet on this surface we know we cannot equal half our old marches, and that for that effort we expend nearly double the energy. The great question is, What shall we find at the depôt? If the dogs have visited it we may get along a good distance, but if there is another short allowance of fuel, God help us indeed. We are in a very bad way, I fear, in any case.

Saturday, March 10. – Things steadily downhill. Oates' foot worse. He has rare pluck and must know that he can never get through. He asked Wilson if he had a chance this morning, and of course Bill had to say he didn't know. In point of fact he has none. Apart from him, if he went under now, I doubt whether we could get through. With great care we might have a dog's chance, but no more. The weather conditions are awful, and our gear gets steadily more icy and difficult to manage. At the same time, of course, poor Titus is the greatest handicap. He keeps us waiting in the morning until we have partly lost the warming effect of our good breakfast, when the only wise policy is to be up and away at once; again at lunch. Poor chap! it is too pathetic to watch him; one cannot but try to cheer him up.

Yesterday we marched up the depôt, Mt. Hooper. Cold comfort. Shortage on our allowance all round.

This morning it was calm when we breakfasted, but the wind came from the W.N.W. as we broke camp. It rapidly grew in strength. After travelling for half an hour I saw that none of us could go on facing such conditions. We were forced to camp and are spending the rest of the day in a comfortless blizzard camp, wind quite foul. [R. 52.]

Sunday, March 11. – Titus Oates is very near the end, one feels. What we or he will do, God only knows. We discussed the matter after breakfast; he is a brave fine fellow and understands the situation, but he practically asked for advice. Nothing could be said but to urge him to march as long as he could. One satisfactory result to the discussion; I practically ordered Wilson to hand over the means of ending our troubles to us, so that any one of us may know how to do so. Wilson had no choice between doing so and our ransacking the medicine case. We have 30 opium tabloids apiece and he is left with a tube of morphine. So far the tragical side of our story.

Scott continued (passage deleted): 'I don't know that anyone is to blame, but generosity and thoughtfulness has not been abundant.' The fact was that, by changing plans at such a late stage, he had, in Huntford's words, 'disturbed the whole organisation' of the depôts. Instead of taking prepared packages of rations, the return parties had had to break them open as best they could. Huntford explains that Scott's instructions concerning the dogs, which were supposed to have got them back to base, were also 'diffuse, ill-conceived and contradictory'. Meares did not arrive with his dogs at base until Jan 5th, and though he then awaited orders, these did not come. When the news came through that Lieut. Evans was dying of scurvy, someone in the base party, says Huntford, should have realised that Scott's polar party might be in similar trouble and would need the dogs urgently, but they did not. Even if they had, says Huntford, Scott had left specific instructions that he was *not* to be relieved on any account. With naval discipline paramount, Atkinson, now in command, followed orders. On Feb 5th the *Terra Nova* arrived. Simpson went on board for the journey home. Meares was also intent on catching the ship. Atkinson felt obliged to stay and look after Evans instead of going south with the dogs again.

Dimitri, an experienced dog handler, and Cherry-Garrard, who was not, were left to go south. Neither could navigate. The two started with the dog teams on Feb 25th, and reached One Ton camp on Mar 4th, having done 20 miles a day without trouble under the experienced eye of Dimitri. A blizzard broke out, keeping them from moving for four days. The dogs could not then go on, because there was a shortage of dog food, though there was enough on their sledges for them to continue for a day or two. Cherry-Garrard, not being able to navigate, dared not go on in case he missed Scott, travelling the other way. Altogether the two men and their dogs remained at camp for 10 days before deciding on Mar 10th to turn round and return.

For some reason there is no entry for Tuesday, Mar 13th. Thursday, Mar 15th is also missing, perhaps because, as Scott recorded on the 16th/17th, he had lost track of dates. On Mar 17th, Oates' 32nd birthday, Scott wrote his famous description of Oates' walking out to his death. There has been controversy ever since about whether or not he intended to commit suicide, and for what reason – whether to relieve his own suffering or to give his companions an extra chance. Certainly Oates' mother appears never to have forgiven Scott, believing that he had driven a subordinate 'to the extremities of suffering'. Wilson left a letter for Mrs Oates, saying that her son had died like a man and a soldier, without a word of complaint.

The sky was completely overcast when we started this morning. We could see nothing, lost the tracks, and doubtless have been swaying a good deal since – 3.1 miles for the forenoon – terribly heavy dragging – expected it. Know that 6 miles is about the limit of our endurance now, if we get no help from wind or surfaces. We have 7 days' food and should be about 55 miles from One Ton Camp tonight, 6 x 7 = 42, leaving us 13 miles short of our distance, even if things get no worse. Meanwhile the season rapidly advances.

Monday, March 12. – We did 6.9 miles yesterday, under our necessary average. Things are left much the same, Oates not pulling much, and now with hands as well as feet pretty well useless. We did 4 miles this morning in 4 hours 20 min. – we may hope for 3 this afternoon, 7 x 6 = 42. We shall be 47 miles from the depôt. I doubt if we can possibly do it. The surface remains awful, the cold intense, and our physical condition running down. God help us! Not a breath of favourable wind for more than a week, and apparently [we are] liable to head winds at any moment.

Wednesday, March 14. – No doubt about the going down-hill, but everything going wrong for us. Yesterday we woke to a strong northerly wind with temp. –37°. Couldn't face it, so remained in camp till 2, then did 5¼ miles. Wanted to march later, but party feeling the cold badly as the breeze (N.) never took off entirely, and as the sun sank the temp. fell. Long time getting supper in dark.

This morning started with southerly breeze, set sail and passed another cairn at good speed; halfway, however, the wind shifted to W. by S. or W.S.W., blew through our wind clothes and into our mitts. Poor Wilson horribly cold, could [not] get off ski for some time. Bowers and I practically made camp, and when we got into the tent at last we were all deadly cold. Then temp. now midday down –43° and the wind strong. We *must* go on, but now the making of every camp must be more difficult and dangerous. It must be near the end, but a pretty merciful end. Poor Oates got it again in the foot. I shudder to think what it will be like tomorrow. It is only with greatest pains rest of us keep off frost-bites. No idea there could be temperatures like this at this time of year with such winds. Truly awful outside the tent. Must fight it out to the last biscuit, but can't reduce rations.

Friday, March 16, or Saturday 17. – Lost track of dates, but think the last correct. Tragedy all along the line. At lunch, the day before yesterday, poor Titus Oates said he couldn't go on; he proposed we should leave him in his sleeping-bag. That we could not do, and we induced him to come on, on the afternoon march. In spite of its awful nature for him he struggled on and we made a few miles. At night he was worse and we knew the end had come.

Should this be found I want these facts recorded. Oates' last thoughts were of his Mother, but immediately before he took pride in thinking that his regiment would be pleased with the bold way in which he met his death. We can testify to his bravery. He has borne intense suffering for weeks without complaint, and to the very last was able and willing to discuss outside subjects. He did not – would not – give up hope till the very end. He was a brave soul. This was the end. He slept through the night before last, hoping not to wake; but he woke in the morning – yesterday. It was blowing a blizzard. He said, 'I am just going outside and may be some time.' He went out into the blizzard and we have not seen him since.

Oates and Scott

Scott's relationship with others on the expedition seems to reflect his general attitude to society in general. His Royal Navy background was paramount and if he had no great experience in commanding a ship, at least when he was on the *Terra Nova* he seems to have acted as he thought a commander *should* act. As with any close-knit group, cliques built up, in spite of the hierarchical framework. Examples of this come through in other people's correspondence and diaries. Perhaps the most revealing and the best known of these relationships is the Scott/Oates interaction, characterised at one extreme by the latter's statements to his mother.

For example, in October 1911, waiting for the start of the expedition, he wrote to her that the party 'get on very well [but] I dislike Scott intensely and would chuck the whole thing if it was not that we are the British expedition and must beat the Norwegians. Scott has always been very civil to me and I have the reputation of getting on well with him. But the fact of the matter is that he is not straight, it is himself first, the rest nowhere, and when he has got what he can out of you, it is shift for yourself.' On the face of it a damning indictment indeed.

The fact is that Oates' mother destroyed most of his letters to her, bar some saved by his sister, so we are unable to make a balanced assess-

Oates was one of the youngest members of the party. He died on his birthday, 17th March, 1912, at the age of 32.

ment of Oates' real feelings. We are told by Huntford that he often complained to his mother about those in positions of authority above him; we are also told that he came to conclude that he did not really want to continue to the Pole, which would go somewhat to explain his desire to 'chuck it'. As for his complaint that Scott is not 'straight', it might be asked if any leader of such a perilous enterprise could be 'straight' in the sense understood by an old Etonian and cavalry captain. Scott had shown himself capable of ruthlessness, for instance in the matter of firing Skelton, the engineer who worked for years on the tractors – and it would be naïve of Oates, or rather in character, for him to find that kind of leadership offensive.

He had, after all, he said 'a fairish chance' of being in the final party 'if Scott and I don't fall out . . . It will be pretty tough having four months of him [as] he fusses dreadfully [everyone said the same].' Scott was, thought Oates, dissembling about his future plans after the race to the Pole, and tells his mother: 'If Scott was a decent chap I would ask him bang out what he means to do.' He even told her that he would not attend their religious service 'as Scott reads the prayers'.

Elsewhere in the notes to the book something has been said about the nature of Oates' end. Huntford says that, to give it its proper name, it was suicide, and that for public consumption the 'story was contrived that Oates had sacrificed himself to save his companions'. A review of Diana Preston's book adds a third theory: 'It is remotely possible Oates went in search of the little boy's room and became lost. Normally, a tent corner sufficed for this purpose, but in Scott's presence the men stepped outside to expose themselves to the biting cold that was capable of locking their joints. The presence of Innuit dogs [at this stage] would have rewritten the [Oates] story. Such is their appetite for human excrement that attending to calls of nature is almost intolerable without a companion to keep [the dogs] away. Oates would have swallowed his pride and stayed inside [the tent].'

Oates had the arrogance both of comparative youth and of upbringing, coupled with fixed ideas about what was proper behaviour. There is little doubt that he thought it right to sacrifice yourself for the good of your companions, but I believe that enough emerges from the accumulation of data to enable readers to form their own opinion as to the nature of his relationship with Scott and the manner of his death.

Huntford suggests that there was in fact a 'more or less unconscious attempt to abandon Evans when he was left behind to tie up his boots, something he could not now do unaided'.

I take this opportunity of saying that we have stuck to our sick companions to the last. In case of Edgar Evans, when absolutely out of food and he lay insensible, the safety of the remainder seemed to demand his abandonment, but Providence mercifully removed him at this critical moment. He died a natural death, and we did not leave him till two hours after his death. We knew that poor Oates was walking to his death, but though we tried to dissuade him, we knew it was the act of a brave man and an English gentleman. We all hope to meet the end with a similar spirit, and assuredly the end is not far.

I can only write at lunch and then only occasionally. The cold is intense, −40° at midday. My companions are unendingly cheerful, but we are all on the verge of serious frost-bites, and though we constantly talk of fetching through, I don't think any one of us believes it in his heart.

We are cold on the march now, and at all times except meals. Yesterday we had to lie up for a blizzard and today we move dreadfully slowly. We are at No. 14 pony camp, only two pony marches from One Ton Depôt. We leave here our theodolite, a camera, and Oates' sleeping-bags. Diaries, etc., and geological specimens carried at Wilson's special request, will be found with us or on our sledge.

Sunday, March 18. – Today, lunch, we are 21 miles from the depôt. Ill fortune presses, but better may come. We have had more wind and drift from ahead yesterday; had to stop marching; wind N.W., force 4, temp. −35°. No human being could face it, and we are worn out *nearly*.

My right foot has gone, nearly all the toes – two days ago I was proud possessor of best feet. These are the steps of my downfall. Like an ass I mixed a small spoonful of curry powder with my melted pemmican – it gave me violent indigestion. I lay awake and in pain all night; woke and felt done on the march; foot went and I didn't know it. A very small measure of neglect and I have a foot which is not pleasant to contemplate. Bowers takes first place in condition, but there is not much to choose after all. The others are still confident of getting through – or pretend to be – don't know! We have the last *half* fill of oil in our primus and a very small quantity of spirit – this alone between us and thirst. The wind is fair for the moment, and that is perhaps a fact to help. The mileage would have seemed ridiculously small on our outward journey.

Monday, March 19. – Lunch. We camped with difficulty last night and were dreadfully cold till after our supper of cold pemmican and biscuit and a half a pannikin of cocoa cooked over the spirit. Then, contrary to expectation, we got warm and all slept well. Today we started in the usual dragging manner. Sledge dreadfully heavy. We are 15½ miles from the depôt and ought to get there in three days. What progress! We have two days' food, but barely a day's fuel. All our feet are getting bad – Wilson's best, my right foot worse, left all right. There is no chance to nurse one's feet till we can get hot food into us. Amputation is the least I can hope for now, but will the trouble spread? That is the serious question. The weather doesn't give us a chance – the wind from N. to N.W. and −40°temp. today.

Wednesday, March 21. – Got within 11 miles of depôt Monday night; had to lie up all yesterday in severe blizzard. Today forlorn hope, Wilson and Bowers going to depôt for fuel.

Tuesday, Mar 20th is also missing from the journal entries.

Although Wilson and Bowers hoped to march on to get help for Scott, the weather made this impossible. For nine days the three men lay in their tent. Scott wrote a number of letters, curiously not to Markham, though he sent a message via Kathleen, 'I thought much of him.'

Scott was too close to death to be able to write entries for the week Mar 23rd to Mar 29th. It is believed he died shortly after the latter date, but not certain if Bowers died later. The exact cause of death was not established, and although Atkinson later examined the bodies in the tent, he always refused to divulge any details.

22 *and* 23. – Blizzard bad as ever – Wilson and Bowers unable to start – tomorrow last chance – no fuel and only one or two of food left – must be near the end. Have decided it shall be natural – we shall march for the depôt with or without our effects and die in our tracks.

[Thursday] March 29. – Since the 21st we have had a continuous gale from W.S.W. and S.W. We had fuel to make two cups of tea apiece and bare food for two days on the 20th. Every day we have been ready to start for our depôt 11 *miles* away, but outside the door of the tent it remains a scene of whirling drift. I do not think we can hope for any better things now. We shall stick it out to the end, but we are getting weaker, of course, and the end cannot be far.

It seems a pity, but I do not think I can write more –

R. Scott

Last entry. For God's sake look after our people.

Farewell Letters

[To Kathleen Scott]

The Great God has called me and I feel it will add a fearful blow to the heavy ones that have fallen on you in life. But take comfort in that I die at peace with the world and myself – not afraid.

Indeed it has been most singularly unfortunate, for the risks I have taken never seemed excessive.

. . . I want to tell you that we have missed getting through by a narrow margin which was justifiably within the risk of such a journey. . . . After all, we have given our lives for our country – we have actually made the longest journey on record, and we have been the first Englishmen at the South Pole.

You must understand that it is too cold to write much.

. . . It's a pity the luck doesn't come our way, because every detail of equipment is right.

I shall not have suffered any pain, but leave the world fresh from harness and full of good health and vigour.

Since writing the above we got to within 11 miles of our depôt, with one hot meal and two days' cold food. We should have got through but have been held for *four* days by a frightful storm. I think the best chance has gone. We have decided not to kill ourselves, but to fight to the last for that depôt, but in the fighting there is a painless end.

Make the boy interested in natural history if you can; it is better than games; they encourage it at some schools. I know you will keep him in the open air.

Above all, he must guard and you must guard him against indolence. Make him a strenuous man. I had to force myself into being strenuous, as you know – had always an inclination to be idle.

There is a piece of the Union Jack I put up at the South Pole in my private kit bag, together with Amundsen's black flag and other trifles. Send a small piece of the Union Jack to the King and a small piece to Queen Alexandra.

What lots and lots I could tell you of this journey! How much better has it been than lounging in too great comfort at home! What tales you would have for the boy! But what a price to pay!

Tell Sir Clements I thought much of him and never regretted his putting me in command of the *Discovery*.

If this letter reaches you, Bill and I will have gone out together. We are very near it now and I should like you to know how splendid he was at the end – everlastingly cheerful and ready to sacrifice himself for others, never a word of blame to me for leading him into this mess. He is not suffering, luckily, at least only minor discomforts.

His eyes have a comfortable blue look of hope and his mind is peaceful with the satisfaction of his faith in regarding himself as part of the great scheme of the Almighty. I can do no more to comfort you than to tell you that he died as he lived, a brave, true man – the best of comrades and staunchest of friends.

My whole heart goes out to you in pity. . . .

Scott's journal (last entry), with its famous plea, 'For God's sake look after our people'.

[To Mrs E. A. Wilson, wife of Dr Wilson]

[To Mrs Bowers, mother of Lieut. Henry Bowers]

I am afraid this will reach you after one of the heaviest blows of your life.

I write when we are very near the end of our journey, and I am finishing it in company with two gallant, noble gentlemen. One of these is your son. He had come to be one of my closest and soundest friends, and I appreciate his wonderful upright nature, his ability and energy. As the troubles have thickened his dauntless spirit ever shone brighter and he has remained cheerful, hopeful, and indomitable to the end.

The ways of Providence are inscrutable, but there must be some reason why such a young, vigorous, and promising life is taken.

To the end he has talked of you and his sisters. One sees what a happy home he must have had, and perhaps it is well to look back on nothing but happiness.

He remains unselfish, self-reliant and splendidly hopeful to the end, believing in God's mercy to you. . . .

177

[To Sir James Barrie]

We are showing that Englishmen can still die with a bold spirit, fighting it out to the end. It will be known that we have accomplished our object in reaching the Pole, and that we have done everything possible, even to sacrificing ourselves in order to save sick companions. I think this makes an example for Englishmen of the future, and that the country ought to help those who are left behind to mourn us. I leave my poor girl and your godson, Wilson leaves a widow, and Edgar Evans also a widow in humble circumstances. Do what you can to get their claims recognised. Good-bye. I am not at all afraid of the end, but sad to miss many a humble pleasure which I had planned for the future on our long marches. I may not have proved a great explorer, but we have done the greatest march ever made and come very near to great success. . . . We are in a desperate state, feet frozen, etc. No fuel and a long way from food, but it would do your heart good to be in our tent, to hear our songs and the cheery conversation as to what we will do when we get to Hut Point.

Later. – We are very near the end, but have not and will not lose our good cheer. We have had four days of storm in our tent and nowhere's food or fuel. We did intend to finish ourselves when things proved like this, but we have decided to die naturally in the track.

As a dying man, my dear friend, be good to my wife and child. Give the boy a chance in life if the State won't do it. He ought to have good stuff in him. . . . I never met a man in my life whom I admired and loved more than you, but I could never show you how much your friendship meant to me, for you had much to give and I nothing.

[To Vice-Admiral Sir George le Clerc Egerton, Scott's commanding officer in the Royal Navy]

I fear we have shot our bolt – but we have been to the Pole and done the longest journey on record.

I hope these letters may find their destination some day.

Subsidiary reasons of our failure to return are due to the sickness of different members of the party, but the real thing that has stopped us is the awful weather and unexpected cold towards the end of the journey.

This traverse of the Barrier has been quite three times as severe as any experience we had on the summit.

There is no accounting for it, but the result has thrown out my calculations, and here we are little more than 100 miles from the base and petering out.

Message to the Public

The causes of the disaster are not due to faulty organisation but to misfortune in all risks which had to be undertaken.

1. The loss of pony transport in March 1911 obliged me to start later than I had intended, and obliged the limits of stuff transported to be narrowed.

2. The weather throughout the outward journey, and especially the long gale in 83° S., stopped us.

3. The soft snow in lower reaches of glacier again reduced pace.

We fought these untoward events with a will and conquered, but it cut into our provision reserve.

Every detail of our food supplies, clothing and depôts made on the interior ice-sheet and over that long stretch of 700 miles to the Pole and back, worked out to perfection. The advance party would have returned to the glacier in fine form and with surplus of food, but for the astonishing failure of the man whom we had least expected to fail. Edgar Evans was thought the strongest man of the party.

The Beardmore Glacier is not difficult in fine weather, but on our return we did not get a single completely fine day; this with a sick companion enormously increased our anxieties.

As I have said elsewhere, we got into frightfully rough ice and Edgar Evans received a concussion of the brain—he died a natural death, but left us a shaken party with the season unduly advanced.

But all the facts above enumerated were as nothing to the surprise which awaited us on the Barrier. I maintain that our arrangements for returning were quite adequate, and that no one in the world would have expected the temperatures and surfaces which we encountered at this time of the year. On the summit in lat. 85°, 86° we had −20°, −30°. On the Barrier in lat. 82°, 10,000 feet lower, we had −30° in the day, −47° at night pretty regularly, with continuous head wind during our day marches. It is clear that these circumstances came on very suddenly, and our wreck is certainly due to this sudden advent of severe weather, which does not seem to have any satisfactory cause. I do not think human beings ever came through such a month as we have come through, and we should have got through in spite of the weather but for the sickening of a second companion, Captain Oates, and a shortage of fuel in our depôts for which I cannot account, and finally, but for the storm which has fallen on us within 11 miles of the depôt at which we hoped to secure our final supplies. Surely misfortune could scarcely have exceeded this last blow. We arrived within 11 miles of our old One Ton Camp with fuel for one last meal and food for two days. For four days we have been unable to leave the tent—the gale howling about us. We are weak, writing is difficult, but for my own sake I do not regret this journey, which has shown that Englishmen can endure hardships, help one another, and meet death with as great a fortitude as ever in the past. We took risks, we knew we took them; things have come out against us, and therefore we have no cause for complaint, but bow to the will of Providence, determined still to do our best to the last. But if we have been willing to give our lives to this enterprise, which is for the honour of our country, I appeal to our countrymen to see that those who depend on us are properly cared for.

Had we lived, I should have had a tale to tell of the hardihood, endurance, and courage of my companions which would have stirred the heart of every Englishman. These rough notes and our dead bodies must tell the tale, but surely, surely, a great rich country like ours will see that those who are dependent on us are properly provided for.

R. Scott

The Finding of the Dead

[Account by Lieut. Atkinson, R.N., the expedition's surgeon]

Preston writes: 'It seemed sacrilege to move the bodies. The months during which they had lain beneath their canopy of snow had made them as one with the white and hostile world on which they had trespassed. Instead, the bamboos of the tent were removed and the tent collapsed over them. The men then built a cairn on which they placed a cross made by Lashly from Gran's skis.' Cherry-Garrard wrote: 'I do not know how long we were there, but when all was finished, and the chapter of the Corinthians had been read, it was midnight.' The cairn remains today but will eventually disappear.

Eight months afterwards we found the tent. It was an object partially snowed up and looking like a cairn. Before it were the ski sticks and in front of them a bamboo which probably was the mast of the sledge. The tent was practically on the line of cairns which we had built in the previous season. It was within a quarter of a mile of the

remains of the cairn, which showed as a small hummock beneath the snow.

Inside the tent were the bodies of Captain Scott, Doctor Wilson, and Lieutenant Bowers. Wilson and Bowers were found in the attitude of sleep, their sleeping-bags closed over their heads as they would naturally close them.

Scott died later. He had thrown back the flaps of his sleeping-bag and opened his coat. The little wallet containing the three notebooks was under his shoulders, and his arm was flung across Wilson. They had pitched their tent well, and it had withstood all the blizzards of an exceptionally hard winter. Each man of the Expedition recognised the bodies. From Captain Scott's diary I found his reasons for this disaster. When the men had been assembled I read to them these reasons, the place of death of Petty Officer Evans, and the story of Captain Oates' heroic end.

We recovered all their gear and dug out the sledge with their belongings on it. Amongst these were 35 lbs of very important geological specimens which had been collected on the moraines of the Beardmore Glacier; at Doctor Wilson's request they had stuck to these up to the very end, even when disaster stared them in the face and they knew that the specimens were so much weight added to what they had to pull.

When everything had been gathered up, we covered them with the outer tent and read the Burial Service. From this time until well into the next day we started to build a mighty cairn above them. This cairn was finished the next morning, and upon it a rough cross was placed, made from the greater portion of two skis, and on either side were up-ended two sledges, and they were fixed firmly in the snow, to be an added mark. Between the eastern sledge and the cairn a bamboo was placed, containing a metal cylinder, and in this the following record was left: –

November 12, 1912, lat. 79 degrees, 50 mins. South. This cross and cairn are erected over the bodies of Captain Scott, C.V.O., R.N., Doctor E. A. Wilson, M.B., B.C. Cantab., and Lieutenant H. R. Bowers, Royal Indian Marine—a slight token to perpetuate their successful and gallant attempt to reach the Pole. This they did on January 17, 1912, after the Norwegian Expedition had already done so. Inclement weather with lack of fuel as the cause of their death. Also to commemorate their two gallant comrades, Captain L. E. G. Oates of the Inniskilling Dragoons, who walked to his death in a blizzard to save his comrades about eighteen miles south of this position; also of Seaman Edgar Evans, who died at the foot of the Beardmore Glacier. "The Lord gave and the Lord taketh away; blessed be the name of the Lord."

This was signed by all the members of the party. I decided then to march twenty miles south with the whole of the Expedition and try to find the body of Captain Oates.

For half that day we proceeded south, as far as possible along the line of the previous season's march. On one of the old pony walls, which was simply marked by a ridge of the surface of the snow, we found Oates' sleeping-bag, which they had brought along with them after he had left.

The next day we proceeded thirteen more miles south, hoping and searching to find his body. When we arrived at the place where he had left them, we saw that there was no chance of doing so. The kindly snow had covered his body, giving him a fitting burial. Here, again, as near to the site of the death as we could judge, we built another cairn to his memory, and placed thereon a small cross and the following record:

Hereabouts died a very gallant gentleman, Captain L. E. G. Oates of the Inniskilling Dragoons. In March 1912, returning from the Pole, he walked willingly to his death in a blizzard, to try and save his comrades, beset by hardships. This note is left by the Relief Expedition of 1912.

It was signed by Cherry-Garrard and myself.

On the second day we came again to the resting-place of the three and bade them a final farewell. There alone in their greatness they will lie without change or bodily decay, with the most fitting tomb in the world above them.

In the following January, when the *Terra Nova* returned for the last time to bring the survivors home, those who had taken part in the search for Captain Scott sledged out to Hut Point to erect a cross in memory of him and his companions.

This cross, 9 feet in height, which was made by Davies of Australian jarrah wood, now stands on the summit of Observation Hill, overlooking the Great Ice Barrier and in full view of the *Discovery* winter quarters.

The line chosen from Tennyson's 'Ulysses' was suggested by Cherry-Garrard.

Amundsen's epitaph, quoted by Huntford, is somewhat more charitable than that of some more recent commentators: 'Bravery, determination, strength they did not lack. A little more experience . . . would have crowned their work with success.'

In
MEMORIAM
Capt. R. F. Scott, R.N.
Dr E. A. Wilson, Capt. L. E. G. Oates, Ins. Drgs.,
Lt. H. R. Bowers, R.I.M.
Petty Officer E. Evans, R.N.
who died on their
return from the
Pole, March
1912.
To strive, to seek,
to find,
and not to
yield.

The men on the fringe

Scott's *Journals* for the final part of the journey returning from the Pole could not, of course, record what was happening, from mid-January onwards, elsewhere, to the remainder of the party. These notes give some of this information from the diaries of those left behind.

January 17th 1912. Ponting, looking through his glass, suddenly saw the *Terra Nova* about 30 miles away across the ice. It was not until February 3rd that she got near enough for Meares to drive out with a dog team to communicate with those on board. He returned with two great bags of mail from home. Two days later the ship moored half a mile from the Glacier and unloaded stores. Ponting and his gear went on board without delay as they feared a blizzard might drive her out to sea again. The ship proceeded to the glacier at the foot of the Western Mountains to pick up the Geological Party. Then she headed out of the Sound, northwards, to pick up Campbell's party at Terra Nova Bay in South Victoria and, some 150 miles north of Ross Island, where they had been landed by the ship on her way south, to enable Priestley to do a few weeks' geological work at the foot of Mount Melbourne. Unfortunately the ice had changed and the ship found it hard to navigate. Indeed it took more than 30 hours to extricate her from the newly-formed pancake floes which were heaped up on the sea for miles.

The *Terra Nova* had to return to Cape Evans, where they found Lieut. Evans seriously ill with scurvy. They took him on board so that he could be tended by Surgeon Atkinson—Lashly and Crean also now came on board. The ship headed

Return of Atkinson's party.
Jan 29th 1912.

once more for Terra Nova Bay to reach Campbell's party, but the ice had not improved and they could get no nearer than on the last attempt. So once more they sailed back to Cape Evans, where Simpson, Taylor, Meares, Day, Forde and Clissold came on board, and two men were landed. *Terra Nova* then headed for Hut Point to land Atkinson and Keohane; they would wait for Cherry-Garrard and Dimitri, who had taken dog teams to One Ton Camp in the hope of meeting the returning Scott and party. Atkinson now took charge of the Cape Evans party.

March 5th 1912. In a final effort to reach the Northern Party, *Terra Nova* left McMurdo Sound for one last stop before heading off for New Zealand. But the ice was even thicker and it was doubtful if the ship could force a way through. All hands had to assemble on deck and run from side to side in an endeavour to sway the ship slightly and so keep her from freezing in. This strenuous work continued for several hours while the engine was used to back and fill. The worry was that the *Terra Nova* would be crushed in the ice. 'Slowly we battered our way fighting hard for every yard,' wrote Ponting. At last 'we crashed through the remaining prison walls and were out in the ice-scattered but open sea'. Once more they headed for the Bay, but the ice was thicker than ever, and they were 10 miles further out than at the last attempt. Pennell was reluctantly compelled to give up further efforts to relieve the party, so laid course for New Zealand.

The story of the Northern party is 'almost incredible', wrote Ponting. They were marooned in the Antarctic and short of food and clothing in the winter—for they had landed with only a few weeks' supplies. 'In this unprecedented predicament they burrowed into a glacier with their ice-axes, and lived in that icy dungeon for six months, subsisting on the flesh of seals and penguins [so escaping scurvy]. It almost surpasses belief that human beings could survive under such conditions and in such temperatures.' A full account is given in Raymond Priestley's book *Antarctic Adventure* and in Scott's *Journals* Volume II. They describe how, with the return of daylight on October 1st 1912, they left the ice cave and set out for Cape Evans with two sledges, arriving there safely on November 7th, some eight months after those who sailed on the *Terra Nova* were back in New Zealand, where they had heard the news that the Norwegians had reached the Pole.

Ponting, then back in Europe, wrote 'We had always known that if all went well with the rival expedition, the chances were all in favour of their being the first at the goal, as their base of operations was so much nearer than ours, and they had more rapid means of transport. Though we all felt much disappointed at this news, we were proud to know that the greatest of the earth's remaining geographical problems had been solved, and that the South Pole was a mystery no more. And we, who had spent more than a year in the Great White South, could perhaps, better than anyone else, realise the magnitude of Amundsen's achievement.'

Ponting's review

Writing in early 1921 for his book, published that autumn, Ponting felt obliged, in his words, to give *some account of the attainment of the primary object of the Expedition— the reaching of the South Pole.* He may have been a member of the Scientific Party but he did not put science first, even though in his letter to *The Times* he had claimed that it had priority.

Ponting had the greatest admiration for Scott. For example, discussing the first sighting of the Norwegian's camp, he quotes Scott's comment *It is a terrible disappointment, and I am very sorry for my loyal companions,* adding 'the greatness of the Leader shines out in that immortal sentence. In that tragic hour it was for his companions that he felt, not for himself, and the blighting of his own hopes.' When Scott actually reached the Pole, again Ponting's thoughts are all for his leader and 'the tremendous effort of those eleven weeks that had passed [which] is felt in that one momentary cry to the Almighty:

Great God! this is an awful place

It is the cry of a strong man out of whose heart hope is crushed. But in such a heart as Scott's it was human endeavour that mattered not the ambition to succeed. The crushing of hope could not long depress such dauntless spirit as his; and the next day found him full of appreciation for his rival's successful work.' Ponting continues: 'In the photographs which they took that day, it is magnificently eloquent of the manner in which the explorers took the frustrating of their hopes, that one of the films shows four of the party laughing—obviously at some mishap to Bowers, just as he released the shutter, for the negative is blurred.'

As Scott set off to return, facing '800 miles of solid dragging and good-bye to most of the day-dreams . . . a desperate struggle', Ponting comments that the pages of the journal contain 'an account of the most heroic and self-sacrificing struggle in the history of Polar exploration'. He begs his readers 'to bear in mind that *not withstanding the infinite striving of each day—striving for dear life itself—and the gradual weakening of the party, the Leader yet found time each night to record the day's doing fully* . . . one of the most remarkable attestations of devotion to purpose and duty in the history of our race. It is all the more remarkable when we think of the simple beauty of the language used . . . and still more so when we remember that, after all, this was *only a diary*—mere notes from which the Leader had intended, later, to write his book in comfort at home.'

When Ponting comes to write about the final tragedy he recounts 'a memorable conversation that Oates had with Nelson and me in my dark room during the winter of 1911. The point was raised as to what a man should do if he were to break down on the Polar journey, thereby becoming a burden to others. Oates unhesitatingly and emphatically expressed the opinion that there was only one possible course—self-sacrifice. He thought that a pistol should be carried [actually, they carried opium] and that "if anyone breaks down he should have the privilege of using it". We both agreed with this; but little did we think that within six months, one of us, and that one Oates himself, would be put to the test . . . But his was not the act of one goaded by suffering into a last distracted, frenzied impulse. It was the deliberate act of a man who had thought out his duty to his companions beforehand, and in cold blood. There can be no question about the quality of Oates' sacrifice. It was sublime.'

When Scott's body was found in November 1913, says Ponting, 'beside the notebooks were the little camera and two rolls of film. In these films were latent, amongst others, the three photographs produced herein which show the explorers at the South Pole—probably the most tragically interesting photographs in the world. They were taken with a quarter-plate film camera; and in the case of the groups, the shutter was released by a long thread, so that all might appear in the picture. Dr. Wilson can be seen pulling this thread in one of the groups and Lieut. Bowers in the other. The films were nearly two years old at the time they were exposed . . . and for eight months those two roles of film lay on the snow.' After they were found by the search party, they were developed by Debenham in the hut at Cape Evans. Their survival seems 'almost incredible', he added.

At the end of his book Ponting wrote 'Twenty, fifty a hundred, five hundred years hence, the story of the Immortal Five who perished after conquering the South Pole will inspire our youth just as it does today.' He did not know that in the year 2000, if it were not for this simple account, Scott's journals would not be in print in the land of his birth.

This maquette of Scott and his companions at the Pole was executed by Mr Derwent Wood c.1914. The full-size sculpture was commissioned to be created in London but in fact the project was never fulfilled.

Glossary

Barrier The Great Ice Barrier, an immense sheet of ice, over 400 miles wide and of still greater length, which lies south of Ross Island to the west of Victoria Land. Now called the Ross Ice Shelf.

Brash Small ice fragments from a floe that is breaking up.

Finnesko Fur boots.

Flense, flence To cut blubber from a skin or carcase.

Hoosh A thick camp soup with a basis of pemmican.

Ice foot Properly the low fringe of ice formed about Polar lands by the sea spray. More widely, the banks of ice of varying height which skirt many parts of the Antarctic shores.

Nunatak A lone peak of rock in the midst of the ice; when rounded by glacial action, a nunakol.

Pemmican Lean, ground, dried meat mixed with melted fat. Originated with the Chree Indians.

Piedmont Coastwise stretches of the ancient ice-sheet which once covered the Antarctic continent, remaining either on the land, or wholly or partially afloat.

Pram A Norwegian skiff, with a spoon bow.

Ramp A great embankment of morainic material with ice beneath, once part of the glacier on the lowest slopes of Erebus at the landward end of Cape Evans.

Sennegras A kind of fine Norwegian hay, used as packing in the finnesko to keep the feet warm and to make the fur boot fit firmly.

Sastrugus An irregularity formed by the wind on a snow-plain. 'Snow wave' is not completely descriptive, as the sastrugus often has a fantastic shape unlike the ordinary conception of a wave.

Skua A large gull.

Tank A large canvas hold-all for sledge use.

Working crack An open crack which leaves the ice free to move with the movement of the water beneath.

Acknowlegements

I have referred in my Introduction to the encouragement given to me by Richard Kossow, without which this book would not have been written. In addition I want to thank the Director and staff of the Royal Geographical Society, in particular Nigel Winser (Deputy Director), Andrew Tatham (Keeper) and Joanna Scudden (Picture Library Manager), all of whom have been most helpful. Similarly, I must thank Robert Headland (Archivist) and Philippa Smith (Picture Library) of the Scott Polar Research Institute at Cambridge.

Both editor and publisher are grateful to those whose editorial material has been referred to, in particular Roland Huntford and Diana Preston (quotation does not necessarily imply concurrence with the sentiments expressed in the original work).

In his book *Scott and Amundsen* (Weidenfeld, 1979), on which I have drawn widely, Huntford notes that the late Sir Peter Scott, son of the explorer, 'totally' disassociated himself from that book, which he did not see before printing. Later, Wayland Young, Sir Peter's stepbrother, wrote a critique of Huntford's book in *Encounter* magazine. I personally found this rather unconvincing and, as I say, my own view is that Huntford should be read alongside the work of Ponting and other contemporaries of Scott, as well as modern commentators like Diana Preston and Ann Savours. Readers will also enjoy Beryl Bainbridge's *The Birthday Boys*. I have, in addition, drawn from Huntford's *The Amundsen Photographs* (Hodder, 1987) which features his original plates. Those who wish to study the subject in more depth could do no better than refer to the list of sources in Huntford's *Scott and Amundsen*.

Finally I must thank Deborah Blake, my editor at Duckworth, and Katherine Lambert for their help in preparing the manuscript and illustrations for printing. Angie Hipkin kindly supplied the index. My apologies if I have overlooked anyone else I ought to have thanked or acknowledged.

P.K.

Picture credits

The illustrations reproduced in this book were obtained from the following sources: The Royal Geographical Society: illustrations on pp. 6, 13 (right), 16, 22, 23, 25, 26, 28, 29, 30, 31, 33, 34, 35, 36, 38, 41, 42, 43, 44 (below), 46, 47, 48, 49, 50, 51, 52, 53, 54, 55, 56, 57, 58, 60, 61, 62, 64 (top), 65, 66, 67, 69, 70, 71, 72, 74, 81, 82, 83, 84, 85, 86, 87, 88, 89, 90, 92, 93, 95, 97, 99, 100, 101, 102, 103, 104, 105, 107, 108, 111, 112, 115, 118, 119, 120, 121, 122, 123, 127, 128, 130, 131, 132, 135, 138, 141, 142, 143, 144, 146, 148, 150, 151, 154, 173, 183, 186; The Scott Polar Research Institute: illustration on p. 129. The Challenge of Antarctica by Eleanor Honnywill: illustration on p. 177. Scott's Last Expedition: frontispiece. All other photographs are from The Great White South by H.G. Ponting.

Further Reading

Amundsen, R., *The South Pole* (London: Murray, 1912)

Bainbridge, B., *The Birthday Boys* (London: Duckworth, 1991)

Cherry-Garrard, A., *The Worst Journey in the World* (London: Chatto & Windus, 1965)

Debenham, F., *Antarctica* (London: Herbert Jenkins, 1959)

Fisher, M. and J., *Shackleton* (London: Barrie, 1957)

Gran, T., *The Norwegian with Scott* (Gran's diary) (London: HMSO, 1984)

Huntford, R., *Shackleton* (London: Hodder, 1985)

Ponting, H.G., *The Great White South* (London: Duckworth, 1933)

Huntford, R., *Nansen* (London: Duckworth, 1997)

Huxley, Elspeth, *Scott of the Antarctic* (London: Weidenfeld, 1977)

Preston, D., *A First Rate Tragedy* (London: Constable, 1997)

Savours, A., *Scott's Last Voyage* (London: Sidgwick, 1974)

Savours, A., *The Voyage of the Discovery* (London: Virgin, 1994)

Scott, R.F., *Scott's Last Expedition. The Journals* (New York: Carroll & Graf, 1996)

Scott's Diaries 1910 in facsimile edition (Bucks: University Microfilms Ltd., 1968)

Scott's Last Expedition, being the journals of Captain R.F. Scott, arranged by Leonard Huxley
    (London: Smith, Elder & Co., 1913)

Seaver, G., *Edward Wilson of the Antarctic* (London: Murray, 1933)

Seaver, G., *Scott of the Antarctic* (London: Murray, 1940)

Shackleton, E. H., *South*, ed. Peter King (London: Century, 1992)

Shackleton, E. H., *The Heart of the Antarctic* (London: Heinemann, 1909)

Wilson, E., *Diary of the 'Terra Nova' Expedition to the Antarctic* (London: Blandford
    Press, 1972)

Films

90° South by H. G. Ponting (Academy Video, BFI, 1933)

Scott of the Antarctic (Ealing Studios, 1948)

Index

Index